38057

D1544903

PAYOFFS IN THE CLOAKROOM

THE GREENING OF THE MICHIGAN LEGISLATURE, 1938-1946

PAYOFFS IN THE CLOAKROOM

THE GREENING OF THE MICHIGAN LEGISLATURE, 1938-1946

Bruce A. Rubenstein
and
Lawrence E. Ziewacz

Michigan State University Press
East Lansing
1995

All Michigan State University Press books are produced on paper which meets the requirements of American National Standard of Information Sciences— Permanence of paper for printed materials ANSI Z39.48-1984.

Michigan State University Press
East Lansing, Michigan 48823-5202

02 01 00 99 98 97 96 95 1 2 3 4 5 6 7 8 9

Library of Congress Cataloging-in-Publication Data

Rubenstein, Bruce A. (Bruce Alan)
Payoffs in the cloakroom : the greening of the Michigan Legislature, 1938-1946 /
  Bruce A. Rubenstein and Lawrence E. Ziewacz.
p. cm.
Includes bibliographical references and index.
ISBN 0-87013-387-X (alk. paper)
1. Political corruption—Michigan—History—20th century. 2. Michigan.
  Legislature—History—20th century. 3. Michigan—Politics and government—
  1837-1950. I. Ziewacz, Lawrence E. (Lawrence Edward) II. Title.
JK5845.R83 1995
364.1'323—dc20
94-48041
CIP

To the memory of

MADISON KUHN

who made Michigan's history come
alive to thousands of students at
Michigan State University

CONTENTS

ACKNOWLEDGEMENTS

We are indebted deeply to many individuals for assisting us in bringing an idea to a printed reality. Special thanks go to Don Gardner whose recollections of the Capitol scene were so insightful and vivid that they transformed names into lively characters. Likewise, Al Kaufman, Richard Foster, Victor Anderson, and Marvin Salmon willingly gave in-depth interviews regarding their roles in the grand jury period.

As they had done with our previous book on the grand jury era, *Three Bullets Sealed His Lips*, LeRoy Barnett and John Curry of the Michigan History Division of the Michigan Department of State manifested tremendous willingness to assist us in what must have seemed at times to be endless requests for source materials and photographs. Staff members of the State of Michigan Library, the Bentley Historical Library of the University of Michigan, and the Waldo Library of Western Michigan University guided us to many valuable sources and were most patient in spending much time answering our additional queries. As well, the staff of the Ingham County Clerk's Office must be commended for ferreting out transcripts, long buried in storage, of trials held nearly fifty years earlier. Dr. Fred Bohm and Julie Loehr of Michigan State University Press were unfailingly supportive, and once again they receive our heartfelt thanks. We are also indebted to Glenda Burgett, secretary for the History Department of the University of Michigan-Flint, for typing the manuscript.

Finally, heartfelt appreciation and affection go to our colleagues, friends, and families for accepting the vicissitudes of temperament which we displayed while researching and writing. Most of all, however, we thank them for listening patiently for countless hours as we related our latest discoveries, expounded theories, read to them newly written chapters, and then anxiously awaited their critical review. While we bear the final accountability for this book, unquestionably they share in its coming to fruition.

Bruce A. Rubenstein
Lawrence E. Ziewacz

AUTHORS' NOTE

All quotations in this book were taken directly from published accounts, private correspondence, personal interviews, trial transcripts, or sworn statements made before either the Michigan State Police or members of the Ingham County Grand Jury. The only liberty assumed was the deletion of certain questions posed by attorneys during the examinations and trials so that the witnesses' response would read as a coherent story; the quotations themselves, however, were altered in no way from the original source. Likewise, all descriptions of individuals, events, or places were taken from published accounts, trial transcripts, sworn testimony, or interviews with persons well acquainted with the individuals, events, or places involved. Multiple citations were required before descriptions were considered for inclusion.

CAST OF CHARACTERS

VICTOR C. ANDERSON
Ingham County prosecutor who tied his career to the tailor-made coattails of Kim Sigler

BYRON BALLARD
an attorney who tried to serve one too many masters

CHARLES BOHN
multimillionaire Detroit industrialist who dove into legislative waters and nearly drowned

LELAND W. CARR
respected mid-Michigan jurist who hoped his one-man grand jury probe into legislative corruption would earn him the seat he coveted on the state supreme court

LOUIS COASH
successor grand juror who doused Sigler's flame

CHARLES DELANO
state senator who never saw a bribe he could refuse

SIMON DENUYL
Bohn's right-hand man and intermediary with lobbyist Charles F. Hemans

FLOYD FITZSIMMONS
Michigan sports promoter who was turned into a patsy by Sigler

RICHARD B. FOSTER
Sigler's successor as grand jury special prosecutor who could not pry open Hemans' lips

WILLIAM GREEN
rural legislator who should have stayed down on the farm

CHARLES F. HEMANS
premier lobbyist and giver of bribes who made his Olds Hotel bathroom the most notorious gathering spot in Lansing

WARREN G. HOOPER
a legislator who knew too much about graft-givers and was silenced permanently before he could testify in open court

CHESTER M. HOWELL
a state senator who knew better, but took the money anyway

IVAN JOHNSTON
head of a senate subcommittee that bared Sigler's books, if not his soul

FRANK D. MCKAY
the oft-indicted, but never convicted, multimillionaire boss of Michigan's Republican party

WILLIAM MCKEIGHAN
five-time mayor of Flint and McKay's chief lieutenant in political machinations

HERBERT J. RUSHTON
Michigan's attorney general who tried to close his eyes to legislative malfeasance but finally was compelled to let his conscience be his guide

KIM SIGLER
flamboyant clotheshorse who expected that his role as grand jury special prosecutor would catapult him into the governorship and possibly the White House

JOHN SIMPSON
circuit judge who let Sigler run fast and loose during the first five grand jury trials, but clamped down on the theatrics when McKay was the defendant

MURRAY D. VANWAGONER
Michigan governor who refused to admit that anything improper happened during his administration, even though his lieutenant governor was indicted for taking a bribe

INTRODUCTION

Since the publication of *Three Bullets Sealed His Lips* in 1987, which resolved the more than four decade old question of who murdered State Senator Warren G. Hooper four days before he was scheduled to testify against Republican kingpin Frank D. McKay regarding graft in the Michigan legislature, many exciting events have occurred. Scores of people have contacted us regarding their recollections of the Purple Gang, individuals highlighted in the book, especially Ingham County Grand Jury Special Prosecutor Kim Sigler who was the star of the probe, reminiscences regarding the times, or simply requesting information as to our detective methodology. Thus, our book not only "unsealed" Hooper's lips, but those of many citizens of Michigan.

To our surprise, while we had answered the question of who had assassinated Hooper, how it had been accomplished, and what the motives had been, the shroud of mystery refused to relinquish its grip on the case. This first became evident when George Weeks, the gifted political correspondent for the *Detroit News*, related that because of his interest in the book he had requested, and received, permission from the Michigan Attorney General's office, as had we, to examine the grand jury records, long thought to have been destroyed, which we had unearthed in the archives of the Michigan History Division of the Michigan Department of State. We had explained to Mr. Weeks that as we had poured over these documents, which had never been intended to become public, we had become the only persons since Sigler to have been privy to all the evidence gathered by the State Police, local law enforcement agencies, and the grand jury secret investigative staff, which reported solely to Sigler. These transcripts had revealed the Special Prosecutor's ruthlessness, his reasons for not cooperating fully with the State Police, and the degree of misinformation he had deliberately fed the press concerning the investi-

1

gation. Seeking to examine these treasures for himself, Mr. Weeks was told by History Division officials that his desire could never be fulfilled as within two months of our seeing them the records had been inadvertently shredded. Therefore, we had been the first, and last, people, except for members of the Attorney General's staff, who had glimpsed the keys which unlocked the door to the Hooper murder conspiracy.

A second unexpected incident occurred in the Spring of 1988 when Professor Ziewacz received a late night telephone call from the grandson of Frank D. McKay, who intimated that he was in possession of a weapon which might have fired the three slugs that took Senator Hooper's life—a .38 calibre Colt revolver belonging to his grandfather. Furthermore, he expressed a willingness to send the gun to the Michigan State Police for a ballistics comparison with the bullets removed from Hooper's corpse. Eager to drive home the final nail in our case, we notified the State Police, who stated they would investigate their records regarding evidence in their safekeeping.

Within two days, our hopes were dashed when the State Police contended that all ballistic records in the Hooper file had been ordered destroyed in 1952. That enraged State Police Lieutenant David Townshend, who had been our main contact person within the force and who possessed not only the exceptional talents of a dedicated law enforcement officer but also those of an historian. Knowing that no evidence should ever be destroyed in an open murder investigation, on his own time he began to track down clues as to what happened to other records and evidence regarding the Hooper slaying. In a few days, he telephoned us and related that he had discovered four boxes of material labeled "Hooper Murder" which had been stored in the State Police Annex and not opened since 1952. With his dry sense of humor, he inquired if we would care to be present when he opened them, and, with the enthusiasm of amateur detectives, we blurted out some form of affirmative and agreed to meet him the following day.

Feeling like Geraldo Rivera on one of his erstwhile quests, and hoping that unlike Rivera the vault we opened would not be as barren as that of Al Capone, we entered the storage room with Lieutenant Townshend. Once again, fortune smiled on us. There before us as we carefully pulled back the lids were Hooper's bullet-riddled, blood-encrusted crushed hat, the contents of his Senate desk, more than one hundred mug-shots and autopsy photographs, and even a tape recording of an interview with Henry Luks, one of the hired assassins who had turned state's evidence. While none of these items affected our conclusions, it was a sobering moment to see and touch this "living history." However, buried in a corner of the final box was what we had only dared to discover—a small box containing two bullets recovered from Hooper's body. Now, even without the lost records, a ballistics check could be made, and the State Police requested that we contact McKay and have him forward the revolver.

Suffering from either an attack of conscience or a severe dose of family pressure, McKay ceased to be cooperative, refusing to answer either telephone calls or letters. After weeks of frustration, we turned to Ralph Turner, retired head of the Criminal Justice Department of Michigan State University, who set up an interview for us with Colonel Richie Davis, then Director of the Michigan State Police. Following an hour conversation, Colonel Davis consented to attempt to track down the elusive Mr. McKay.

Located in California, McKay reluctantly agreed to submit the gun he possessed to testing by California authorities. Since the time of the initial telephone call to Professor Ziewacz, however, the revolver suspiciously and miraculously had transformed from a more than fifty year old .38 calibre Colt into a .32 calibre weapon manufactured after McKay's grandfather had died in early 1965. Yet, this was not unexpected, as the younger McKay denied to police interrogators virtually the entire story he had related previously to us.

Meanwhile, both the *Detroit News* and the Booth Newspaper Syndicate were notified of these developments, and the latest State Police probe into the once-forgotten Hooper murder was headlined across the state, while wire service accounts engendered national interest. Director Davis assigned Detective Lieutenant Chester Wilson to the case, and for more than a year he questioned every individual who had been involved, even remotely, with the Hooper murder. Among those whom he tracked down were Mike Selik, the Purple Gang lieutenant who, with Harry Fleisher, had been an architect of the original plot to silence the lawmaker, and Harry Keywell, another Purple Gang member, who was involved, as shown in *Three Bullets Sealed His Lips*, in the actual assassination. Both were living in exclusive suburban Detroit nursing homes and refused to say anything about their past. In fact, in his best Edward G. Robinson fashion, Selik sneered to Detective Wilson: "I didn't rat on my pals forty years ago, copper, and I ain't gonna rat on 'em now." Closing his investigation, Lieutenant Wilson stated: "I can hardly argue with the conclusions they [Rubenstein and Ziewacz] draw." This was in keeping with previous comments by Lieutenant Townshend, who had remarked: "These guys [Rubenstein and Ziewacz] are like super sleuths. Maybe they're frustrated policemen. Whatever, they've done one heck of a job. I wish there were more guys out there like them."

3

This flurry of activity not only kept alive interest in the Hooper slaying, but also afforded us the opportunity to accomplish something we had wished to do from the onset of our research—delve into the issue of corruption in Michigan during the period 1938-1946. During the course of our research, we had been struck by the obvious irony of the state known during World War II as the "Arsenal of Democracy" being governed by men intent on lining their own pockets while their sons and daughters were waging a struggle overseas for freedom, and we sought to tell this sordid tale. Yet the murder which resulted from the grand jury probe into legislative malfeasance overshadowed the causes of the crime.

With the murder resolved, readers and Capitol correspondents, such as Hugh McDiarmid of the *Detroit Free Press*, expressed a desire for more information on the overall scenario of graft and corruption of the times, which, while not unique to Michigan, seemingly was more flagrant in the Wolverine State. Moreover, the topic of legislative graft became extremely timely during the early 1990s as the nation was shocked by revelations of widespread irregularities by congressmen utilizing the House of Representatives' banking privileges and a savings and loan scandal implicating five United States senators in questionable ethical behavior while serving on the Senate Banking Committee. As several Michigan congressmen and the state's senior United States Senator, Donald Riegle, were among those whose actions had come under scrutiny, Michigan's residents eagerly sought the truth about the actions of their elected officials, as well as expressing a desire to investigate the propriety of the remainder of the state's delegation in the nation's capitol.

These issues barely had begun to fade when in January, 1993 *Detroit News* correspondent Jim Mitzelfeld reported widespread corruption in the Michigan House Fiscal Agency, which advises the legislature on budget and tax issues. While the Michigan officials charged in the federal cases had emerged with little more than sullied reputations, the state irregularities resulted in the resignations of Representative Steve Shepich, who pleaded guilty to obtaining more than $100 under false pretenses while he was a fiscal analyst at the agency, and John Morberg, the dapper director of the agency who pleaded guilty to federal racketeering and tax evasion. As of May 1994 four others, including the agency bookkeeper, had been convicted on felony charges.

These convictions, as well as the reputed $2,500 bribe offer by a lobbyist to State Representative Ed Giese in 1989, raised the volume of demand from dismayed citizens for a comparison of current misdeeds with those of the past. As George Weeks tantalizingly noted in a column: "It [the House Fiscal Agency disclosure] is the worst scandal since the

1940s, when a grand jury investigation produced more than forty convictions. . . . How far [investigators] go will determine if today's burgeoning scandal matches the one that rocked the Capitol more than a half a century ago."

We believe this book will further the ease by which that comparison may be made. As with *Three Bullets Sealed His Lips*, it is our intention to recreate for the people of Michigan in particular, and all those seeking a better understanding of the legislative and criminal justice systems in general, events which badly tarnished both the state of Michigan and the reputations of prominent public figures, so that armed with the truth a vigilant populace can seek to assure that such a situation may never occur again.

Bruce A. Rubenstein
Lawrence E. Ziewacz

CHAPTER ONE

THE DEN OF CORRUPTION

I The corruption that tainted the Michigan legislature in the late 1930s and early 1940s had its origins in the waning days of the unparalleled prosperity of the "Roaring Twenties." During the post-World War I decade, Michigan's booming automobile industry was the core of economic expansion which seemed destined to bequeath permanent wealth to the nation. Unfortunately, many of the state's lawmakers did not view their $3 per working day stipend as an accurate reflection of their worth in this decade of prosperity, and gossip of bribe-taking ran rampant throughout the Capitol City of Lansing. A favorite story of Booth newspaper correspondent Guy Jenkins was the recollection of Fred Green, an austere rural Republican who served as governor from 1927 to 1931, standing with correspondents viewing group portraits of members of the state house and senate. "Fine pictures," someone remarked, and Green shot back solemnly, "Yes, sir. That's one of the finest legislatures that money can buy."[1]

The crash of the stock market and subsequent decline of the country's economy hit Michigan extremely hard. As the depression deepened, tens of thousands of the state's residents lost their jobs and unemployment in 1932 reached 46 percent, nearly double that of the nation as a whole. Disgruntled workers, who were having their wages cut and were threatened with layoffs should they object, began to unionize, and confrontational strikes often led to physical violence against management and its property. By 1937, the prevailing philosophy of Michiganians was to survive by any means possible, and this precept was nowhere more prevalent than with their elected officials.

The ultimate weapon utilized to wage war on malfeasance was the grand jury, which, unlike the attorney general's office, possessed subpoena power. While other states utilized a similar system for uncovering political corruption, Michigan was peculiar because it favored a one-man grand jury rather than the more common multi-member structure.

Most spectacular of the early grand jury probes was that of Judge Homer Ferguson who conducted an explosive investigation into illegalities in Wayne County during the years 1939-1942. The unlikely event that triggered Ferguson's probe was the suicide of Mrs. Janet MacDonald, who, with her eleven year old daughter, was found dead in her automobile on Wednesday, August 9, 1939 from carbon monoxide poisoning. What transformed this personal tragedy into sensational headlines throughout the state was that the thirty-six year old divorcee, despondent over being jilted by her lover, a drunken bagman for the mob who delivered protection money to Detroit police officers, left a packet of letters addressed to local newspaper editors and the Federal Bureau of Investigation in which she set forth detailed accounts of her personal knowledge of widespread payoffs and "easy money which flowed from a system of graft and civic corruption."[2]

Despite possessing the damning evidence, Wayne County Prosecutor Duncan McCrea chose not to pursue the case, saying cryptically that he did not wish to be a party to a whitewash of the police department. Frustrated by McCrea's indifference, Detroit City Councilman Philip H. Breitmeyer presented his colleagues a resolution which was passed unanimously recommending a grand jury investigation. Consequently, on August 21, 1939 Homer Ferguson was chosen by his fellow Wayne County Circuit Judges to act as a one-man grand juror to ascertain the validity of MacDonald's charges. Former Berrien County Prosecutor Chester P. O'Hara was designated by the jurist to be his special prosecutor.[3]

Collection of evidence and taking of testimony was painstaking and tedious, but all the hours of toil proved worthwhile when on February 22, 1940, based on information submitted by the grand jury, indictments were handed down against twenty-five individuals, including McCrea, his three chief assistants, former Detroit Police commissioner Fred W. Frahm, two Detroit patrolmen, and Wayne County Sheriff Thomas Wilcox, alleging each was engaged in a conspiracy to protect gambling, prostitution, and other forms of vice through the bribery of public officials. After a January 7, 1941 trial date was established by Circuit Judge Earl C. Pugsley who had been assigned to preside over the proceedings, the beaming short, stocky O'Hara pronounced ebulliently to reporters that this "was only a starting gun, and a pop gun at that."[4]

The two main characters in this drama, McCrea and Wilcox, were colorful local figures whose exploits had achieved, in the eyes of many local residents, the level of folklore by the time of their removal from office by Governor Luren Dickinson in 1940. The fifty-six year old McCrea had been a former lumberjack, railroad brakeman, and self-described "rambler" before moving to Detroit, where he decided to study law at night school while working at a clerical job by day. A bulbous nosed, big cheeked man, violence seemed natural to him and physical altercations became his trademark as both an assistant under Robert S. Toms and Harry S. Toy and during his own tenure as Wayne County's "fighting prosecutor."[5]

Lanky Thomas Wilcox, sixty-one years of age, had come to Detroit in 1917 as a federal agent tracking down draft dodgers. In the mid-1930s he was the city's police commissioner and then was elected Wayne County sheriff. Sporting a diamond studded badge, purchased through involuntary contributions from staff members who complained they had donated an amount far in excess of the worth of the glittering symbol of authority, the bespectacled sheriff was a comedic caricature of a lawman, once piously proclaiming to a chortling audience that he wished to reduce the theft of chickens by having each bird identified by a tattoo.[6]

What would prove to be the prosecution's first big break came a day prior to the trial's onset when Wayne County Undersheriff Barney McGrath, a defendant in the case, turned state's evidence. This shocking admission of wrong-doing created a domino effect, as shortly thereafter Gustave Pines, self-confessed collector for Wilcox, admitted his guilt and was followed quickly down the path of soul-cleansing by Sam Block, a collector for McCrea.[7]

Devastating testimony against McCrea was offered almost immediately by Bernard A. Boggio, an assistant Wayne County prosecutor, who swore that he had turned over to his employer $1,000, which he had received from Everett Watson, a leader of the rackets in Detroit. Rising with a lurch from his chair, the bushy-browed, gap-toothed McCrea vehemently refuted this allegation, shouting: "You know that's a lie. I never saw Watson before this inquiry. I never took a dollar from a gambler in my life."[8]

As the three-month long trial neared its conclusion, forty-three year old Harry Colburn administered the knockout blow to the former Wayne County Prosecutor by turning state's evidence. On April 3, the puffy cheeked former tailor took the stand to bare his soul.

"How did you handle the graft money for McCrea?" O'Hara asked the ill-at-ease, chalky-complexioned witness.

"I generally did it in person and in cash and generally in McCrea's office," Colburn said so softly that he had to be instructed by Judge Pugsley to speak louder. "The money was in cash, not even in envelopes. It was paid each month. Sam Block would give me the slips showing where the money came from and who paid it, but McCrea never looked at the slips. He would say, 'Oh, keep those. It'll be all right. I'm not worried.'"

"When did this racket start?" inquired O'Hara.

"It all started in 1935, shortly after McCrea became prosecutor," Colburn said, refusing to look at his former friend who sat placidly with his thumbs hooked in his vest pockets while he chewed gum. "He decided to set up a graft agency. McCrea said if we're smart, we could make some money together and not get hurt."

"How could you make this money?" interrupted the Special Prosecutor.

"McCrea explained by collecting from illegal enterprises without promising too much. I was supposed to make the collections, but after one attempt in which I failed, I suggested that we should get someone we could trust who could handle it for us. It was then that graft collections from gambling and bawdy houses was turned over to Block, who worked on a ten percent commission. Of the balance, I received one-third and McCrea the remainder."

"How much did you receive?"

"My share was $52,000," admitted the witness, running his hands through his dark hair.

"Then McCrea's cut was $104,000," calculated O'Hara, as he walked away. "No further questions, but I reserve the right to recall Mr. Colburn."[9]

McCrea, acting as his own counsel, awkwardly rose to his feet and began cross-examining Colburn in a gentle tone. "Harry," he cooed, "you and I have been friends for many years, haven't we?"

"Yes, Dunc."

"I even loaned you $1,000 before you came to work for me, didn't I?"

"Yes."

"And up until ten minutes before you pleaded guilty you were saying I was innocent of all these charges, weren't you?" McCrea asked, a smile etched on his ruddy face.

"Yes," replied Colburn, his eyes clouding with tears.

"You've been sick a long time, haven't you, Harry?" asked McCrea.

"Well, not really sick," the witness hedged.

"Well, Harry," McCrea went on, "didn't I suggest to you several years ago that you should go to the Mayo Brothers Clinic for treatment of your nerves?"

"Yes."

"And haven't you visited two Detroit psychiatrists for treatment?"

"Yes."

"No further questions today, Harry," chortled McCrea, unwrapping a new stick of gum as he returned to his seat.[10]

As he stepped down from the witness box, Colburn broke into tears and collapsed into a nearby chair, where he was consoled by his eldest son. "It was a terrible ordeal," he gasped between choking sobs. "I love that man [McCrea]. I hope nobody thinks I was drilling it into him."[11]

Several days later, on rebuttal questioning by O'Hara, Colburn was much more composed. "McCrea approached me on March 24 after the testimony of Bernard A. Boggio," Colburn related in a steady voice. "McCrea told my wife, 'I don't like the look of things. Harry hasn't got a chance. He'll be convicted and get a long prison sentence.' I told McCrea that he had always led me to believe I had a fighting chance. He replied that he didn't want to upset me. He told me: 'You are a sure pop to go to prison. You are a sick man, and you've got to be sick so we can get a mistrial or neither of us has a chance. You go to bed and stay there. Now I've given you a chance.'"

"What did you do then," commanded O'Hara.

"I objected because I said I would be found out by the doctors," Colburn stated frankly. "McCrea replied: 'Tell the doctors you've got a humming in your head. Pound the walls and tear your hair. In six months you'll have a better chance in a trial than now.'"[12]

After O'Hara concluded, McCrea stepped forward once again to confront his old ally. After repeatedly failing to shake Colburn's testimony, McCrea lost his temper.

"You know you never gave me ten cents in your life, Harry," McCrea sneered. "But never mind that. What about all the previous testimony you gave supporting me?"

"God," Colburn said in anguish, "you know that was all false, Dunc. I did it to try to save you."[13]

When put on the stand by O'Hara, McCrea was asked why he had not initiated a probe into the allegations of graft. "I lacked sufficient investigators," was the lame response.

"Wasn't the real reason," O'Hara shot back fiercely, "that you had been taking dough along with other officers in the Detroit Police Department?"

"No," McCrea responded softly.

"Why were hundreds of gambling warrants found in bank safety deposit boxes owned by you, Mr. McCrea?" O'Hara inquired.

"I don't recall," came the feeble retort.[14]

On April 24, McCrea, no longer self-assured and arrogant, made his final argument to the jury. In an often disjointed four hour discourse, McCrea asserted that Block kept any graft money for himself or, if not, gave it to Colburn who retained it to pay off a judgment against him by the Internal Revenue Service. Fearful that he may have bored the veniremen over the duration of the trial, McCrea concluded by pleading that they "forget and forgive" anything he may have said and base their verdict entirely upon the facts as he had pointed them out.[15]

After McCrea, Wilcox's attorney, George S. Fitzgerald, made an impassioned plea on behalf of his client. "Does the average man wait to go crooked," he shouted, "until he is fifty-seven years of age? That's the story they would like to have you believe about Tom Wilcox. This is more than just another lawsuit with me. I've known Tom Wilcox since 1924 when he was connected with the Federal Bureau of Investigation and I was a member of the Customs. I have known this man throughout the years, and I have never heard that he was connected with any business that wasn't open and above board."[16]

In his summation to the jury, O'Hara hammered on the purpose of the trial. "I have no apologies to make to you, to the people of Wayne County and the State of Michigan, for the case we have presented here. We have attempted to bring to you the story—the true story—of what corruption went on between racketeers and public officials," he said earnestly. "We cannot delve into a situation where gamblers and women of shame are involved and get the true story by bringing in substantial citizens as witnesses. We must go to those places and bring the people who work in those places to testify. I have no animosity in this case. I know that I have been abused at times when personalities have been injected into the trial. The prosecutor always has to take that when the case of the defense is weak. And I know my neck has turned red. This is my nature. I'm Irish, and I flare up easily. But I do not hate McCrea, as he would like to have you believe. I don't hate Wilcox, as he would like to have you believe. I simply seek justice for them."[17]

Judge Pugsley began his charge to the jury at 3 p.m., Saturday, April 26, concluding with the admonition: "A man's good character should be given consideration by the jury, but if you find beyond a reasonable doubt that a man is guilty as charged, his character, however grand and noble in the past, must give way to the inevitable result of crime, for crime washes out and gives blank the past history of good character."[18] At 5:12 in the afternoon, the jury began its deliberations, and the following morning it brought in guilty verdicts against all but one of the twenty-five defendants.[19]

After accepting congratulations from well-wishers, O'Hara held a brief press conference. "I am naturally pleased that the jury has placed its stamp of approval on our work," the smiling Irishman stated. "There is still much to do. Of course, it does not make me happy to see these persons suffer. Their difficulties, however, are of their own making. We are merely doing a job and will continue to the best of our ability."[20]

McCrea grabbed reporters as they passed to profess his innocence. "The verdict returned by the jury was not only contrary to the weight of the evidence, but to that of the law," he railed. "It is based on the unsupported testimony of a self-confessed criminal. I shall continue to fight for vindication to the highest court of the land, if necessary. I am confident that the verdict will be set aside. The law is very clear on the point that the unsupported testimony of a criminal must be disregarded if other witnesses deny it."[21]

Wilcox, demonstrably shaken by the outcome, sputtered: "Of course, I'll appeal this case to the United States Supreme Court, if need be." His chief deputy, Carl J. Staebler, raised the post-trial commentary to a higher plane when he offered a thoughtful explanation as to why guilty verdicts had been rendered against the defendants: "The jury has been influenced by the chaotic conditions and unrest brought about by the war, and all public officials are now under suspicion."[22] For whatever reason, the message had been sent forth: Michigan would no longer ignore graft and corruption committed by its public officials.

III Emboldened by the success of Judge Ferguson, the search for improprieties among lawmakers moved beyond the confines of Wayne County when, on August 13, 1943, six members of the Detroit Citizens' League petitioned Attorney General Herbert J. Rushton to establish a one-man grand jury to look into charges that members of the state legislature had been accepting money from lobbyists. "We are convinced," contended Citizens' League secretary William P. Lovett, who had spearheaded the movement against McCrea and Wilcox, "after a careful investigation for six months, that graft was paid to certain members of the legislature to defeat the anti-chain banking bill, which prohibits the establishment of any more chain banks in Michigan. During the last three sessions there have been reports about the buying and selling of votes to defeat this bill. As a result of our own investigation, we were able to present voluminous reports in writing, with facts, figures, and overt acts of corruption, to the State Attorney General."[23]

The sixty-six year old, silver-haired Rushton, himself a former member of the state senate during the time of the purported corruption, initially turned a deaf ear to Lovett's plea and berated the Detroiter for being rash by making public his request for a probe "before we know where we are going."[24] The attorney general was compelled to reassess his stance, however, when William C. Stenson, who represented Rushton's home district in the state house, blurted to reporters an incredible tale of a blatant attempt to purchase his vote on the bank bill.

"During the 1941 session," the former upper peninsula automobile dealer related to the press, "$1,000 in fifty dollar bills was placed in my overcoat pocket in an envelope which also contained a note scribbled on a scrap of paper which read: 'Vote against number one.' Well, since Senate Bill 1 was the anti-chain bank bill, I assumed that was what the message meant. Later I returned the money to a man in a gray suit whom I suspected had put it there."

"I didn't know the man, and I still don't know his name, although I probably would recognize him if I saw him again," Stenson explained, adding self-righteously: "I voted for the bill partly because that was the way I felt and partly because I didn't want to vote the way the note had told me to." In a vain attempt to look sheepish, the first term Republican, whose reputation for veracity was suspect by his peers, concluded: "It's kind of late now, but I wish I had stood right up to him during the session and announced to the entire membership I had this $1,000 on my desk and how it came into my possession, but I was excited and didn't think fast enough."[25]

His hand forced by Stenson's recitation, as well as that of State Treasurer D. Hale Brake, who in 1941 had been in the state senate, that a "barrel of money" had been spent to kill the bank bill, Rushton reluctantly ordered the Circuit Court of Ingham County, where the alleged bribe had occurred, to convene a one-man jury.[26] "Verbal request has been made by certain citizens, as well as members of the legislature, that a grand jury be called to investigate rumors current throughout the state that lobbyists and others interested have corrupted, or attempted to corrupt, members of the legislature," Rushton's mandate stated. "As to the truth of these rumors or statements, I have no knowledge. But the people of this state are entitled to know if this is true, and if it is true the offenders should be punished. We cannot have clean government when members of a legislative body are being influenced either by promises or by payment of money to pass or defeat legislation. I have been assured that necessary funds to cover expenses of such an investigation will be forthcoming, and that Governor Harry Kelly is in full accord with the investigation in the interests of clean government."[27] To his pals in the media, the feisty former district attorney stated his goals in a more earthy manner: "This is an attempt to clean out these fellows who hang around the Capitol to try to corrupt members of the legislature."[28]

IV Senate Bill 1, which was at the root of all the commotion, had been introduced by State Senator Brake and had as its goal remedying a loophole in Michigan's banking laws. Under existing statutes, branch banking was prohibited in Michigan except when the home bank was within the same county or within a radius of twenty-five miles. Michigan National Bank circumvented these stipulations by purchasing banks in Lansing, Flint, Battle Creek, Marshall, Port Huron, and Saginaw, all of which were then made part of the Michigan National system.

After court rulings upheld Michigan National's practice, small banks across the state which had formed the Michigan Bankers' Association were fearful that they could not compete with rates offered by their conglomerate competition and sought legislation to prohibit chain banking. The measure easily sailed through the House and narrowly passed the Senate, but was vetoed by Democratic Governor Murray D. VanWagoner, largely on the advice of his legal aide Byron Ballard, who also represented Michigan National Bank.[29]

In a spate of partisanship, leaders of the Republican majority in both houses demanded that the governor not exert pressure on his fellow Democrats and a few wavering Republicans to sustain his veto. With the majority party refusing to adjourn unless it got its way, and the minority equally insistent on not buckling under, a nearly five month impasse ensued. Finally on October 10, after failing to override the veto, Republicans temporarily conceded defeat.[30]

The following year, VanWagoner, in the heat of a re-election bid, flip-flopped and said if the legislation reached his desk again, he would affix his signature to it.[31] This selling out of Michigan National Bank in an effort to curry favor in rural areas and small towns was not enough, however, to forestall the governor's repudiation at the polls. In 1943, a similar bill was defeated, but in 1945 an anti-chain banking law cleared both houses and was signed into law by VanWagoner's Republican successor, Harry F. Kelly.

VOn Monday, August 23, senior Ingham County Circuit Judge Leland W. Carr named himself one-man grand juror and announced that he would not only issue any arrest warrants emanating from the grand jury, but also would preside over subsequent trials.[32] Rushton quickly clarified his role, stating that he expected to call between 400-500 witnesses and would personally interrogate them. While he would employ both Republican and Democratic special prosecutors to assist him to assure that the probe could not be construed as a partisan witch hunt, he insisted that he would hold the reins over his team. "I will see to it," he pontificated, "that the guilty, whoever they may be, are punished. This may lead to high places and to low places, but wherever it leads we will go. Nothing will be covered up, and no-one will be spared who has participated in the corrupting of the legislative branch of the government."[33]

Despite Rushton's assertions, most Capitol insiders knew that whatever success the probe might garner would come from Carr, not the attorney general. A member of the circuit court since 1921, the hulking sixty-year old jurist had achieved legendary status in Ingham County for his strict adherence to the letter of the law. Al Kaufman, a reporter for the *Detroit Times* recalled that Carr was "Mr. Jurisprudence . . . a jurist who wore blinders. If the law said you shall get fifty years for killing a man, you went to prison, notwithstanding the fact that he had raped your mother, your grandmother, and your three sisters. The law was the law, and you should have called the police."[34] Don Gardner, another youthful member of the Lansing press corps at the time, remembered Carr as a man who "spent his whole life aiming for the Supreme Court, and he didn't care how he got there."[35] Despite his hardline meting out of justice, Carr's integrity was unquestioned, and every newspaper editorial in the state concurred that Leland W. Carr was the best man to ferret out grafters who were in the taxpayers' employ.

Even before Governor Kelly ordered the Emergency Appropriation Commission to assemble on September 1 for the purpose of authorizing $150,000 to finance the grand jury, Carr had begun calling witnesses into his chambers in the Lansing City Hall. On Monday morning, August 30, State Treasurer Brake, while emphasizing that his testimony was hearsay, related that a senator and a representative had told him of being offered money to vote against the anti-chain bank bill, and that they knew of other lawmakers who had been approached with similar offers.[36]

Speaking to newsmen hovering outside Carr's office, Brake downplayed the value of what he had said to the judge. "My information concerning the men who offered to sell their votes might be of some help, but

I'm not too sure about it," he vacillated. "The information came to me in a rather roundabout fashion and mentioned two groups of three legislators each, both of which were willing to vote against the bill if they were paid. I have no information that the money actually was paid to them. I do know that not a dime was spent to influence votes in favor of the bill, and that I was never offered any money as the bill's sponsor."[37]

Following Brake's revelation, the *Michigan State Digest*, a Lansing political weekly edited by Edwin Goodwin, asked two questions which were doubtless on the minds of many of his fellow Michiganians: (1) Why did Brake not come forward with his story until two years had passed? and (2) If Brake was wilfully concealing evidence of a crime, should he not be considered an accessory after the fact in prosecuting those crimes?[38] The State Treasurer's response to these queries was a stony silence.

Goodwin also sought to impugn Stenson's tale of the mysterious man in a gray coat slipping money into the lawmaker's overcoat as it hung in the cloakroom of the House of Representatives. "Mr. Stenson is peculiarly susceptible to freak experience," wrote the vitriolic political satirist, who not coincidentally was a crony of Michigan National Bank Vice President and Republican kingpin Frank D. McKay. "Back a few months, having returned from a hurried trip to Washington, D.C., he explained to his constituents that he had 'talked with Navy Secretary Frank Knox' and that he now knew 'important naval secrets.' When the FBI caught up with him, he begged off. He had not talked with Knox and knew no secrets. He merely had hoped to impress his constituents with his importance. As a member of the House Committee on Corrections he purchased considerable furniture at the Ionia State Reformatory and had it delivered to his home in Greenland in Ontonagon County. When the invoice came, he did not pay. He expostulated that as a lawmaker he had 'done much for the Reformatory.' His inference was that he should not pay. The state repossessed his goods. On weekends during the legislative sessions, the State Police relayed him from post to post, all the way from Lansing to Ontonagon. On his third request for this hitchhike favor, the police declined. Up Ontonagon way he had trouble renting a building to the State Liquor Commission for a state liquor store. That he, oddly, finally found '$1,000' which someone in a naughty mood tucked in his conveniently hung overcoat appears as mere continuity of an increasingly remarkable and somewhat exciting career."[39]

VI

Snide remarks and smug tittering about Stenson's tale dramatically ceased among the Capitol denizens when, shortly after 9:00 a.m. on September 13, Lansing Municipal Judge Louis Coash, upon orders from Rushton, issued warrants against Republican State Representative William Green and Michigan National Bank Vice President Francis P. Slattery. The former, a sixty-three year old farmer and former lumberman affectionately referred to by his colleagues as "the little gray man of the House," was charged with soliciting a $600 bribe in 1939 from Floyd Trumble, a past president of the Lansing branch of the National Hairdressers Association, in return for casting a favorable vote on House Bill 364 which would have created a State Board to regulate cosmetology. The Grand Rapids financier was accused of offering a bribe "of great value" to State Representative George N. Higgins in May, 1941 in an effort to purchase a nay vote on the anti-chain bank bill.[40]

Escorted by State Police troopers, both men appeared before Coash at 2:30 that afternoon. After pleading not guilty and being released on $2,500 bond each, Green and Slattery faced reporters and passionately professed their innocence. "I never asked anybody for any money in connection with any legislation," insisted the lawmaker, his eyes showing both sadness and anxiety through his six-sided wire framed spectacles. "I might know Trumble if he came in here right now, and I might not. That's how well I knew him. I might have talked to Trumble because cosmetologists in my district asked me to, but I can't even remember whether he wanted me to be for the legislation or against it."[41]

Slattery, with Michigan National Bank counsel Byron Ballard at his side, was far more belligerent. Pressured by reporters to respond to being positively identified by Higgins as the man who had offered bribe money, the dapper banker, looking his role in a black three-piece suit with a gold watch chain draped across the vest, blurted: "I never paid anyone." Before his emotional client could elaborate, Ballard silenced him. "The charges are the most absurd thing I ever heard of," Ballard said. "I, as his attorney, will authorize him to make that statement."[42]

"Didn't you come to Lansing to lobby against the branch banking bill, both during the 1941 and 1943 sessions of the legislature?" hollered a member of the press.

"No," cut in Ballard before his client could utter a word. "He came down here to get information, but not as a lobbyist."

"You came down here as a representative of Michigan National Bank, didn't you?" burst forth another question.

"Yes."

"As a representative of Michigan National wasn't it your job to at least talk to legislators and try to get them to vote in your favor?" pressed the reporter

"Oh, sure," Slattery said sardonically.

Frustrated by the banker's reticence, Ken McCormick, the acerbic Capitol correspondent for the *Detroit Free Press*, bore into the heart of the issue, shouting: "Did Michigan National have a slush fund for the purpose of influencing legislators to vote against the bank bill?"

Momentarily caught off guard by the blunt query, Slattery stammered that if there had been such a fund he had never heard of it. Racing to his client's defense, Ballard said with legal suaveness: "What my client means to say is that there never had been such a fund and therefore he could not have been aware of one. No more questions."[43]

As Slattery was bustled off by his legal mouthpiece, reporters, perhaps for the first time, realized the seriousness of the graft investigation and the glory which would accrue to the members of the press corps most diligent in gleaning out information. The probe's offensive had now opened a second front, and the legislative enemy on the home-front, like the Axis powers overseas, was caught in a deadly pincer movement.

VII Heat turned into fire on September 23 when Floyd Trumble took the stand in a preliminary hearing before Coash. Under interrogation by Rushton, the hairdresser positively identified Green as the legislator who had tried to extort money from him.

"In April, 1939, I received a mysterious telephone call from a man who refused to identify himself," the witness said in a soft, hesitating voice. "He summoned me to a room in a Lansing hotel and cautioned me to come alone."

"Did you follow those instructions," Rushton growled.

"Yes, sir. I was admitted to the room by Representative Green. He demanded $600 for his vote and told me that was the least he would accept. Then he warned me that I should not mention the meeting and conversation because, he said, 'in a court I can state that you're a liar, and you can swear I'm a liar.'"

"Did you see Mr. Green after that?"

"Yes, sir," the witness nodded. "he later came to me and said that the deal was off."[44]

When Trumble concluded his recitation, the hearing was recessed to permit Green time to retain permanent counsel.[45] Rushton consented to the delay, saying that evidence was mounting so rapidly against Green and other potential legislative lawbreakers that "we have to stop and gather up all the loose ends of testimony so we won't go too fast and fall all over ourselves."[46]

One of the dangling issues was neatly tied up in October when State Representative Warren G. Hooper, an Albion Republican, took the stand before Judge Coash to testify that William J. Burns, executive secretary of the Michigan State Medical Society, had offered him a bribe to kill a health insurance bill (House Bill 215) in committee in the 1939 session. According to the witness, Burns had been opposed to the law including osteopathic practitioners, and he went to Hooper because the lawmaker also served as executive secretary of the Michigan Association of Osteopathic Physicians and Surgeons.

Under direct examination, Hooper admitted having several conversations with Burns regarding the proposed legislation and meeting with him in the House chambers, the lounge of the Lansing City Club, the Olds Hotel, and in Hooper's apartment.[47] He said that Burns told him: "Now I understand that your mother and father live in California. If this bill comes out of committee the way we want it to, without the inclusion of osteopaths, I could make it possible for you to go to California for a vacation with your family."[48]

"I told him I would not have a part in that," the balding, fish-eyed solon said with an air of moral superiority. "He very quickly turned to me, extended his hand, and said: 'I am glad to have met you, Mr. Hooper, but you are too honest.' I said, 'Thank you, Bill, that's the best compliment I ever had in my life,' and walked away."[49]

On cross-examination, defense counsel harped on the sensitive issue that had been raised previously against Brake: why did it take a grand jury probe to bring disclosure of lobbying irregularities? The chain-smoking Hooper, perspiring and doubtless in need of a cigarette to sooth his nerves, fidgeted as the initial loaded query was fired at him.

"Mr. Hooper, did you realize a crime had been committed when you made the statement you claim Mr. Burns made to you?"

"I'm not an attorney or law enforcement officer."

"No, you are not. But didn't you know that if anyone offered you a gratuity to influence your position on a matter pending before the legislature, that would be a crime?"

"I have heard that bribing is criminal," the witness admitted, wiping his shining brow with a handkerchief.

"So you did know," defense counsel reiterated for emphasis, "in March, 1939 that if anyone offered you a gratuity to influence your position in the legislature, that individual would be committing a crime?"

"Yes."

"Then, Mr. Hooper, as a public officer of the State of Michigan, why didn't you report it to the Ingham County Prosecuting Attorney or the Attorney General?"

"I did not report it," Hooper said thoughtfully, "because I felt it was a personal matter between myself and Mr. Burns, and I did not want to cause any trouble for him."

"Is that the only reason?"

"Well," Hooper blurted, as though insulted by the query, "it is not regarded as good form for the members of the legislature to report to the public authorities if anybody offers them a bribe, unless they are compelled to."[50]

With this simple statement of Lansing ethics, Hooper had opened the Pandora's box of graft. He was now a marked man, not only by the colleagues he had betrayed, but also by those afraid of what he might tell the grand jury in the future.

VIII

Yet another turning point for the grand jury occurred on the afternoon of November 30, 1943 when five-term State Representative Stanley Dombrowski, who earlier had told the grand jury that a lobbyist named Charles Hemans had summoned him to a room in the Olds Hotel in 1941 and promised to pay him $350 in two installments if he would vote against the anti-chain banking bill, repudiated his testimony. Standing before Ingham County Circuit Judge Charles F. Hayden, the burly ex-professional boxer wiped away tears while listening to the jurist recite his sworn statement.[51]

"You intended to go into court at the time of the trial of the case and repudiate your testimony?" Hayden inquired sternly.

"Yes, sir," the red-eyed legislator admitted, his face flushed. "I committed an awful crime. I didn't tell the truth when I testified before the grand jury."

"Have you been coerced into this action?"

"No, sir," Dombrowski said. "I am doing this voluntarily to get it over with."

"For the record, Mr. Dombrowski," Hayden asked angrily, "you are now saying that Charles F. Hemans never approached you in 1941 or any other time, and that the conversation which you told the grand jury never occurred?"

"Yes, sir."

"Will you later change this repudiation, too?" inquired Hayden sarcastically.

"I couldn't change it," the Detroit Democrat stated, "because it's the truth."[52]

Hayden peered down at the apparently contrite lawmaker, who had never even removed his overcoat during the proceedings. "I don't want to be vindictive or show any malice," the judge declared, "but the crime of perjury is one which subverts our whole system of government and justice. If things like this were permitted, chaos would result and dishonesty would run rampant. Your conduct is so far-reaching, so poisonous, it cannot be overlooked or dealt with lightly. I have no alternative but to sentence you to no less than three and one-half nor more than fifteen years in Southern Michigan Prison."[53]

While in the Ingham County Jail awaiting transfer, Dombrowski told Kenneth McCormick of the *Detroit Free Press* that he had perjured himself deliberately before Judge Hayden because he sought the sanctuary of incarceration to protect himself from his political enemies.[54] Nervously pacing his cell and wringing his hands, the haggard forty-two year old legislator told McCormick that he had become frightened when his grand jury testimony leaked out. "I was questioned by grand jury investigators on November 21," the reporter said Dombrowski had told him. "I told them I had accepted $150 from Hemans and had been promised $200 more after I voted on the bank bill. Then I went before the grand jury and made that statement. Then I went to my part-time job as a guard in the Wayne County Building and everybody seemed to know that I'd been before the grand jury. They pestered me so much that I had to quit. I took a job at the Ford Highland Park Plant. But this thing bothered me. Then last Friday [November 26] as I was driving on Conant I just turned the corner when a black car with two men in it came along. One of them shouted: 'You'd better change your position on that thing—or else.' I was so scared that I went to Lansing to deny what I had said to Judge Carr."[55]

"The truth," Dombrowski told McCormick, "is that during the 1941 session of the legislature I received a telephone call and was asked to go to a room in the Olds Hotel. I went there an hour later, and I understood that it was Hemans' room, and I met a man I don't recall having seen before, but who, as I remember it, or who as I understood, represented Hemans. He offered me $150 to vote against the anti-chain bank bill and promised I would receive $200 more after I voted. So what I told Judge Carr was a lie only because it wasn't Hemans who bribed me. I didn't even know I was pleading guilty to perjury. I thought it was contempt of court."[56]

The Dombrowski saga continued when Rushton and Hayden, having been told by McCormick of the new version of the story, paid a brief visit on the lawmaker. This time, Dombrowski repeated the yarn spun to McCormick, except he identified the mysterious bribe-giver as fellow Wayne County Democratic representative Walter N. Stockfish.[57] As he left the jail, Rushton shook his head ruefully. "You know," he confessed, "I can't tell when Dombrowski is telling the truth and when he's lying. But Judge Carr and I will get to the bottom of this strange case."[58]

Stockfish, a thirty-five year old five-term lawmaker, emphatically denied the validity of his colleague's claim. "I did not bribe him or anyone else or act as a payoff man," he asserted. "I am willing to appear before the grand jury at any time."[59]

Meanwhile, Dombrowski's attorney, Frank G. Schemanske, appeared before Hayden and moved to have his client's perjury sentence set aside. "My client," the barrister intoned, "is not guilty of perjury. He thought he was pleading guilty to a contempt charge. Moreover, he did not have counsel when he was sentenced, and no probation report was requested by Your Honor. His grand jury testimony was made under duress after he had been grilled for nine hours by grand jury investigators. He was in a complete state of fatigue and highly nervous as the result of methods used by questioners. His testimony that he was bribed by Charles Hemans was made solely to be freed from serious injury to his health."[60]

Rushton responded, by affidavit, that the legislator was fully aware that he had been cited for perjury and that no mention of contempt had been made. Roy E. Smith, the grand jury stenographer who took Dombrowski's statement, stated, also by affidavit, that Dombrowski had been "treated as a gentleman" and that he had "exhibited no nervousness."[61] After having the state's declarations read into the record, Hayden recessed court until December 21 at which time he would deliver his opinion.

Even though Dombrowski gave Lansing attorney, lobbyist, and former University of Michigan regent Charles F. Hemans a clean bill of health, his name resurfaced when Stenson tentatively identified the army major from a photograph as the mysterious stranger clad in a gray suit who had attempted to bribe him by stuffing money into his overcoat pocket. To attain absolute certainty, a grand jury investigator took Stenson to Washington, D.C., where Hemans was serving in the Provost Marshal's office. While Hemans dined at the Mayflower Hotel, Stenson hid in a nearby telephone booth peering at him. After several minutes, he emerged and positively fingered Hemans as the would-be dispenser of graft.[62]

Upon being informed of Stenson's statement, Hemans issued an immediate perfunctory denial. "I never saw Stenson to know who he was, and I do not know him," the stocky, dapper officer claimed. "I never talked with him, and it is my idea an attempt is being made to try me in the newspapers."[63] Suddenly an infectious smile burst across his countenance. "Besides," he chuckled, "anyone who knows me knows I haven't worn a gray suit in twenty years. And I haven't eaten in the Mayflower Hotel in ten years."[64] His protestations notwithstanding, Hemans knew it was simply a matter of time before he, too, would be summoned before Carr and Rushton, and that it would take more than personal charm to convince them of his innocence.

Four days before Christmas, Judge Hayden put the expected lump of coal in Dombrowski's stocking by denying his appeal. "There are no crimes that are more insidious and far-reaching in their evil effect than the crime of perjury and that of bribery to which the respondent testified," the judge stated. "Unlike crimes which affect only the individual or property, they defeat the administration of justice and the enactment of legislation in the interests of good government."[65]

IX Because of the purported leak in the Dombrowski case, Carr insisted on as much secrecy as possible. "We wanted little publicity," he explained to newsmen, "because a grand jury always functions best when its witnesses are not stirred up by headlines."[66] Oblivious to what the jurist had said, an over-eager reporter asked Carr to name his investigative staff. "It would be improper to disclose the identity of these investigators or for me to tell you how many of them we employ," he lectured the assembled press corps. "Moreover, contrary to what some may believe, we have never said we were through with our investigation. If some persons drew the conclusion we were through simply because we did not advertise what we were doing, that is not our fault. We have been hard at work, and we have covered a broad field of inquiry which I cannot discuss at this time. A grand jury must protect its secrecy."[67]

By this time, however, a public rift between the jurist and the attorney general already threatened to undermine, or possibly even destroy, the entire investigation. The dispute began on December 7, 1943, when Rushton, without prior consultation with Carr, appointed Jay W. Linsey, a prominent Grand Rapids barrister, to be chief grand jury prosecutor at a salary of $2,000 per month. The *Detroit Free Press* assailed the selection as an attempt by the attorney general to sabotage the probe before it could uncover the roots of legislative corruption.[68]

The crux of the tirade was not Linsey's legal prowess, but rather his one-time association with fellow townsman Frank D. McKay, whom the

Free Press had railed against for years because of his domination of Republican state politics.[69] So intent was the Detroit morning daily on impugning McKay at every opportunity, that before the first warrant was served by the grand jury, it ran a story predicting the imminent arrest of a prominent Grand Rapids financier—an obvious implication of McKay rather than the obscure Slattery.[70]

The politically astute out-spoken attorney general grasped the potential danger caused by his impetuous act, but characteristically opted to pursue a frontal assault against his critics, rather than a strategic retreat. "Jay Linsey is just the man I've been looking for. I'm convinced he can do a good job, that he has no prejudice, and is not a Republican politician or a tool of the McKay machine," he said gruffly to newsmen gathered at his office. "I have established that Linsey was never a regularly employed attorney for McKay. I find there is nothing whatsoever to the story that he was so friendly with Frank McKay that to appoint him would amount to handing the grand jury over to McKay. Besides, we can't hire a lawyer who has never had a client. I even discussed his hiring with Governor Kelly first."[71]

Unfortunately for the attorney general, his final comment brought an instantaneous denial from the chief executive. "I have not talked with Mr. Rushton about Mr. Linsey—period," Kelly replied hotly. "I'm not running the grand jury."[72] This denial from the popular and highly respected governor, coupled with the equally beloved Carr's icy "no comment" when asked about the hiring, placed Rushton in an even more precarious position in the public's mind.[73]

X The eye of this tempest, of course, was not Linsey, but rather McKay. A self-made banker, real estate magnate, and general entrepreneur whose estimated wealth at the time of his death in 1965 was $50,000,000, McKay was, above all else, the long-time political czar of the Michigan Republican party.

After serving three terms as state treasurer, he left office in 1931 under the cloud of a grand jury looking into his handling of state funds. During his stint in office, McKay claimed to have "smartened up" as a politician, driving across the entire state to gain support, especially in the often neglected upper peninsula.[74] At this time, he also mastered the art of political revenge by leading an intraparty revolt against three-term liberal governor Alex Groesbeck, who had opposed the conservative McKay's nomination for treasurer. Consequently, in the 1926 gubernatorial primary the incumbent was ousted by lightly-regarded Fred Green, who subsequently easily bested Democrat William Comstock in the general election.[75]

The new governor thanked his benefactor by appointing him chief legislative lobbyist and chairman of the highway and finance committees on the State Administrative Board. To further increase his influence, McKay used his ties with Green to manipulate Republican politics through control of party conventions. Joining with G.O.P. kingpins Edward Barnard of Detroit and William McKeighan of Flint, the three formed a triumvirate which dictated Republican fortunes for nearly two decades. So absolute was their authority that McKay could boast with complete truth: "Reporters who covered those conventions had an easy time of it. I would tell them the night before the convention what the ticket was going to be, and they could play cards all night."[76]

His ever-expanding power was accompanied by insinuations of corruption from foes in both parties. It was charged that McKay, as the guiding force behind Republican Governor Frank Fitzgerald (1935-1937, 1939), had urged his affable fellow Irishman to ignore widespread illegal gambling operations in several of the largest, and most Republican, counties, and that Fitzgerald had instructed the State Police to curtail their investigations into such crimes.[77] Furthermore, stories circulated that "The Boss" had utilized his clout to have friends appointed to such key positions as state purchasing director, chairman of the Michigan Liquor Control Commission, and chairman of the State Corrections Commission, and that he was extorting trade from banks and private businesses for his surety bond company through the use of state contracts. Moreover, as founder of the General Tire Company, McKay made certain that all state vehicles were fitted with his product. Worse than the obvious conflict of interest was the discovery that, while state treasurer, he had purchased from his own company—with state funds—hundreds of obsolete, flawed, and otherwise unusable tires which he then stored—also at state expense—in a local warehouse.[78]

Beginning in 1940, McKay was the subject of three federal grand jury probes charging him with receiving money from distillers in exchange for his influence in getting their products on the shelves of state liquor stores; using the mails to present the City of Grand Rapids with fraudulent bids on municipal bonds; and extorting $9,918 from Edsel Ford, president of the Ford Motor Company, on the pretense that the sum was necessary to defray party campaign debts. In each instance he was acquitted as his attorneys argued, with probable validity, that their client was the target of a political vendetta by United States Attorney General Frank Murphy, whose defeat for re-election as Michigan's governor in 1938 had been orchestrated by McKay.[79]

His reputation greatly sullied by the trials, by 1943 McKay had become anathema even to his protege Governor Kelly who was threatening to oppose his renomination as Republican National Committeeman the following year. McKay, however, steadfastly proclaimed his innocence of any wrongdoing, explaining to reporters: "I always played politics hard. We gave appointments to those who were loyal. That's the way you stay on top, and those are the rules of the game. But I never took anything from the state. I never gave money to a legislator in my life. Why should I have? I was doing pretty well for myself outside of politics."[80] Regardless of this disclaimer, by late 1943 Frank McKay was perceived by many Michiganians as an evil genius, and political fame and national acclaim would belong to the man who put him behind bars.

XI Following the Linsey appointment, Carr silently seethed for three days mulling over what he considered an unwarranted intrusion by Rushton into grand jury affairs. Then, on December 11, he announced his intention to name a special prosecutor of his own choosing. In a carefully worded release, the jurist set forth his perception of the situation. "Within a few days I shall appoint counsel to assist in the grand jury investigation," the proclamation read. "This is entirely satisfactory with Attorney General Rushton and also has the approval of Governor Kelly. This arrangement will give Mr. Rushton more time for the regular work of his department, which is particularly heavy at this time, and will be even more so when the legislature is convened in special session. He has given a large part of his time to the grand jury and, of course, will continue to take part in proceedings as much as possible. We worked together in close co-operation and our relations have been at all times friendly and congenial. I respect his ability and integrity and capacity for hard work. I do not want it construed that he has been shoved out of the picture. I have not thought that anyone could or would ever construe it in that way."[81]

Piqued, Rushton responded with resentment to what he considered a blatant invitation by Carr to divorce himself from the probe. In a formal written reply, the attorney general was noble. "I am only a citizen, and if my not being too prominent in these proceedings will help the court to gain its objectives, then I feel I should not appear very often," the letter stated with apparent altruism. "In view of the attitude of some of the newspapers and the unfounded accusations made, I believe it is just as well for you to take full charge. This will prevent those people who are trying to sabotage the grand jury from going any further. Therefore, I am making available to you the unspent balance of $24,126.23 from the legislative appropriation of $40,000 from one account and $100,000 from another."[82]

To newsmen gathered at his office, however, Rushton vented his true feelings. "I'll be delighted to step aside if that is the court's wish," he said, his eyes unable to hide the pain and fury welling within his outward composure. "Remember, I receive no additional compensation for serving with the grand jury. My payment has been hard work, unjustified criticism for some of my decisions, and slanders upon my character by persons outside the grand jury. I have the highest respect and deep affection for Judge Carr, whom I know to be an able judge. But it now seems that my presence in the grand jury room is embarrassing because of attacks that have been made upon me. This seems clear from the language in the judge's statement. What happens to me is not so important as having a successful grand jury. Rather than embarrass the grand jury investigation, especially one as important as this one, I'll be tickled to death to step aside and once more devote full time to the job of being attorney general—and believe me, this should be a full-time job. Of course, I shall continue to co-operate in every way I can with the grand jury and the conduct of any resulting trials."[83]

For his part, Carr chose to ignore Rushton's verbal insincerities and replied with an equal lack of candor that he appreciated the attorney general's promise of assistance.[84] "Our relations in the past have been wholly congenial and harmonious, and I certainly do not want any change in this regard," Carr assured Rushton through an impersonal press release. "I am confident that the present situation will work itself out within a very short time and that the investigation will proceed in a manner satisfactory to all of us who are so vitally concerned in it."[85]

In the meantime, the grand juror closeted himself with several prominent attorneys, including Burritt Hamilton of Battle Creek, to discuss possible choices for special prosecutor. Hamilton, one of the most respected legal minds in the state, urged consideration of his junior partner Kim Sigler. In deference to his old friend, Carr agreed to interview Sigler, and he came away deeply impressed with the dapper forty-nine year old barrister's enthusiasm.[86] On December 14, Carr made Sigler's appointment official, describing his newest assistant as "one of the most noted criminal lawyers in Michigan" and a man who possessed "a splendid background of twenty-five years of courtroom experience."[87] Unable to resist a jab at Rushton's nominee, Jay Linsey, the judge added that Sigler had established "a very good reputation in the legal profession."[88]

Tracked down by avid reporters, Rushton was hounded into commenting on Carr's selection. "He is a capable lawyer and a good trial attorney," Rushton sneered. Wheeling abruptly, he added as he slammed the door to his inner office behind him: "That's all I have to say."[89]

XII Kimber Cornellus Sigler, whose name had been shortened in his youth as a reflection of the popularity of Rudyard Kipling's *Kim*, was the complete opposite of his new employer. Carr viewed the law as his entire life, whereas Sigler, the son of a wealthy Nebraska cattle rancher, had pursued a variety of careers as a cowboy, boxer, football player, and factory worker before settling into the legal profession. Carr was humorless and stern, while Sigler was a garrulous, flamboyant, astute courtroom technician who reveled in theatrics before juries. The gray-haired, pachydermatous jurist wore clothes merely to cover his frame and was so careless of his appearance that he earned the sobriquet "Old Gravy Vest" from the Lansing press corps. The handsome Sigler, by contrast, chose clothing to adorn his broad-shouldered, trim-waisted physique. Selected from a wardrobe reputedly containing forty-seven different suits, a typical Sigler ensemble would be a wide-billed coal black hat, light gray fitted Chesterfield topcoat with a black velvet collar, blue pinstripe suit, starched white shirt, flaming maroon tie and matching pocket handkerchief, pearl gray vest with white piping, ruby cuff links, two-tone gloves matching his shoes, spats, and a walking stick. Thus garbed, and with his Barrymore-like profile and iron gray hair, Sigler cut a dashing figure. It was for these differences that Ingham County Prosecutor Victor C. Anderson, a protege of Carr, expressed reservations to his mentor concerning the new special prosecutor. The jurist urged patience, and soon Anderson was echoing Carr's admiration for Sigler's diligence and skill.[90]

Always confident to the point of arrogance, Sigler harbored no doubts as to his mission. Judge Carr informed the new special prosecutor that the reason for his appointment was that the jurist distrusted the Rushton-Linsey intimacy with Frank McKay. Sigler, who already thought of the Grand Rapids politico as a personification of every evil that plagued American government, correctly interpreted the judge's remarks to mean that the ultimate target of the grand jury probe was to be McKay.

Invigorated by the thought of eradicating malfeasance, Sigler threw himself into his work, writing his long-time friend and political advisor William R. Cook, editor and publisher of the *Hastings Banner*, that the job was terrific and "so completely all-absorbing that it demands and receives every second of my time from awakening in the morning until falling asleep."[91] In other correspondence with Cook, Sigler had expressed the awesomeness of his duties in different terms, saying: "I've gone into this job with a feeling inside of me that I've never had before. It seems as if from somewhere there comes an impelling force that leads me on with greater political strength and determination than I've ever known before. Political considerations seem as nothing. Publicity seems infinitesimal. Somehow I feel obsessed with but one ambition, and that is to go down through the middle of this thing with all I've got, without the slightest regard for whom it may hit. I want to so conduct the affairs of this grand jury so that you, Cook, and the other friends who believe in me, will always be proud of it."[92]

As to the contrast with Carr, Sigler wrote: "In many ways, he [Carr] is a great, big wonderful man. He has the greatest knowledge of fundamental law of any judge or lawyer I've ever come in contact with. He is so stalwart and strong, patient, conservative, kind, and somehow seems to possess those qualities which I need. I guess it is generally being understood that he and I make a team, and I suppose this is because we are so entirely different. I know what 'my mission' is, and it seems as if every expression of my entire life has been training me to accomplish that mission."[93]

When Cook cautioned Sigler that, as a former Democrat, he ought to go easy on assailing McKay and other prominent Republicans if he hoped to advance within that party, Sigler, whom Kenneth McCormick described as having the "guts of a burglar," dismissed any fears and explained his strategy airily. "You spoke of Frank McKay and some other big shots," he wrote his friend. "Don't worry, Old Top. I have my heavy artillery constantly trained on them, and one of these days I expect to blow them out of the water. It may take some time, and there may be a number of other indictments in the meantime, but you can rest assured that I'm going to give them all I've got, and the funny thing about it, Bill, is that they all know it."[94]

XIII Less than a week after Sigler's appointment, the grand jury was racked again by dissension when Rushton proclaimed he was standing by his intention to employ Linsey. To rub salt in the wound, Rushton told reporters that Linsey would start work immediately at a salary of $2,000 a month, and that since he did not have the funds in his budget to pay that amount, "the money will have to come from the grand jury appropriation."[95] Asked if he had conferred with Judge Carr regarding the decision, the crusty attorney general snarled: "Oh, sure. I asked everybody, including the Supreme Court. It doesn't make any difference what Judge Carr thinks. After the grand jury is finished and some people are indicted, then the attorney general takes charge and begins prosecution. The two phases are separate and distinct."[96]

As might be expected, Carr's stance was at variance with that of Rushton. "The grand jury rests solely in my hands, and I will leave no stone unturned until this matter is cleared up to the satisfaction of the people of the state of Michigan. I believe the man who goes through the detail work of the grand jury investigation is far better prepared to proceed with the prosecutions than someone brought in from the outside," the grand juror decreed sharply. "I refer, of course, to Kim Sigler, whom I appointed last week to carry on the grand jury work. After the indictments are made, Sigler would be a better prosecutor than anyone else. Perhaps the best way to settle this would be an opinion from Governor Kelly."[97]

While the decision was pending, Sigler sought to influence the chief executive's decision by making public a recommendation to Carr that John Dalton, a forty year old grand jury investigator who had been hired by Rushton at a stipend of $400 monthly, be removed because he had chauffeured Frank McKay from Lansing to Grand Rapids in the attorney general's state-owned Buick on grand jury time. Sigler related that Dalton had admitted making the trip on orders from Rushton and that McKay had asked him about the grand jury probe. According to the Special Prosecutor, Dalton recalled that the G.O.P. boss stated that he "didn't like grand juries because you never know where they're going to stop, and they are a lot of trouble to people."[98]

Acting upon Sigler's evidence, Carr released Dalton from duty but refused to be quoted regarding the specific reasons for his action. When reached by reporters, the portly Dalton, who carried more than 250 pounds on his rather squat frame, said only that he had been taken to the grand jury "hideout" at Jackson on December 18 and had been questioned at length that night about the McKay incident. Wavering between anger and tears, he ran his hands through his red hair and shouted that he was "tired of being bullied, questioned, and interviewed." Defensively, he added that he had not disclosed any grand jury secrets because he did not know any, and that the car was not Rushton's, but a "borrowed red Pontiac."[99]

To no-one's surprise, Rushton was beside himself with rage. His face florid, he fairly screamed to reporters that he had never given any orders to Dalton, saying that his position was merely to suggest that if Dalton were going to Grand Rapids it would be a kind gesture to invite McKay. "The whole thing is really too silly to talk about," he said. "But as to Mr.

Sigler and his role, I will say again that as far as I'm concerned, the attorney general is the state's prosecutor. I have already appointed Linsey as special assistant attorney general, and he will try the grand jury cases."[100]

Linsey, busily at work in the attorney general's suite, said simply that he was determined to prosecute the upcoming graft cases and did not care if Carr preferred another attorney. "I don't think that will make any difference," he smiled. "The decision rests with the attorney general and Ingham County Prosecutor. I don't know what part Sigler might play in the trials. I consider him a very good man, but his work is in connection with the grand jury and mine will be in connection with the trials."[101]

As newspapers trumpeted the controversy across the state, it seemed that Lansing was treating the citizens to an expensive pre-Christmas farce. Yet, behind the scenes, Sigler, having been named as an Assistant Prosecutor for Ingham County, was working at a furious pace, often putting in twenty-hour days, in an effort to centralize and co-ordinate grand jury power within his control.[102]

XIV During the Carr-Rushton-Linsey-Dalton imbroglio, Sigler spent hours quizzing legislators to uncover details of alleged corruption. Despite the mandatory cloak of secrecy surrounding grand jury proceedings, astute observers predicted an impending explosion. Bleary-eyed, sullen, stoop-shouldered lawmakers from both political parties emerged from Sigler's office suite in a seemingly endless procession. An "official leak," possibly from Sigler, relayed that even Judge Carr, who had been holding court across the street from the Capitol for twenty-five years, was amazed to find that more than half of the senators and representatives interviewed admitted to accepting bribes and that, if the trend continued, by the time the legislature convened on January 31, 1944 more than one-third of its members could be under indictment.[103]

Despite bipartisan involvement in wrongdoings, it was also forecast that Republicans would gain from the grand jury revelations. Frank Morris, veteran *Detroit Times* Lansing correspondent who was whispered by his colleagues to be "friendly" with McKay, predicted that the grand jury would elevate Carr to his long-coveted seat on the state supreme court, and that Sigler, whom he described as a man with the "homely philosophy of a small town, the glamour of brightly lighted streets, the self assurance of a Texas cowboy, the meekness of a guy checking his hat at an expensive hotel, and the emphatic honesty of a mirror," would be the successor to Harry Kelly as governor.[104] Neither man cast a frown or issued a disclaimer to the prognostication.

XV

The dawn of a new year ushered in the fading away of both Rushton and Linsey as viable participants in the grand jury when Frank McKay offered them his moral support. "According to what happened to John Dalton," McKay fumed, "anyone who even shakes hands with me is forevermore contaminated. Both Linsey and Rushton are victims of gross injustice."[105]

Having received this kiss of death, on January 3, 1944 the attorney general bitterly announced his withdrawal from all pending and future grand jury prosecutions. "I will not intervene in any cases, even though it is my right as attorney general," he stated tersely. "If I am asked for legal assistance by Ingham County Prosecutor Victor C. Anderson, I will send any assistant from my office that he wants. He and Sigler can take care of everything. I am doing this so that there cannot be the slightest inference that I may be interfering with the grand jury. After all, Judge Carr is responsible for the successful outcome of this grand jury, and Judge Carr doesn't want me in the court room."[106]

As to Linsey, Rushton was apologetic. "It grieves me that I got him into this mess," the attorney general said, his eyes brimming with scorn. "The trouble all arose because he handled a couple of minor cases for McKay. Linsey is now at work in Grand Rapids on his own private law business, and he is not likely to return to Lansing to work for the state unless I call him. Linsey doesn't want to participate in the grand jury prosecutions now. The whole thing is embarrassing to him. He cannot afford to have his name smeared by insinuations, nor can he come to Lansing to work permanently at the $500 per month salary my other assistants receive. I never had any agreement with him about salary. I asked what he could come to Lansing for and permanently work for the grand jury, and he said $2,000 per month and expenses. If he had worked for the grand jury that salary would have been possible. The $100 a day that Sigler is receiving as Judge Carr's assistant is fair for a man of his experience, but I just can't pay Linsey $2,000 a month."[107]

When asked by reporters if he intended to seek re-election to a third term, Rushton was ambivalent. "I don't intend to," he said thoughtfully. "I have been much happier in private practice than in public and political life. I don't care to go through this again. I'll run only if I am compelled to by this unwarranted criticism."[108]

Before the press conference concluded, Rushton detailed his views on the causes of legislative graft and what punishment he felt would be appropriate for the crime. "I would recommend all sentences be for no more than six months and fine of no more than $200," the six-year veteran of the state senate said somberly. "The $200 fine will pay the cost of bringing them to Lansing for questioning—or to confess. With pay fixed at $3 a day for the members of the legislature, how can the state expect them to be immune from bribery? These poor guys come down to Lansing to perform a public service. They grope around for a dollar-a-day room and for ten cent dinners. They are honest men when they get here. But along comes a man with a satchel full of $100 bills. So what do they do? They help themselves and then go to church on Sunday and offer thanks for this bounteous life. Don't forget that they have wives and children at home who they must feed and house and clothe. How can the state expect honesty at $3 a day."[109]

"The question of penalties is one cause of my differences with Judge Carr," he continued, aiming well-placed barbs at both the grand juror and Sigler. "I have been insisting that six months in jail is sufficient penalty. The bribe takers would suffer the greater penalty of being publicly disgraced, and they would be prevented from holding public office for the rest of their lives. That is enough. Let them serve six months and then go home to feed their families. Judge Carr contends that they have violated their constitutional oaths of office. Constitution—Hell! These poor guys don't know the difference between the Constitution and the Declaration of Independence. My make-up wouldn't allow me to gloat over sending even one of them to jail. I would feel worse than they would. The real trouble in this grand jury is that too many people are parading in the hope of capturing newspaper headlines."[110]

With his opponents cast aside, Sigler had an open field and for the first time his well-known arrogance, which he had sublimated since his appointment, burst forth. When asked by reporters what he intended to do about newspapers that had editorialized against the grand jury, Sigler's eyes shone with malicious glee. "To hell with them," he sneered. "I know there will be efforts to besmirch me and frustrate the grand jury. But if anyone thinks they can stop the grand jury, they will get a big surprise party. We've got a big job to do, and believe me, we are going to do it."[111]

CHAPTER TWO

CHARLIE AND HIS LITTLE
BLACK BOOK

The new special prosecutor's mettle was soon tested, as on January 22, 1944, just nine days before the opening of the special legislative session called by Governor Harry F. Kelly, Judge Carr ordered State Police troopers to serve arrest warrants on twenty members of the 1939 legislature and six finance company executives for their purported roles in the largest payoff scandal in Michigan's political history. The alleged bribes, which Sigler stated exceeded $25,000, were in connection with Senate Bills 85 and 166, which tightened regulations on automobile finance companies in an effort to afford car buyers greater protection. Upon enactment, these measures compelled finance companies to: 1) hold a repossessed automobile for ten days before disposing it so that the original owner had a chance to redeem his purchase; 2) hold a public auction sale on the automobile if the original owner had paid more than 50 percent of the contract price; and 3) notify the original owner of the time and place of the sale. Bribery was also said to have taken place on Senate Bill 41 which cut small loan interest rates, including those on automobiles, from a flat three percent per month to a rate of three percent monthly on loans under $100 and 2.5 percent on loans above that amount.[1]

All three Detroit newspapers as well as virtually every outstate daily devoted a full page to biographical sketches of the accused lawmakers, with each blurb accompanied by an unflattering photograph. By nightfall of January 23, the state's residents were familiar with every man charged with violating his public trust. Objects of this unwanted notoriety were Detroit Democrats William G. Buckley, Adam W. Sumeracki, Walter N. Stockfish, Stanley Dombrowski, Martin A. Kronk, Joseph J. Kowalski, Francis J. Nowak, Earl C. Gallagher, and Edward J. Walsh, all of whom were still serving in the House of Representatives, and former Detroit

Democratic House members Joseph L. Kaminski, Ernest G. Nagel, and Michael J. Clancy. State Senators Charles C. Diggs, the sole black in the legislature, Leo J. Wilkowski, and ex-Senator William F. Bradley, all Detroit Democrats, were also charged, as were three upper peninsula Democrats, ex-Senators D. Stephen Benzie, Henry F. Shea, and former Representative Isadore A. Weza. Republicans named in the warrant were Representative Miles M. Callaghan, who had been in the Senate in 1939, and Senator Jerry T. Logie. Finance company officers cited were Abraham Cooper, Mark S. Young, Ernest W. Prew, and Samuel Hopkins, all of Detroit, and John Hancock and George Omacht of South Bend, Indiana.

Reaction to the news of the grand jury warrant came quickly. Abraham Cooper, President of the Union Investment Company, declared his innocence in a hastily called news conference. "My company has had two attorneys in Lansing to keep us informed on legislation that might affect us, but that is common practice," he asserted. "Neither I nor my associates have anything to conceal, and we will co-operate fully with the grand jury in whatever they may wish of us."[2] Former Representative Kaminski, previously indicted with William Buckley for allegedly splitting a $100 bribe on a chiropody bill, said he was "surprised" he was named, but beyond that refused comment.[3] Ex-Senator Bradley laughingly stated: "I'm entirely innocent. This is the first time I've ever been in trouble— excepting, of course, that time I slugged a policeman."[4] Callaghan, one of the deans of the Capitol in years of service, remarked softly: "Well, if Judge Carr and Mr. Sigler believe the warrant is the right thing for them to do, I have no complaint. But I know nothing about vote buying in the Senate."[5] Nagel, a fifty year old former balloonist and pugilist, was drunk and unable to post bail when he was brought in and spent two days in the Ingham County jail before his colleagues collected a sufficient sum to extricate him.[6]

Unlike Nagel, who posed for photographers and chatted amiably with the press, other indicted elected officials either would not talk to reporters or, like Benzie who was in New Mexico on lumber business, could not be found.[7] As a public display of support for good government, Wayne County immediately suspended Nowak and Bradley who were employed as clerks in the Tax Research Department, Gallagher who was serving as a Deputy County Clerk, and Wilkowski and Kronk, both tax clerks in the County Treasurer's office.[8]

The *Flint Journal* captured the essence of public reaction in an editorial entitled "These Graft Charges." After reminding its readers that those named were entitled to a presumption of innocence, it placed the blame for the alleged corruption squarely on the shoulders of the voters. "The public can be impressed with its own responsibility," the *Journal* lectured, "especially with the approach of a general election. Too little attention is paid to the qualifications of aspirants to political office and too little encouragement is given worthy citizens who might be induced to serve. The mess at Lansing will prove worth the price if it awakens every township, village, and city in the state to a determination that the best available timber be enlisted for public service."[9] With such noble aspirations being attributed as its ultimate goal, the worth of the grand jury as a tool of democracy now was unquestioned in the popular psyche. Lawmakers who doubted its value were engulfed by a cloak of suspicion that they feared discovery if the probe progressed.

The validity of the prosecution's blockbuster allegations was strengthened when, within forty-eight hours of the warrant's issuance, Ernest W. Prew, Vice President of the General Finance Corporation of Detroit, and his attorney, Guy Bratton, appeared at Sigler's office. After a brief consultation, the three men strode into Judge Carr's courtroom. The distinguished forty-nine year old defendant stood before the judge, removed a sheet of paper from the inside pocket of his gray business suit, and in a steady, deliberate voice read his prepared statement. "In my effort to assist in the prevention of certain proposed legislation adversely affecting the interests of our business, I, unwittingly, became the victim of vicious circumstances existing in the legislative halls of our state," he declared. "Although I had considered that my participation in such effort had been within the law, my counsel now advises me that my conduct amounted to participating in the doing of a lawful thing in an unlawful way, so that I am technically guilty as charged. Finding myself in the predicament of being engulfed within the meshes of legislative graft, I foolishly permitted myself to become a part of this without realization of the legal significance of it. It moved with such rapidity and was so involved that I did not do what I should have done, namely communicate all the facts to my officers and directors. The whole thing has bothered me for some time, and I believe it is my duty in the interest of this government to plead guilty and save further expense and effort on the part of the state. Therefore, I plead guilty."[10] Carr accepted the plea and placed Prew under $2,500 bond. The phalanx of denial had been blown apart and Lansing observers anxiously awaited the fallout.

II Before the grand jury could progress, however, it had to surmount a formidable obstacle. When the special session of the legislature met it had to vote on whether to grant Judge Carr latitude to use the $150,000 grand jury appropriation to investigate allegations of malfeasance in all state agencies or to confine the probe to the legislature. A potential floor fight arose when Attorney General Rushton, still smarting over what he considered to be his forced resignation, informed the twenty-five man State Emergency Appropriation Committee, known in Lansing political circles as the "Little Legislature," that Carr was exceeding the authority granted the grand jury by permitting Ingham County Prosecutor Victor C. Anderson to examine the records of the highway department and liquor control commission. "No prosecuting attorney can broaden a complaint made by the Attorney General," Rushton blustered. "He can file such a petition only on behalf of his county. You have no authority to defray the expenses of such an investigation."[11]

Republican Senator Otto W. Bishop of Alpena sought clarification. "If we have the authority to appropriate the money," he inquired, "can't we allow it to be used for a broadened investigation and to cover the cost of trials?"

"No, sir, you cannot," Rushton shot back sarcastically. "My original petition was for an investigation of the legislative branch. Broadening of the scope was not included in my petition and must be an obligation of Ingham County. This commission has no authority to do as Judge Carr wants."[12]

Sigler, barely able to contain his scorn for his obdurate predecessor, sought permission to speak. "Gentlemen," he said, his handsome features locked in grim determination, "if the state doesn't want to appropriate the necessary funds to let Judge Carr and myself clean up this dirty mess in Michigan, I'll try the cases for nothing a day."[13] He then resumed his seat amid an eruption of spontaneous applause emanating primarily from the Republican members.[14]

Senator Don VanderWerp, Republican of Fremont, asked Rushton if the legislature itself could appropriate the money specifically to meet Carr's request. "There is no limitation on the powers of the legislature," the Attorney General reluctantly admitted. "It can even appropriate money for private purposes."[15] Smiling, VanderWerp stated, "Well, if we have the authority to handle this matter in a special appropriation bill, we will see that this is done."[16]

Representative John Espie of Clinton County, chairman of the G.O.P. dominated House Ways and Means Committee, stated that such a measure had already been discussed and would be viewed with favor in the lower chamber. In somewhat less than altruistic terms, Espie urged his fellow solons to muster support for the grand jury. "We've started the clean up so let's do a thorough job," he urged. "Until it is done, every member of the legislature is under suspicion. Any member who opposes the bill will be in an awful spot back home and here when he tries to explain his position."[17]

A hush fell over the committee when aged Miles Callaghan, still respected and beloved despite his indictment, sought recognition. "Nothing should be done by this body that would hamper Judge Carr or his associates in carrying on a full and complete investigation," he insisted with sincerity. "I surely want him to have the funds to do all that is necessary to make a thorough and complete investigation, no matter whom it hurts. I have confidence in Judge Carr and his associates that it will be done. We must give him any support that we can."[18] Following this dramatic plea, there seemed to be little doubt as to the course to be pursued, but even though Judge Carr's position won an easy victory in the House, the margin in the Senate was an ominously narrow four votes.

The following day, Saturday, January 29, Callaghan, whose once husky frame had wasted away to that of a skeleton barely covered with flesh, appeared before Carr. Flanked by his attorney, Claude Marshall, and Sigler, the state representative explained his presence in court. "Judge," he began in a quavering voice, "I'm seventy-seven years old. I've made some mistakes in my life, like all people who have lived a long time. I've been fifteen years in the legislature. At my age I can't hope to live too many more years. I'm not in very good health and neither is my wife. If I can make a contribution to good government by helping to clean up what appears to be a dirty mess, I desire to do so. For that reason I am pleading guilty to the charge."[19] Like Prew, Callaghan was released on $2,500 bond and was given by Sigler both immunity and a fee of $100 a month, under the alias of "Herb Cook," to be a grand jury informant.[20]

III The grand jury was confronted by another potential crisis on February 1 when famed New York columnist and radio newscaster Walter Winchell reported that Carr and Sigler had employed Charles Spare as a special investigator. "Nightshirt Charlie" was a former member of both the Ku Klux Klan and Black Legion and was well-known for defaming Jews, Blacks, and Catholics. In the state senate, Democrats futilely beseeched their colleagues to curtail further funding for the grand jury until Carr explained Spare's hiring. Senator Stanley Nowak, a Detroit labor organizer, passionately recounted Spare's role in instigating disgruntled white factory workers, particularly at the Packard plant, to strike, causing the loss of millions of man-hours of war production.[21] Charles C. Diggs, a black, expressed doubt whether he or any of his Roman

39

Catholic co-defendants could expect justice from an account submitted by a Klansman.[22] To assure that Spare's employment could not be denied, Rushton, ever willing to hurl a barbed lance at Carr, volunteered the information that Spare was listed on grand jury records as "Charles Allen."[23]

Both Carr and Sigler angrily refused comment, but within the week they announced that Spare had been relieved of his duties. However, six months later Sigler, who for reasons known only to himself considered Spare invaluable, secretly rehired the purported bigot and for nearly seven months paid him a total of $3,947.32 in salary and expenses under the pseudonym of "Mary Duke." Only when Sigler was removed from office was Spare's name permanently deleted from grand jury ledgers.[24]

Having weathered this turmoil, Sigler devoted his efforts to interrogation of those indicted in the finance conspiracy warrant. One by one, defendants were compelled to peer into the Special Prosecutor's steely eyes and listen to him state in a harsh, bitter voice: "Come clean, fellow. You might as well confess. I'm going to convict you anyway, because you're guilty. I'm going to send you to prison."[25]

On the eve of the pre-trial examination, Sigler instructed Capitol correspondents on what to expect at 9:00 a.m. on Monday, February 28 when Judge Carr assumed the bench in his familiar Circuit Court room and rapped his gavel to signal the onset of the pre-trial examination. The state had only to produce enough evidence to hold the defendants for trial, the Special Prosecutor explained, thus some of the state's key witnesses might not be called to testify. Futhermore, he continued, because the legal procedures had been established by the Ferguson grand jury in Detroit and points of law regulating graft indictments had been clarified by the Michigan Supreme Court through the numerous appeals filed from that grand jury's convictions, the examination should not consume more than two weeks. It would be a sensational, ugly story, Sigler promised, but one that had to be revealed.[26]

The drama began thirty minutes late and with six defendants not in court. Two absentees were Prew and Callaghan who would be state witnesses. The others were Representatives Stockfish, Sumeracki, and Weza, to whom the United States Army refused to grant leaves of absence, and Stephen Benzie, upon whom the arrest warrant had not yet been served. The missing faces notwithstanding, there was no shortage of activity at the defense area, as fifteen attorneys and their aides crowded around the counsel table inside the railing. On the prosecution's side of the aisle, Sigler was joined by Lansing attorney Harold H. Warner, who had been assigned by Carr to assist the Special Prosecutor in preparation of evidence, and Ingham County Prosecutor Victor C. Anderson.[27]

As expected, before the first witness could be called, the battery of defense counsel challenged the authority of Carr who had issued the arrest warrants to preside over the hearing. The judge tersely denied the motions, citing a Michigan Supreme Court ruling which sustained the right of a one-man grand juror to be the examining magistrate at preliminary hearings of those whose arrest the grand jury caused.[28] Following the ruling, Sigler rose, smiled wanly at his throng of antagonists, and inquired mockingly: "Is the atmosphere all cleared now so we can proceed?"[29]

Receiving nothing but icy glares in response, the Special Prosecutor launched into an opening statement. "This will be a shocking story told in morning, afternoon, and even night sessions," he pledged. "It will be a story of votes bought and sold; of the use of money, liquor, beautiful women, and lavish entertainment to sway the votes of pliant legislators to the will of selfish special interests which had the money and contacts to obtain their way in the making or killing of laws. The State will produce surprise witnesses and a mass of evidence to substantiate its case, but we'll keep some of our stuff in reserve for the actual trial."[30]

Before calling his first witness, Sigler, uncharacteristically attired in a conservative blue-green business suit, introduced thirty-five deposit slips bearing the signature of John E. Hancock, Detroit manager for the American Discount Corporation, to show that $8,270.59 had been placed in a special account in the National Bank of Detroit during the period from January 2 to July 31, 1939, which corresponded to the legislative session. He also introduced eighty-two cancelled checks, including one made out to "J. E. Hancock, legislative committee," which had been endorsed by Hancock and deposited in his special account and more than 150 letters written by Hancock, many of which were addressed to lobbyist Charles F. Hemans.[31]

When defense attorney Joseph W. Planck objected to the introduction of these documents, Sigler, unperturbed, walked toward the defense table. "Be patient, brothers. If counsel doesn't get nervous, we'll get along very well," the Special Prosecutor said, forgetting that he had a partially filled glass of water in his hand as he flamboyantly flung open his arms in a gesture of friendship and nearly doused his startled adversaries. "Everything will tie up eventually. I'm just pouring concrete to create the foundation of a house of corruption in Lansing."[32] The motion was denied, and a parade of "verification witnesses" ensued.

Frederick B. Robinson, then manager of the National Bank of Detroit branch in the Maccabees Building, was called to identify Hancock's signatures on the checks and deposit slips and to swear that Hancock had opened the special account. Warren Whitehead, senior clerk of that bank branch, testified that Abraham Cooper opened a special account during the 1939 legislative session and identified numerous checks deposited into said account by Cooper, as well as more than twenty pieces of correspondence signed by the Union Investment Corporation head. Cooper's secretary, Mrs. Luella Earnest, admitted that her boss had met at least six times during December 1938 and January 1939 with defendants Prew, Hancock, Young, and Omacht. Adolph Demmer, catering manager at the Statler Hotel, stated that the finance company officials seated before him as defendants met several times in December, 1938 and January, 1939 at the hotel, while Wayne Otis, manager and treasurer of the Citizens Loan and Investment Company of Lansing, revealed that he had attended three or four of the meetings at the Statler.[33]

Having devoted the initial day to demonstrating the existence of a slush fund to purchase votes, Sigler, who was spectacularly adorned in a light brown suit and tan flannel vest with pearl buttons, used the second session to relentlessly pursue the trail of the money from the time it arrived in Lansing. Self-assured to the point of arrogance, Sigler turned to the press table, rubbed his hands together in glee, and said with a grin: "Put the nuts back on the buggy, Mary Ann. Here we go!"[34]

His first witness was fifty year old Ralph W. Smith, president of the Community Finance Company of Niles, Michigan, who testified that he and twenty-five or thirty other small loan company officials had been summoned by Abraham Cooper to attend a "congress" being held at Detroit's Statler Hotel on December 1, 1938. The purpose of the gathering, according to Cooper's invitation written on his firm's letterhead stationary, was to organize a special legislative committee to raise money with the intent of protecting the interests of small automobile finance firms which were threatened by detrimental bills in Lansing supported by Household Finance Company and other large lending institutions.[35]

"How was the money to be raised," Sigler asked the slender, well-tailored businessman.

"Cooper said we'd have to chip in—$50 for small companies and $100 for large ones. That unless we did this we would remain at the mercy of the big firms and always be behind the eight ball."

"For what purpose was the money to be used?" Sigler inquired, leaning toward the witness expectantly.

"The first round was to be used to hire a representative in Lansing to look after our interests," Smith said softly, stroking his thin gray mustache. "The next rounds would be used to contact legislators and doing whatever was necessary to get votes, like entertaining and other things."

42

"What other things?" Sigler inquired, still leaning on the rail by the witness.

"For buying votes, if necessary," was the matter-of-fact response.[36]

Defense counsel strenuously objected to the assertion that the funds would be used to bribe lawmakers. Carr agreed that the statement would be stricken unless further evidence brought out that the money actually had been given to one or more of the legislative defendants. Sigler smiled confidently and offered no argument.[37]

"Did you meet with George Omacht, counsel for the Associates Discount Corporation of South Bend, Indiana, at a later date?"

"Yes," Smith replied, remaining stiff in his chair, yet not giving an impression of being ill-at-ease. "George met me at Niles and said he was smoking out the Household Finance Company by offering so many amendments to the small loan bill Household was sponsoring that the objectionable features would be removed."

"Were you told the Household Finance Company was prepared to spend $50,000 to ease its bill through the legislature?" Sigler probed.

"It was said Household would spend a large sum, but I don't recall the specific amount."

"Did Omacht tell you at a later date that he had reached a compromise with Julian Thompson, Household's lobbyist in Lansing?"

"Yes," Smith stated. "Thompson said Household would help us defeat other detrimental legislation if we would help on a major small loan bill after certain amendments had been made."

Prancing before the defense attorneys, Sigler paused, and asked reflectively: "Oh, Mr. Smith, were there any names brought up as to a possible lobbyist for your group?"

"Yes," the witness replied with scorn, "Charlie Hemans was mentioned, but I objected because of his reputation. Besides, he was said to be representing other conflicting interests in Lansing. But it was decided to hire him anyway. Another Lansing lawyer, Claude Marshall, was named as being a good person to form laws and amendments of interest to us."[38]

On cross-examination, Walter Nelson tried in vain for more than two hours to break Smith's story. Finally, he asked the witness: "Don't you know that it is the duty of a lobbyist to talk to the members of the legislature and argue the merits of his proposition and that such action does not mean that money is being passed?" Indignantly, Smith countered: "That's true, but it was made plain when Hemans was hired that there should be more to the job than that."[39]

With the courtroom filled past seating capacity, Smith resumed the stand the following day to complete his testimony. Sigler then introduced a series of letters allegedly sent by Hancock to Hemans purporting to show that money had been sent to the lobbyist. Two were singled out by the Special Prosecutor, who dubbed them the "Old Mother Hubbard" and "Blood Pressure" correspondence. The first read: "Old Mother Hubbard's cupboard is bare, but I am enclosing herewith our check for $1,000 which is all we have today. As soon as I get sufficient funds to pay the balance you can rest assured I will send you a check promptly." The other was supposedly a reply to an urgent telegram from Hemans seeking money and said, in part: "I received your telegram and was very sorry to hear of the serious illness of the old exchequer. I am sure he will get well again—he always does. I have just $73.09 in the bank, so I am sending you $70, which is running the blood pressure of the old exchequer's brother very high and to the danger point. I have put through a few telephone calls for blood donors, and I hope to have in a supply of new energy within the next few days, at which time I hope we can make the transfusion."[40]

Claude Marshall was called to the stand to be the next target for Sigler's stinging jabs and jibes. "Mr. Marshall," Sigler asked, leaning forward and twirling his pince-nez spectacles by their black ribbon, "did you know that Charles Hemans was acting as a lobbyist for your finance company clients? That he maintained a two room suite at the Olds Hotel in Lansing, where he wined and dined lawmakers before securing their votes through payoffs made in the bathroom of his suite?"

"No, I did not."

"Did you ever talk to any of the sixteen legislative defendants here in court?"

"No, I did not," repeated Marshall.

"Did you know that defendant Francis A. Nowak was a constant visitor at Hemans' room and acted as an informer for Hemans?"

"No, I did not," came the familiar refrain.

"Did you know that Stockfish, Sumeracki, and Dombrowski received checks from Hemans for their votes on the very thing you were working on?"

"No, I did not," echoed again through the courtroom.

"But," Sigler inquired, "isn't it true that you thought you were leading the fight for those gentlemen who employed you?"

"Yes," Marshall stated, his lips pursed tightly, "I thought I was doing the work."[41]

Sigler then read into the record a letter written in March, 1939 by Marshall to Hancock, in which the Lansing barrister said: "I am more convinced than ever that Senate Bill 41 was perfectly lubricated before it was let loose in the Senate. I see that Senator [Felix] Flynn appointed on the committee of conference Senators [Earl] Burhans, the introducer of the bill, and [Earl] Munshaw, chairman of the State Affairs Committee."[42]

"Didn't you know at the time you wrote this letter that Hemans was paying money to the legislators and that is why you used the word lubricated?" Sigler shouted.

"I did not," snarled the witness. "A number of people had gone to the State Banking Department and presented their case in a very satisfactory manner and convinced the department through hard work. I don't wish to infer that the word lubricated had anything to do with Hemans or shady practices."[43]

On March 2, Miles Callaghan, wearing dark glasses, took the stand briefly to assist Sigler in setting the stage for what the Special Prosecutor knew would be the show-stopping witness. "In the 1939 session of the legislature," Sigler asked the white-haired gentleman who had just days before resigned his seat in the House, "did you accept $150, in the form of a cashier's check, from Major Charles F. Hemans to influence your vote?"

"Yes," Callaghan said in a low voice with head bowed .

"Was it in connection with Senate Bills 41, 85, and 166 that you accepted money from Mr. Charles F. Hemans?"

"According to the record, yes," replied Callaghan, adding, "I pleaded guilty to that offense. I found that I needed money and needed it badly because the depression had dissipated what once was a good income from my farm. I took the check with the understanding that I would go along with Hemans in support of a bill limiting maximum interest rates on small loans. I found out afterward that he expected me to support him on the finance bill, too."

"Did you know Hemans prior to January, 1939?"

"Yes, as a lobbyist for the meat packers and the cigarette interests at one time, but that was on the other side from the people I represented. I was interested in the farmers' problems. I wish to add that most lobbyists I have known have been lawyers, and some have been very high-grade men."

"Were you ever in Room 516 of the Olds Hotel—Mr. Hemans' room?"

"Yes," the witness said, a slight blush reddening his sallow cheeks. "I was there once that I remember. There was an elaborate bar and some whiskey bottles lying around. There were six or seven other legislators there, and they seemed to be doing pretty good."[44]

The Special Prosecutor had now completed the overture, and the audience eagerly anticipated the arrival of the maestro's heralded soloist. At

9:00 a.m., March 3, the courtroom aria began as Charles Fitch Hemans, wearing the uniform and insignia of a Provost Marshal Major marched forward to be sworn in, stopping to greet and shake hands with the defendants.

IV The Hemans family had a long record of public and community service. Lawton T. Hemans, a Mason farmer, had been a lawyer, member of the Constitutional Convention of 1908, author of a history of Michigan, member of the Michigan Historical Commission, chairman of the Michigan Railroad Commission, and unsuccessful Democratic gubernatorial candidate in 1908 and 1910. His son Charles, an affable, suave, dapper youth, quickly became a fixture in the Ingham County social whirl. After service in World War I, the younger Hemans graduated from the University of Michigan and received a degree from Detroit College of Law in hopes of following in his father's illustrious, and very large, footsteps. He practiced his profession in Detroit, Eaton Rapids, and Howell before hanging out his shingle in Lansing in 1928.

Charlie, as he was affectionately known by all who met him, had thought he would return to the Capitol City two years earlier, but was defeated in a bid for the state legislature. In 1933, his fortune took an upward turn when, riding on his father's statewide fame, he captured a seat on the University of Michigan Board of Regents. Three years later, however, he destroyed whatever chance he had of a career in politics when he threw an errant punch at Frank Murphy after the former Governor informed the brash barrister that the State Democratic Convention had denied him the nomination for attorney general.[45]

Not wishing to leave the glamour of the Capitol scene, Hemans utilized his charm and gregarious personality by becoming a lobbyist, peddling his services, like the prostitutes he frequented, for money.[46] Because he had numerous employers, he meticulously recorded all payments made to legislators in a mysterious little black book, which he never showed anyone. Possibly flushed with patriotism after the war had turned in the Allies' favor, but more likely because he feared the rising clamor for a probe into legislative graft, in 1943 Hemans enlisted in the army, using his legal training and past service in World War I to secure a cushy desk job with the Provost Marshal's staff in Washington, D.C. at the rank of major.

When the Ingham County grand jury convened, Rushton urged Carr to indict Hemans, whose unethical practices were by then legendary among Lansing insiders, but Carr refused.[47] The attorney general's insistence that

Hemans was a key figure was one of the underlying causes in the animosity between Rushton and the grand juror. Following Rushton's resignation, Sigler, cognizant of the value of Hemans to the prosecution's cases, urged Carr to offer immunity to the lobbyist in return for his testimony.

The grand juror, still bedazzled by his new associate, consented, but only if the rumored "little black book," which Hemans denied possessing, could be found. Sigler assigned the grand jury's chief sleuth, Leo Wendell, to recover the ledger. Wendell tracked down Heman's former secretary in Fort Wayne, Indiana, and she revealed that her former boss had moved all his business material to his family's farm near Lansing. Wendell braved a pitchfork-wielding caretaker and, in the hayloft, uncovered cardboard boxes stuffed with yellowing pages. Buried near the bottom was the black book. Sigler then accompanied Wendell to Washington, D.C. and induced the lobbyist to return to Michigan and testify.[48] Appearing before Carr on February 11, 1944, Hemans agreed to trade his information on the finance company bills in return for immunity.[49]

Over the course of the next two years, Sigler and Hemans developed an unusual relationship. The Special Prosecutor knew that Hemans could solve the mystery surrounding the anti-chain bank bill, the task for which the grand jury had been established. The egotistical witness was equally aware of his importance and made a series of escalating demands, including full immunity from all prosecution, threatening to turn mute if his conditions were not met. Despite the crudeness of such extortion, Sigler continually acquiesced and, immediately upon the major's arrival in Lansing, put him on the grand jury payroll under the assumed names of R. Millard and F. Benson. Through February 1945, Hemans received $150 monthly, with Sigler laundering the money by authorizing checks to the Chief of his State Police detail, Detective Sergeant Leo VanConant, who cashed them and delivered the funds to the would-be witness. In March, Hemans upped the ante to $450, and then for the following eleven months the lobbyist raked in $600 per month from grand jury coffers.[50]

The explanation as to why Sigler would make payoffs to acquire testimony to convict others who committed the same crime for far less money was simple: he honestly enjoyed Hemans' company and urbanity. Thus, to keep his new-found friend contented, the Special Prosecutor also authorized expenditures of $1,337.10 to house the lobbyist in an Olds Hotel suite, $601.04 for meals, valet service, and long distance telephone calls, $2,000 for travel to such diverse places as Washington, D.C., Cleveland, Texas, and Mexico, and unspecified amounts to provide high-priced Scotch whiskey and equally expensive prostitutes. The taxpayers even had to foot a $16 bill to replace a mattress ruined when Hemans, in a drunken stupor, urinated.[51] By contrast, the legal state expenditure for witnesses was $2 per day plus meals in the jail dining hall, the same was afforded jurors. Moreover, since Michigan statutes forbade use of paid testimony, Sigler was compelled to conceal the payments.[52]

The irony of this unholy alliance, which was the worst-kept secret in Lansing, virtually destroyed Sigler's credibility, which already was suffering as tales of his longstanding extra-marital relationship with his secretary Ruth Prentice and his reputation in his hometown for never paying his bills became common items on the gossip menu. Edwin Goodwin, never a friend of Sigler, went so far as to publish a poem belittling Hemans' "most-favored status" with the Special Prosecutor:

> The field of battle was not his,
> He never saw a fortress,
> He gained his fame in the Olds Hotel
> On a $16 mattress.
> A sportive army major
> Deluxe in soldier raiment,
> The highest known paid witness
> Was Hell-bent for entertainment.
> He was a lawyer in the Capitol,
> Prime lobbyist for bills,
> Passed laws with gifts of liquor,
> Dinners, cash, and frills.
> A strutful army major,
> With hatred for the Axis,
> But he got confused and fought the war
> On a $16 mattress.[53]

In all, more than $15,500 was spent on the debonair Hemans, who truly proved that the old adage was wrong: you could have your cake and eat it, too.

Beginning what would eventually turn out to be a five hour sordid tale, Major Hemans, whose shiny, slicked-down hair came to a point in the center of his forehead and gave him a Mephistopheles appearance, requested from Sigler the privilege of making an opening address. "The graft which I shall talk about has existed for at least a decade," stated Hemans, a grim expression masking his usually cheerful countenance, "and is all part of the system. It probably was not the fault of these people. Here was a condition in a system, under which logic and reason no longer obtained results in Lansing. I wish to God that the cup might have been passed from me so that I would not have had to do this thing, but it didn't. The condition had to be faced. Many of these members were honest men, perhaps, but because of the system they accepted money for their votes. I am here to tell the truth, which I must do unflinchingly. I am here as an officer in the U.S. Army, and the army is co-operating with the civil authorities to clean up this situation."[54]

Thanking the witness, Sigler then proceeded to have Hemans identify letters addressed to him from the indicted finance company officials and relate the circumstances surrounding his employment by these men as their lobbyist.[55] The groundwork thus laid, Sigler honed in on specific payoffs, and handed the Major the "little black book" to refresh his memory.

"How and where did you line the pockets of these legislative defendants?" the Special Prosecutor asked sharply.

"In small installments, usually in my hotel bathroom, which I called the 'library.'"

"Why was the money not paid in one lump sum?"

"Because if a man has something coming, he will not forget how he promised to vote," Hemans explained. "That is the going practice around here. Later, if their vote made no difference to the final result, I let them vote against my company's interests so that they could impress their constituents back home, if that was the popular way to vote."[56]

"Let us, Mr. Hemans, discuss briefly the money given to each of the defendants," Sigler requested, peering down at the witness through his beribboned glasses. "Did you ever pay Ernest Nagel any money?"

"I regret to say that I gave him $125," said the witness, removing his reading glasses after flipping pages in his black notebook. "And when I say that I regret to say so, I mean that I regret that I made those payments and that those who received them did so. Over a period of years there existed a situation which grew progressively and increasingly into a malignant situation. Probably Michigan is not the only state where it existed. It may have existed in others, but nevertheless such was the situation here in Michigan."

"Can you give us a word description of Ernest Nagel's actions when he would come to your hotel?" Sigler asked.

Staring at the bent-nosed, unkempt, ex-boxer slouched at the defense table, Hemans extended his hand palm upward and said with mirth: "I fear Shakespeare and Barrymore couldn't do that, but I shall do the best I can. I have known Ernest since he came to the legislature in 1933. He didn't talk much. He would usually come into my room, get a bottle, pour himself a drink, and sit beside the dresser. He would sit around awhile, come and go, and have little to say. A few times he said he needed money to pay his hotel bill. Besides giving him money, I bought him a suit of clothes and a hat."

"Former Representative Callaghan?"

"In all, $459," Hemans said. Then, shaking his head slowly, he added: "You know, I've known Miles well since 1929 when we were on opposite sides of the oleomargarine fight. We had a common interest in that we both own orchards. We used to talk about apples. I regard him as a very fine gentleman, but like many farmers, including myself, he found it hard sledding at the time, and I helped him occasionally."

"Earl Gallagher of Detroit?" Sigler continued, pausing to cast a glance at the bespectacled, beak-nosed lawmaker who sat with his head lowered, seemingly impervious to the events around him.

"Oh, I gave Earl a total of $125," Hemans replied airily. "You know, Gallagher would drop into my room about once a day. He drank moderately, but if he could not find a poker game he would stay until the fountain ran dry. Sometimes the libations would hold out until 4:00 a.m. Usually, though, I only put out enough to last until 2 o'clock. That way I could get some sleep because the brethren left when the font ran dry. There was a lot of liquor because we aimed to please. We didn't want to offend anyone just because we didn't have scotch or rye or bourbon. Why not? These finance company gentlemen were paying for it. Earl could usually find a card game though. Charlie Gadd, who was lobbyist for the Detroit Board of Education had one across the hall. The lobbyists for the City of Detroit operated a nightly game and so did Mr. Bonnier, another lobbyist. It wasn't hard to find a card game or an oasis in the Olds Hotel."

Directing his words to the downcast defendant, Hemans bantered: "Remember, Earl, you were going to be a father, and I promised you a baby buggy. It slipped my mind, and months later you wired me to forget the buggy and send a bicycle instead."[57]

After the gallery ceased chuckling, Sigler resumed his legislative litany and elicited from Hemans accounts of payments of $100 each to Representatives Buckley and Kowalski, $150 to Ed Walsh, and $310 to Walter Stockfish. "Stockfish, Kronk, Sumeracki, and Dombrowski called themselves 'The Four Counts,'" the witness recalled. "I never actually paid any money to any of them but Stockfish. Walter would make the arrangements and the others would go along with him. I would give him money with which to pay the others."

"How about Joseph Kaminski?" Sigler inquired, again turning briefly to catch a glimpse of the next victim's reaction. "Wasn't he such a heavy drinker that he would sometimes fall down?"

"I gave Joe $100," Hemans said, adding with a broad smile, "and I don't recall him ever falling, but he sure did bounce around from one end of the room to the other a few times. He was an excessive drinker. He came to my room three or four times a week and always stayed until the whiskey was gone or until somebody took him out to dinner."

"And Michael Clancy?" Sigler said, extending a finger at the pudgy, red-headed Irishman wearing a United States Navy uniform.

"Oh, he's a fine tenor. A happy-go-lucky fellow who did a lot of singing—much to the consternation of the tenants in adjoining rooms. I gave him $100."

"And my young friend, Francis Nowak, who sits there looking so defiant?" Sigler said with sarcasm.

"I gave Frank $150 for the finance bills, but he received other compensation," Hemans revealed. "Nowak was my ear in the House. He would report to me each day exactly what was happening. I got well acquainted with him when he was scheduled to make a radio speech in support of a small loan rate of one percent a month. I called him to my room and we argued. Then we stepped into the 'library' and I gave him some money. He did not make the speech. I got to know him real well."[58]

"And the absent Mr. Weza?"

"That was rather humorous," Hemans recounted, an infectious smile radiating his features. "He was a young fellow and apparently didn't know his way around. He came to my room one day and complained that all the boys were getting money, and he asked me to put him on my list. I kind of felt sorry for him, so I broke my steadfast rule and gave him a lump payment of $100. All the others were in extended payments."

Hemans then rattled off that Senator Diggs, who received $250, was "a perfect gentleman who rarely drank and never more than one when he did," that William Bradley, the recipient of $250, "dropped in a couple of times a week for a nip or two and got overly loud and tough on occasion," and that Senator Wilkowski, who "seldom took a drink" was given his $250 over the course of several trips to the lobbyist's now-famed bathroom.[59]

"What about Henry Shea?" Sigler inquired, slowly pacing before the defendants.

"Senator Shea got $250," Hemans stated, and after a moment of reflection added: "You know, he got so drunk in my room one night that he thought he was in Marquette. The next morning he arose in the Senate and conducted the opening prayer. He was a heavy drinker then, but now he is a tea-totaler [sic] and gives temperance lectures for the state liquor control commission."

Referring to Shea's upper peninsula colleague, D. Stephen Benzie, Hemans asserted that the senator had received $250, but that he did not trust the lawmaker. "Benzie agreed not to vote for a reduced small loan rate," the witness testified, "but when the bill was up, he voted to cut the rate to 1.5 percent a month. This led to a quarrel of considerable size in my room. He explained that he knew the 1.5 percent amendment would not carry, that I did not need his vote, and that he was voting for it to look good back home. The members were authorized to vote against me when I didn't need them, but I didn't like Benzie skating on such thin ice because the score was close. However, the quarrel ended. We went into the bathroom together and peace was restored."[60]

"Finally," asked the Special Prosecutor, flicking an imaginary speck from his brown tweed jacket, "what about Jerry Logie?"

At the mention of the Bay City Republican, Hemans twisted his hands and thought a moment. "He was not part of the group I was using," Hemans said upon reflection. "I think it was my handyman, former Senator Joseph Roosevelt of Detroit, who came to see me one day and said that Senator Logie wanted to be cut in. In any event, I recall sending $100 to Logie in an envelope which Roosevelt delivered. I met Logie a few days later on the sidewalk in front of the Olds Hotel. He acknowledged receiving the money and promised to go along on the finance bills. Later he came to my room and I gave him another $100. That was the only time he was in my room."[61]

Returning to the prosecution table, Sigler was handed a sheet of paper by Warner. The Special Prosecutor wheeled and strode back to the witness. "This is a record of the votes cast on Senate Bill 85," he stated, turning the paper over to Hemans. "You will notice that Nagel, Kaminski, and Stockfish did not vote as you instructed them. How do you explain that?"

"I have no recollection why they went against me," Hemans replied. "It seems to indicate a double-cross."[62]

Lifting the black notebook as though it were some sort of religious icon, Sigler requested that Hemans describe its contents to the Court. "In it are the names of the members whom I believed I could control with money, judging from past experiences," the Major responded in a clear, unwavering tone. "After each name is an amount. The amount represents the sum in dollars which I thought it would be necessary to pay. The list was prepared in regard to the small loan bills—Senate bills 85 and 166—which were then pending. Some of the names are marked with a check, others with an X. These marks indicate those who were paid and those who were not paid. You know, I learned my lesson ten years ago when I was employed to kill a bill taxing oleomargarine. I used every legitimate argument I could, but the bill passed. Later I was told to lean more heavily on payment methods and less on verbal arguments. I have followed that procedure ever since, paying men according to their black market value, shall we say."[63]

"Before I leave you to the tender mercies of my brothers," Sigler said, motioning in the direction of the defense counsel, "I want to know one more thing. Were you aware prior to being subpoenaed that the grand jury was interested in you?"

"Yes, I was," Hemans replied, with a barely perceptible flinch. "I had been kept informed of some of the events behind the grand jury's closed doors by an informant."

"Don't give me his name," Sigler commanded. "I know his identity and permitted this disclosure to let certain persons know that I am aware of what is going on."[64]

After a brief cross-examination in which defense counsel donned "kid gloves" lest they evoke the further ire of the man who had given damning testimony against their clients, Joseph W. Planck, Hancock's mouthpiece, demanded to see the entire contents of the "little black book," and not just a single page selected by the prosecution. Sigler leapt to his feet. "I object," he fairly screamed. "This is just a fishing expedition by counsel. He knows there is other information in that book which might have a bearing on future cases. I don't care to have Mr. Planck rummaging around in this book. The only part of that book which is competent evidence in this case is that sheet which has here been introduced as evidence."[65] Carr concurred with his protege, and Planck, mumbling under his breath, took his seat.

Just as Sigler was about to dismiss the witness, Hemans blurted: "God knows I'm not a reformer. But there is a moral to this thing, and that is we clean Lansing up and keep it clean."[66] Picking up his hat, Hemans tugged at his Eisenhower jacket and crisply strode out of the room.

With Sigler's passionate cry that "these defendants who have sold their lousy souls for a few paltry dollars be brought to the bar of justice" ringing in his ears, Judge Carr retired to his chambers. The horde of reporters mingled with spectators, and the consensus was that Sigler had presented a nearly perfect conspiracy case and there could be little doubt of Carr's ruling. Within forty-five minutes the jurist resumed his place and verified this opinion by ordering all those accused to stand trial in Ingham County Circuit Court before Judge John Simpson on June 12, 1944. Major

Hemans had done his duty and awaited with smug confidence the public acclaim which he self-righteously thought to be his due.[67]

VI Much to the major's chagrin, in the aftermath of his testimony he was not nominated by acclamation for the role of avenging angel. The *Ingham County Press* offered a half-hearted defense of its fellow county resident, saying that Hemans had "some good qualities, among them courage to take the stand and tell things he could have refused to tell." Yet, it was this, his local newspaper—the one which knew him best—that launched the most devastating arrow, because it was aimed at Hemans' heart. "Chuck, as he is called by hundreds of people in this community, is being, and will continue to be, punished by the disgrace he has placed upon a name that has always stood for the best in his community and state," the editorial set forth with small-town candor. "Major Charles F. Hemans is paying the full price for walking in the counsel of the ungodly and standing in the way with sinners. His neighbors here in Mason pity him."[68]

The *Detroit Times*, conversely, saw no redeeming qualities in Hemans and ran a vitriolic editorial portraying the lobbyist as a self-serving "stool pigeon" who tried to "save his own soiled face" by coming forward, but only after the "Judas" had been granted immunity for his dishonest acts. Ironically, these were the same acts which he denied doing in a *Times* interview in November 1943, in which he labelled those who accused him of bribery as "rats who are taking unfair advantage of my absence while in the armed services and artfully insinuating wrong-doing."[69]

The *Times* then opined that the crux of the problem in Lansing rested with the electorate and not those "misfits and dummy representatives of the people, who are, in reality, only stupid tools of cynical political factions."[70] In a powerful conclusion, the Detroit daily lambasted the men and women who were responsible for choosing "nondescripts" to represent them in the Capitol. "When elevator operators and out of work ward healers are sent to Lansing merely because they may have done some spade work for some party precinct organization, it is a sorry reflection upon the public interest of the average citizen. It is a tragic reflection on the honor of the legislature that such inept members are admitted to its halls. But it is basically a reflection on the people of Michigan. If they had the honor of their state more at heart, they would not tolerate for more than a single session the rag-tag and bob-tail character of the men who have proven to have misrepresented them so badly."[71]

Meanwhile, at the very time the presses were rolling out the *Times* story, Hemans was lounging in his now famous Olds suite with *Free Press* correspondent Ken McCormick. In an exclusive interview, Hemans bared his soul in a maudlin recitation to Kim Sigler's favorite newsman and confidante. "I don't want to make a big guy out of myself," Hemans stated to McCormick. "I want to be a little guy. I don't want to be a reformer. Reformers always get caught up in raids. But when I learned that Judge Carr was determined to clean up this mess and had appointed Kim Sigler as Special Prosecutor, my heart was with them. Why, it used to be that every morning when I looked out of my window here in this hotel I would wonder if the Capitol dome was still there. There were times when it was impossible to get anything done unless it was paid for."

Pacing from wall to wall and chain-smoking cigarettes, Hemans continued his sob-sister account. "When you can't get under the fence, you gotta buy a ticket. Its been that way for years. I can remember forty years ago when my father was in the legislature. He used to come home and tell me how some legislator was bought. He used to be madder than Hell. That's why I'm here," the admitted graft dispenser stated with pride, apparently oblivious to the fact that in the elder Hemans' eyes the role of his son would have earned condemnation and dishonor. "Now we have the ground turned up. It's up to those who are interested in good government to cultivate and raise a good crop. But remember—plowing up old sod is tough. The grand jury is doing the plowing. Let those interested in good government do the cultivating and planting."

The lobbyist, who had come to the interview directly from Sparrow Hospital where his mother-in-law had succumbed to a fatal illness, was interrupted by the jangle of the telephone. "To add to everything else," he sighed, "my six year old son got the mumps." Picking up his overcoat, which he had tossed over the arm of a chair, Hemans concluded his oration. "I was in a vicious circle," he asserted in a blatant effort to elicit sympathy from those who would read his tale. "As long as I was in it, I couldn't turn down these good clients. They would have been lost here without someone who knew Lansing. When I left Lansing to go into the army I told my wife 'never again.' After this war is over, I'll go down on the farm and watch the corn grow."[72] Unfortunately, the insincerity of this downhome, farmboy confession, complete with the repentant sinner pledge never to stray again, was made apparent within forty-eight hours.

VII Bitterness and anger gnawed at Hemans as he read again and again the less-than-favorable press reviews of his performance. Unable to contain his wrath, the irate lobbyist telephoned Sigler, ordered the Special Prosecutor to delay departure for a Florida vacation and call a joint press conference. When Sigler demurred, Hemans reiterated his command, disclosing dramatically that he had received a death threat. Then, abandoning his theatrical guise of martyr for the more familiar and comfortable one of extortionist, Hemans warned that if the Special Prosecutor did not consent to being at his side when he confronted reporters, he would withhold his testimony in upcoming graft cases. Knowing the high-strung temperament of his star witness, Sigler, with trepidation, agreed to Hemans' blackmail demand.

At the hastily convened gathering with newsmen, Sigler was treated like a stage prop by Hemans, who only sought the Special Prosecutor's presence to add legitimacy to his comments. Still obviously furious over reaction to his testimony, Hemans took from his briefcase a typed, formal statement, which he later distributed to those present so that his words would reach the widest possible audience. With a dour expression clouding his handsome features, Sigler stood motionless as Hemans, in full military regalia, adjusted his reading glasses and cleared his throat.

"I never paid a dollar to anyone in the belief that it was in the nature of a bribe. I never received or paid a bribe in my forty-seven years," he asserted to the wide-eyed astonishment of all who had heard his courtroom testimony. "What I have done is to pay extortion money to those in the position where they could demand it. Call it a 'shake-down' or whatever you wish. I never read of a victim being prosecuted for bribery who handed over his money to a burglar who held a gun in his back. I do not recall that any member of Congress was ever indicted for having voted to make payments to the Barbary pirates when they demanded tribute for the safe passage of our ships. I do not recall that any grief stricken parents were accused of wrong-doing when they paid ransom to a kidnapper for the return of their abducted child. The situation in Michigan for many years has been anomalous, yet I read that because of my act in doing this, the only thing which could be done under similar circumstances, I am a culprit."

Pausing for effect more than breath, Hemans unctuously continued his tirade. "I have always admonished my children to tell the truth, no matter what the consequences, when confronted by the necessity to do so. What a hypocrite I would be if I failed to observe that teaching! The truth I have told—my reward for public service for so doing—is to be branded as a briber—to suffer the indignity of possible disbarment proceedings. For the giving of the truth, my life has been threatened. I have been offered all the money I need to live the rest of my life to clear out and seek the sanctuary of a distant country. But I do not bluff or scare easily. I had thought that by laying the truth before the uninformed public I was doing an honorable and decent thing. My mind will not be changed. If by disbarring someone who dares to tell the truth they hope to coerce me into silence or stop me from further aiding in cleaning up this mess, they had better adjust their sights while they think it over. If after sober reflection, they come to the conclusion that what I am endeavoring to do is to aid an agency which seeks to make a better and cleaner Michigan, I am sure that they will even lend their assistance to the cause. How can it be expected that good results will follow if those who dare to carry the torch are to be beaten back and criticised."

A wistful, knowing smirk came to Hemans' lips. "Of course, maybe I'm all wrong. If so, I shall say no more and let the poisonous venom continue to eat at the vitals of an otherwise glorious state," he said ominously. "God help her if it is not stopped somewhere, sometime."[73]

As Hemans stepped back, refusing to answer questions, Sigler was asked if the grand jury planned to follow up on the charge that the witness had been bribed to go into exile. "That is for certain," he assured reporters. Peering at Hemans with scorn, Sigler added bitterly: "We have known about the offer of enough money to Major Hemans to keep him the rest of his life if he would leave the country, but we did not want to reveal it until we were prepared to act. The Major has exposed our hand."[74]

Response to Hemans' diatribe was swift in coming. Albert E. Blashfield, executive secretary of the State Bar of Michigan, proclaimed that Hemans had no foundation for the charge that disbarment proceedings had been instituted and stated that none would be made against any attorney cited by the grand jury until after the cases had been tried in open court.[75] A War Department spokesman stated that Hemans would be transferred to non-active status pending investigation of his connection with the alleged bribery of lawmakers.[76] Grand jury attaches huddled with Sigler and tried in vain to convince their employer that Hemans was an irresponsible, lying scalawag who should be abandoned before he left an irreparable stain on the prosecution's credibility.[77] State Treasurer D. Hale Brake, a former member of the state senate, dismissed Hemans' allegation that the system was to blame, saying that bribery would not exist "if persons interested in legislation would spend more time explaining their side of the story to leaders of the legislature instead of relying on support from its weak-kneed members."[78]

The piece de resistance of rebuttal came from the acid pen of Edwin Goodwin in the *Michigan State Digest*. "Mr. Hemans' picture of himself being chased by legislators, over hill and dale, in order, figuratively, that they might rape him, is pathetic," Goodwin wrote petulantly. "His untimely ravishment by them is the one blot upon his otherwise virgin life. He hates money, particularly tainted money. He has not said that nasty lawmakers compelled him to maintain a bar in a hotel and required of him that he provide whiskey, or even women, as pleasures for the piratical legislators, but he infers as much. It may appear yet necessary that reformer Hemans be put in protective personal care of some courageous prison warden to shield him from the legislative mafia who hound him in and out of season, demanding of him money. There should be adequate safeguards to innocent citizens of this great state."[79]

VIII

Promptly at 9:00 a.m. on May 2, 1944, Sigler, natty as always in dark brown slacks and a light brown sport jacket, celebrated his fiftieth birthday by presenting Judge Carr with yet another small loan company warrant for his signature. Named to be rearrested for giving payoffs were Hancock, Omacht, and Cooper, who were joined by first-time offenders Julian Thompson, Household Finance's Lansing lobbyist, and Armand Robichaud, a lobbyist for Beneficial Management Corporation of Newark, New Jersey. The unlucky recipients of their largesse were nine names familiar to devotees of the grand jury: Wilkowski, Diggs, Nagel, Nowak, Walsh, Gallager, Buckley, Stockfish, and Benzie.

The object of the conspirators' desire was Senate Bill 282, introduced in 1939 as an amendment to an intangibles tax proposal. This measure would have levied a specific tax on paper, including currency, certificates of deposit, corporate shares, bonds, and other "hidden wealth," held as security for loans. After much controversy, this feature was stricken from the final bill which was signed into law by Governor Dickinson.[80]

The seriousness of this indictment was shown when, within a week, Eugene Garey of New York, who was G.O.P. boss Frank D. McKay's attorney, and Fred R. Walker of Detroit, who represented McKay's top henchman William McKeighan, appeared as counsel for Thompson and Robichaud. They instantly did battle with Sigler over his promise to file an arrest warrant for Thompson, who failed to appear for his May 12 hearing, and to request extradition from New Jersey for Robichaud, who also was not present. "I have been informed that Thompson will appear on Monday," Sigler announced after conferring with Garey, "but I have not heard anything from Beneficial Management Company. Because this company operates small loan firm offices in Michigan, I had hoped they would respond voluntarily to the warrant. But extradition proceedings are now necessary."[81]

Thompson came before Judge Carr as promised on Monday, May 15 and was released, as had been all the other defendants, on $2,500 bond. Robichaud's attorney informed the Court that his client would fight extradition. This prompted an irate Sigler to proclaim that "Beneficial is doing everything it can to prevent Judge Carr's grand jury from examining records disclosing its legislative activities in Michigan."[82] In the meantime, the hyperenergetic Special Prosecutor leaked word to his press cronies that the grand jury was beginning a probe into irregularities within the highway department and liquor control commission. If Sigler had his way, every day the citizens of Michigan would learn of how the Carr-Sigler broom was sweeping the Capitol clean.[83]

IX Before the onset of the initial finance company trial, the grand juror accomplished what many Capitol observers thought to be impossible—shoving Charlie Hemans from the headlines. In the midst of the lobbyist's testimony in the pre-trial examination of the defendants in the second finance case, Carr issued a warrant citing five men, including former Lieutenant Governor Francis (Frank) Murphy, and two corporations, the Mohawk and Arrow Distilleries, as accepting and/or offering bribes in 1941 to influence the passage of Senate Bill 203, which would have reduced liquor license fees by eighty percent.[84]

Reporters sped to the recently purchased twenty-one room red brick mansion, complete with separate servants' quarters, to quiz the forty-seven year old Murphy, who had ridden to victory in 1940 by capitalizing on the reputation of the popular former governor of the same name, regarding the allegation that he had pocketed $2,500 from distillers in return for political favors. They were greeted by Murphy's wife, who said her husband was visiting a doctor for a recurring heart ailment. Declining to answer questions, Mrs. Murphy, who was seven months' pregnant, did make a brief statement regarding the family's apparent affluence. "I know that this big house certainly looks bad," she stated defiantly, "but people forget that I have an income, too, from an estate. My husband has been in the electrical parts business and has a big contract with the Willow Run bomber plant. Several weeks ago his two partners were killed in an airplane crash near Lansing, so he is now the sole owner. I know Mr. Murphy never took a cent from anyone. I knew everything about my husband's affairs while he was lieutenant governor under Murray VanWagoner, and I can't believe he could ever be guilty of bribe-taking."[85]

After nearly three days of detective work, an enterprising *Detroit Times* newsman ferreted out that Murphy, driving his bright red town car, had left his home prior to the issuance of the warrant and, with the knowledge of Carr and Sigler, had taken residence in a Detroit hotel room. When the reporter went to the hotel to call on Murphy, he found the former Democratic leader propped up in bed, his handsome features contorted in pain from another heart attack. As the apologetic intruder prepared to depart, Murphy called him back and said he wanted to say something to the people of Michigan. "I heard lots of rumors that things were going on in the Capitol, and I was new in politics," he said in a barely audible whisper. "I took the money in three payments from March to May, 1941. It was the only wrong thing I did while in office. I'm ready to take my medicine, and I'm willing to aid Judge Carr and Prosecutor Sigler all I can. They've been decent to me, and that's the least I can do. Above all, I'd like to be allowed to return the money and get as much worry from my mind as I can. Perhaps I can get to Lansing to surrender on Wednesday [June 7]. If I'm able, I will plead guilty. So far though I've just been following my doctor's orders and resting as much as I can."[86] True to his word, on Wednesday, Murphy, his face drawn and body trembling, shuffled into Judge Carr's courtroom, admitted his guilt, and was released on $2,500 bond.[87]

As if following a predictable film script, two men named by Murphy as tendering him money angrily sputtered denials. "I don't know what Murphy is talking about," said Samuel L. Schreier, secretary-treasurer of Arrow Distilleries. "His purported confession is astonishing to me."[88] Abraham H. Weinstein, President of Arrow, was more truculent, snarling: "I'm ready to fight this charge."[89]

Once again, it was the poison pen of Edwin Goodwin which sarcastically set forth the anguished thoughts of many residents of Michigan, who, by now, were becoming dumb-struck by the flood of bribery revelations. "Vice Governor Murphy got $2,500 worth of boodle. He kept it. He covered up. He expostulated that all was honest and rosy in lawmaking. There was no corruption. He could swear to it," railed Goodwin's editorial. "Then the law caught up with him. Immediately he began to drip. He was president of the sedate body of 32 men, good and true—some of them, maybe—and, as their honored president, he took for his part $2,500 in graft from liquor interests. He was paid off. He got it direct. It could be that the liquor boys were unwilling to trust Hemans with that much moola. So they hired their own lawmaking lawbreaker."[90]

X At long last, on Monday, June 12, the conspiracy trial opened at the tree-shaded courthouse in the center of the Ingham county seat's business district. The presiding jurist, John Simpson, was a former state legislator (1927-1929), who, on the eve of the trial, had elicited chuckles from the press corps when he said with solemnity: "I saw no indications of graft during that one term I served in the House of Representatives. If there was bribery in those days, it was well concealed."[91] With Simpson as ringmaster of the legal circus, newsmen were anticipating a display of judicial tartness which would equal that of the barristers. The jovial judge, who was a stickler for decorum, was known for cowing attorneys with icy glares from his piercing blue eyes. An indication of how he would run the trial was given observers when defense attorney Walter Nelson appeared before Simpson to argue that the one-man grand jury system, under which his clients had been indicted, was unconstitutional in several states. "Never mind the other states," interrupted the jurist, "let's hear what you have to say about the Michigan Supreme Court holding the act constitutional." Before the nonplussed Nelson could resume, Simpson added: "I'll let you know now that I won't hold this law unconstitutional. The trial starts Monday. Be there. But I'll listen to you for a short time if you hurry."[92]

For six days, the process of selecting a jury droned on, as everyone in the tiny courtroom sweltered in temperatures which neared ninety degrees. Finally, with only five perspiring spectators as witnesses to the scene, three males and eleven females were sworn in as veniremen, and court recessed until 9:30 a.m., Monday, June 19.[93]

Simpson lived up to his reputation for strict adherence to detail by gavelling court into session promptly at the appointed time. When defendant Charles C. Diggs arrived at 9:32, Simpson chastised him, saying that if he could drive from his home in Jackson and arrive on time, there was no excuse for the defendants being late. If they were tardy in the future, Simpson warned, they would be held in contempt of court.[94]

Sigler, seemingly bored by his own introduction of 285 pieces of preliminary evidence while court was in session, was a bundle of energy outside the courtroom, intimating to reporters that he had "secret witnesses" who would prove that Abraham Cooper "was the mastermind of the scheme."[95] The dashing darling of the media even turned groundskeeper for a day. Seeing the courthouse gardener jockeying a riding power lawn mower, Sigler asked if he could give it a whirl. The city employee readily consented, and, like the former cowboy he was, the lawyer mounted the machine and, to the astonishment of all who saw the spectacle, finished mowing the lawn.[96]

Sigler's unbounded good humor was genuine, as he had been following with glee political activity in Lansing. While the trial was plodding forward in Mason, eleven miles away at the Capitol, two of Sigler's arch-foes had suffered crushing defeats at the hands of Governor Harry F. Kelly. Frank D. McKay, the Grand Rapids G.O.P. boss, had been ousted as Republican National Committeeman and been replaced by Arthur Summerfield of Flint. As well, Herbert Rushton had been forced out as Attorney General, and John Dethmers won the Republican nomination for that post. With a potential friend as Attorney General and Frank McKay no longer holding an official position within the Republican party, Sigler had every reason to believe the gates to fame and power had swung wide to await his entrance.

Once Sigler began to call witnesses, the trial became eerily similar to the examination. Ralph Smith, Ernest Prew, Claude Marshall, and Warren Whitehead all trooped dutifully to the stand and repeated their damning pre-trial testimony. Only when Charlie Hemans, now clad in the trim summer uniform of an army major, was called to testify on Friday, July 7, did the press and spectators arouse themselves from their reverie to pay closer attention.

Guided by Sigler, Hemans related his life story to the jurors, who were enduring yet another day of tropical heat and humidity, while receiving little relief from the electric fan sending an all-too-gentle breeze upon them.[97] Reiterating his previous testimony, Hemans somberly told the jury: "I met with about a dozen finance company officials, including the defendants Mark Young, John Hancock, George Omacht, Ernest Prew, Samuel Hopkins, and Abraham Cooper, on January 26, 1939 in Cooper's office. I told them the kind of legislation they could expect in the session and mentioned the rumor that Household Finance Company was prepared to spend $50,000 for a bill that would hurt the smaller finance companies, and that they would have to spend a considerable sum to combat this threat. It was an open meeting, and I told them money would have to be spent for hotel rooms, lunches, dinners, and payments to legislators to influence their votes. I also told them we would have to have an occasional bottle of whiskey and other expenses normally incurred by lobbyists."[98]

After a weekend recess, during which courthouse custodian Stanley Parker endeared himself to all those in attendance at the trial by installing venetian blinds on the windows to shut out the intense rays of the sun, Hemans resumed the stand for two more days of direct examination.[99]

During Hemans' testimony, three of the defendants learned that they, at least, had something to smile about despite being labelled as grafters by the Major. State Senator Leo J. Wilkowski and Representatives Francis Nowak and Joseph Kowalski won renomination in their Detroit districts, as voters proved themselves either remarkably forgiving or ignorant.[100]

Under cross-examination, Hemans repeatedly defended his actions as a lobbyist. "I was representing clients with what I believed were meritorious cases. It was impossible for them to continue in business with certain legislation which was introduced," he contended. "There was a time in Michigan when it was possible to dissuade the legislature by arguments and reason. But later it became necessary to pay legislators. Surely it is a crime to bribe legislators, but it is also a crime to pay ransom. But when the time comes, it would be disastrous not to pay."[101]

"What is the 'third house' of the legislature, Mr. Hemans?" inquired defense attorney Maurice H. Shillman.

"Oh, it is a group of lobbyists who support most of the members of the House and Senate during the sessions," Hemans replied with a smile.

"And were you not known as the 'Casanova of the Third House?'" asked Shillman with a sneer.

"Not to my knowledge," Hemans said with a hearty laugh. "But it is flattering."

"During the sessions did you not drink so much that your memory was affected?" demanded Shillman.

"Absolutely not," Hemans shot back, his voice filled with indignation.[102]

"You have been divorced, have you not?" asked Shillman

"Yes," responded the witness, doubtless pondering the direction in which the attorney was now moving.

"Did you not make false financial statements in that divorce proceeding, Mr. Hemans?" snapped Shillman, who barely had the words pass his lips before Sigler thundered an objection.

"What is the purpose of this line of questioning, Mr. Shillman?" intoned Judge Simpson. "I don't want to shut counsel off, but I don't propose to have lawyers go on a fishing expedition either."[103]

"I merely wish to discredit Hemans' dependability by establishing that he made false statements under oath at a prior time, Your Honor," the barrister stated with a smile.

"Objection sustained," snapped Simpson, dismissing Shillman with a flick of his wrist.[104]

Hemans, under questioning by defense counsel Harold Bledsoe, related that "there was a going rate in Lansing on payoffs, not only by myself, but by others," and that his finance company clients had hurried to his Washington office once the grand jury probe had begun.[105] "They said that 'the barn's afire' and asked what I was going to do about it," the lobbyist recalled, his chubby face breaking into a broad smile. "I told them they had better buy a fire engine, and that it would have been better had they done so before the fire broke out."[106]

Hemans also told how Senator Wilkowski and Representative Nowak came to him in Washington. "'Are you going to tell the truth or stay out of Michigan?'" they demanded, recalled Hemans. "I told them I would stay out of the state unless specifically told to return by the War Department."[107]

Over the weekend recess, with the trial entering its sixth week, an article in the *Detroit Times* raised a light-hearted issue which had aroused the curiosity of reporters covering the trial. Not once since the trial began had the Special Prosecutor worn the same suit or ensemble twice. Could he continue at such a sartorial pace, he was asked. "Oh, I think I can last out the trial," Sigler replied with a grin, reminding *Times* reporter Al Kaufman, himself a noted "clothes horse," that he owned "more than forty suits, a comparable number of slack trousers, twelve topcoats, a gross of neckties and four-in-hands, several dozen shirts, boxes of hats, and a dozen pairs of shoes."[108] Even staid Judge Simpson came under the sway of the Special Prosecutor's dress code, as showing above his black robe were no longer plain neckties, but rather the flowery types preferred by Sigler.[109]

On Thursday, July 20, each of the legislative defendants took the stand and categorically denied taking money from Major Hemans or any other lobbyist. Swedish-born ex-representative Ernest Nagel, a former sailor, boxer, balloonist, and dishwasher, brought forth gales of laughter when he told of why he entered politics. "Well," he said with a heavy accent, "I woke up one morning without a job in the depression and decided to take a crack at it."[110] As to his honesty, Nagel asserted that "if I wanted to be crooked, I would take a million dollars, not chicken feed."[111]

Representative Joseph Kaminski recalled that he had been inspecting nuts and bolts in a factory when he was induced to seek elected office by his friends. "Practically all Wayne County legislators visited the room of Charlie Gadd to drink and play cards," he insisted when asked if he had frequented the dens of lobbyists. "There was nothing wrong with that or going to Hemans' room for a drink. But I never took any money."[112] Representative Joseph Kowalski said that he became a politician because he did not like working in his father's meat market, and Earl Gallagher ran for public office after losing his assembly line job at Ford Motor Company.[113] During his stint in the witness chair, Gallagher earned the scorn of Judge Simpson by stating that in 1939 he served on "Mickey Mouse committees," such as those governing the University of Michigan and the Ypsilanti State Hospital."[114] After explaining to the jurist that a "Mickey Mouse" committee was one that was unimportant, Gallagher was asked by Simpson why he thought that the operation and welfare of the

University of Michigan and the State Hospital were so unimportant? Stammering, Gallagher admitted his erroneous choice of words to describe a body that met infrequently.[115]

Wilkowski, Nowak, Walsh, Bradley, Logie, and Buckley manfully proclaimed their innocence, as did Martin Kronk, the final legislative defendant. Kronk, a forty-four year old Detroiter who was the only Democrat on the powerful House Ways and Means Committee in 1939, claimed that he took no money from lobbyists and consented to accept "just one drop of whiskey in a glass of soda water" whenever he went to a lobbyist's room.[116]

"Did you measure that out with a medicine dropper?" interrupted Sigler snidely.

"No," admitted the bespectacled witness, "that's just a relative term."[117]

Later, when Kronk innocently stated that he had poor eyesight, Sigler remarked in a loud aside which brought forth laughter from the gallery: "Well, your vision was good enough to get in and out of Hemans' bathroom." Before defense counsel could rise to finish their objection, Simpson sternly ordered the remark stricken from the record.[118]

On July 27 United States Representative Robert A. Grant of Indiana testified as a character witness for George Omacht, general counsel for the Associates Discount Company. The pompous thirty-six year old Indiana attorney, when asked to briefly describe his background, stated: "I am privileged to be serving a third term in the House. I am privileged to be a member of the Naval Affairs Committee, and I am privileged to be sitting alongside that great American statesman. . . . " Interrupting, Sigler shouted: "I don't care what your privileges have been. All I want to know is when you started practicing law and what do you know about Major Hemans' bathroom?"[119]

When Omacht took the stand shortly afterward, he stated that Hemans had been hired solely to draw up one amendment for the finance companies. "You know that in your entire bar experience," Sigler said in exasperation, "no lawyer ever got $7,200 for that kind of performance, don't you?"

"Well," Omacht replied smugly, "I've heard of lawyers getting $100 a day."[120]

Ignoring the jibe, Sigler continued. "Isn't it true that the reason he was paid that much money was to bribe legislators?"

"No," Omacht responded tersely.[121]

On Monday, August 7, defense attorneys began what eventually would amount to twenty-two hours of summation, much of which was personal attacks on Sigler and the grand jury system. The leadoff batter in the defense line-up was George Fitzgerald, representing Buckley, Walsh, Bradley, Kaminski, and Kowalski, who viciously assailed the veracity of Hemans. "Remember, Hemans is the whole conspiracy. Without him there would be no case. And he is dead certain of only one thing—that he paid money to the legislative defendants in 1939," Fitzgerald asserted loudly, "but he was uncertain as to the time and place of payment and to the purpose for which the money was purportedly paid. From that point on it is as hard to bring him down to facts and dates and circumstances as it would be to bring down a game bird with a bow and arrow."[122]

"Hemans had no right to say he paid bribes without remembering and telling when and where they were paid," Fitzgerald continued, his voice a steady roar. "Had Hemans wanted to tell the truth, he would not have asked for immunity from prosecution. No, Hemans built up a front by insisting he was the savior of Michigan. He traded his testimony for immunity. He lied to make sure his skin was not touched. He is a dishonest witness who would not hesitate to put the finger on anyone in order to save himself. Hemans didn't want to work for a living. He was a prominent Democratic official—a Regent of the University of Michigan. Naturally the finance companies wanted all the help they could get in combating legislation affecting them. They thought he was honest. They became his dupes."[123]

Dwight L. Wilson, Nagel's legal mouthpiece, carried on the assault the following day. "I would place more credence in what Hemans said," the barrister declared, "if he had said: 'I am not worthy to wear the uniform of an officer. Give me a dishonorable discharge.' I might have believed him had he resigned from the bar and then taken the stand to testify on his revolting story."[124]

Lloyd Parr, attorney for Nowak and Wilkowski, noted that Republicans had full control of the 1939 legislature, yet all the legislative defendants except one were Democrats. "If Hemans had paid bribes to Democrats who had no authority and who were not members of important committees," Parr said sarcastically, "then he is not as smart as people credit him with being."[125] The attorney, after detailing the charges against his clients, added: "Make no mistake, Charlie Hemans is a gracious man and a flatterer, but he is not the kind of individual that I like."[126]

Milton Johnson spoke on behalf of Mark S. Young and noted that no witness but Hemans had claimed that Young was present at the January 26, 1939 meeting in Cooper's office. "There is not a word in evidence anywhere, except from Hemans, that Young heard or knew of anything improper," Johnson pleaded. "He took no part in the legislative activities of the finance group, was never in Lansing in 1939, and did not know Hemans or anything about his activities in behalf of the finance companies' men."[127]

Next came Benjamin Watson representing Senator Logie, who summed up his one hour and forty-nine minute address with the assertion that Hemans was a "falsifier" and that the entire case against his client "literally smells."[128] Maurice Shillman, counsel for Gallagher, agreed, saying that "Hemans was deliberately falsifying when he claimed to have given money to my client in 1933 and 1935. Mr. Gallagher was not elected to the legislature until 1936. It seems my client is being convicted by Mr. Sigler on the petty claim that he played poker, not that he was part of a conspiracy."[129]

Altering the attack slightly, Roy T. Conley, who had been retained by Shea and Benzie, zeroed in on Sigler rather than Hemans. "Mr. Sigler," he shouted, "bargained with both Hemans and his lackey Joe Roosevelt, giving them grand jury expense accounts and promises that they could walk from the courtroom free men. Sigler and Judge Carr paid their living allowance with your money and mine and granted Hemans a pleasure trip on tires and gasoline you and I probably would like to have. Mr. Sigler coached Roosevelt during a recess, outside the courtroom, to make sure his story jibed with known facts. He wants to convict these defendants by any means at his disposal, fair or otherwise. As far as the prosecution in concerned, everything has not been honest in this case."[130]

Flushed with anger, Sigler leapt to his feet. "Will the stenographer please repeat that statement?" he demanded. After it had been read, the Special Prosecutor requested that it be stricken. Simpson so ordered, and as Sigler retreated to his chair, he glared at his adversary and thrust out a shaking index finger. "In view of this abuse," he thundered, "my dander is up. I, and not my associate Mr. Warner, will now make the State's closing argument."[131]

The onslaught continued against the Special Prosecutor, however, when Walter Nelson, representing Cooper and Hopkins, took his turn at bat. "Mr. Sigler is guilty of trying to frighten you," Nelson bellowed at the jurors. "He is giving sinister means to innocent letters. Mr. Cooper is not a fool, but only a fool would have signed his name to seventy-five letters which carried any implication of conspiracy. Mr. Cooper is old enough to know better and honest enough not to undertake any conspiracy. You cannot believe this bribery talk unless you want to believe it."[132]

"What we have here is a case based on a flimsy web of gossip and suspicion," Nelson said loudly. "The conspiracy may have been beautifully planned, if there was one, but has the prosecution proved it? No, it has not! If no votes were purchased, your verdict must be not guilty. Don't borrow the rod of the Special Prosecutor to rummage around in the ashes of suspicion to convict these defendants. Rather use wisdom, courage, and kindness in making your decision. I shall not call Hemans names. I shall leave him to his conscience and to your verdict."[133]

The final speaker for the defense was James Haggerty, the attorney for Hancock and Omacht, who spoke on Thursday morning. "I am," he smiled, "in the words of Mr. Sigler, the 'last of the Brilliant Brethren' to address you. I wish to speak on the unholy quartet of the prosecution witnesses: Hemans, Roosevelt, Prew, and Smith. None of them have any honesty or fine sensibilities. They are crooks, liars, and swamp denizens. Oh, Major Hemans is resplendent and deceptive. He is worthy of a medal for being a knight, first class, of the Order of the Triple Cross. He truly was the 'Baron of the Bathroom.' Joseph Roosevelt has lived a life of lies and cannot be expected to suddenly start telling the truth when confronted by the Special Prosecutor. Prew wanted to make good the mistakes of his youth, when he embezzled $25,000, but judging from his testimony he didn't achieve his goal. Smith is crafty and sly, and he is an artist in preserving his own hide. Indeed, all four were smart enough to seek favor with the prosecution by lying in order to save themselves."[134]

On Friday morning, August 11, Sigler, symbolically attired in the purity of a white suit, white shirt, white shoes, and a black tie, rose to rebut the summation of defense counsel.[135] "I shall not make a speech, I shall not yell. I shall not rant. I shall not enter the campaign of hate that has been conducted for nine weeks in this courtroom," the Special Prosecutor said in a low voice, standing before the jurors. "I have no hatred in my heart for anyone. I intend to think out loud about this case for a little while because I believe it is high time that was done."[136]

Pacing slowly before the panel, Sigler discussed what the defense had alleged about the State's witnesses. "The statements of my learned brethren were the silliest I have ever heard," he said, shaking his head sadly. "Charles Hemans has been called a crook and a thief and described as dishonest and immoral. He has been called every name that a tongue can use to defame a man's character. Every known adjective of approbation has been used against Ernie Prew. Joseph Roosevelt has been blasted for days. Ralph Smith has been given the same kind of treatment. I expected that the witnesses would be attacked. I believed that certain of the defense attorneys would show their true colors. Yet, I never dreamed they would go to the extent that they did. This man Hemans is the same man today he was in 1937 and 1939 and 1941, and then he had the friendship and confidence of all these men on trial. If

Hemans had a shell, a veneer covering wormy rottenness, these finance company defendants knowingly bought that rottenness in 1939."[137]

The Special Prosecutor then spoke to the issue of the character of his witnesses and the granting of immunity for their testimony. "Hemans was the hub of the conspiracy," he explained, removing his pince-nez glasses and letting them dangle from their black velvet ribbon. "Which was better, to let all the crooks go and not even be able to prosecute Hemans, or to grant immunity and get the record of graft in this case and a lot more that are to come? And why not grant Hemans immunity? Who has done more to help in the investigation?"[138]

"We did not select these witnesses," Sigler went on, a hint of bitterness entering his voice. "We found them as conspirators. They were linked to the natural chain of events. And let me say that the grand jury does not go into churches and Sunday Schools to look for criminals. I hold no brief for Hemans or for Prew. But who would know better what was done by these finance company defendants than Hemans, the man they now say was a mass of rottenness beneath a suave exterior? To assail Prew, they drag in here a mistake he made twenty-five years ago when he embezzled some money. But he went on and raised a family and lived it down to the point where he could get a $150,000 bond from an official of this company. It is only now, after he has testified, that defense lawyers call him a crook. We didn't find Joe Roosevelt, or ask for him. He was a conspirator. Yet, he had been good enough to represent 200,000 Wayne County electors in 1937. He was the finance officials' friend in 1939. Ralph Smith sat in the meetings of the finance executives in 1937, 1938, and 1939, as a trusted ally. No objections were raised against any of these men until they went before the grand jury and told the truth. Then the four became the 'Unholy Quartet.'"[139]

Turning his attention to the personal slanders made against him, Sigler put his head down and spoke barely above a whisper so that the jurors were compelled to listen carefully. "I was troubled by the personal attacks," he said with candor, "until sleepless at night I realized that anything derogatory said about me and Judge Carr hurts the grand jury, and a lot of people want to see it fold up. These attacks were, therefore, more than just personal. In fairness, I want to say that Mr. Haggerty rose above the tactics of his brethren. He conducted himself as a gentleman and uttered not a work that could be considered as personal."[140]

"I wish I could say of Walter Nelson what I said about James Haggerty," the Special Prosecutor added, positioning himself so that he could cast glances at both his adversary and the jury. "Walter Nelson must have many good qualities. He is a good organizer, a good lawyer, but there is something in his soul I cannot understand. There must be something twisted in a man's soul to encourage him to stoop to name-calling in the trial of a case. You have heard the abuse Nelson has heaped upon the prosecution staff and the State's witnesses. Everyone with the prosecution was a so-and-so, and everyone connected with the defense was a magnanimous man. To Nelson the whole prosecution was a bunch of crooks. I feel sorry for a man who comes into a court of justice and acts in this manner. I am not saying this behind Walter Nelson's back. I am saying it here in open court. For nine weeks he has preached the doctrine of hate. The world has enough of that. Certainly hate should never be allowed to enter a court of justice."[141]

"I was never so disappointed in a man before as I was with Roy Conley," Sigler stated, his voice still quiet. "He referred to Judge Carr's grand jury as a boarding school. The last man to say a word derogatory of the courts should be a lawyer. You know, I honor lawyers who will fight in the courtroom, but I do not like to be hit below the belt by an assault gang in desperate straits."[142]

Walking to the jury box, Sigler adjusted his spectacles on the bridge of his nose and leaned on the railing. "For twenty-five years I have been engaged in trying law suits," he related, pausing for effect. "During those twenty-five years I have strived to be an honorable lawyer. I have turned down many cases that my conscience would not permit me to accept. I didn't run for this job as Special Prosecutor. I didn't seek it, nor did I have to take it. Judge Carr and others concerned with the graft charges asked me to serve. They told me it was my public duty. I never dreamed that my motives would be questioned, that abuse would be heaped upon me, that I would be called dishonest and unethical. What have I done to be subjected to such bitter attacks? I have done the duty I was sworn to do when I took my oath before the grand jury."[143]

"I can only say to you," Sigler pleaded to the jurors, "ask yourselves why the affable, good-looking, well dressed finance company officials paid Hemans, a crook, $7,200 and Claude J. Marshall, their other Lansing attorney, $401? The legal advice Hemans gave could have been given by a ten year old child. Ask yourself why Hemans was instructed to sit in his hotel room if he was hired to give legal advice. You know the answer. Hemans was hired to sit in his hotel room because it was there that he served liquor to legislators and bought their votes. Poor Claude Marshall was merely a front man to give the conspiracy an air of respectability, while Hemans, who handled the bribe jackpot from his hotel room, was the real influence. You must remove personalities from this case. Personally, I like certain of these defendants. I would like to take a ride with Mr. Hancock in his overgrown limousine. But he is guilty, and like the average man in the street, he, too, must pay the penalty for his crime. And I am sorry, too, for the legislative defendants. They are all good fellows. But when they had the greatest opportunity of their lives to serve the people, they frittered it away. Good men or not, they are guilty and must pay."[144]

Following Sigler's summation, Simpson adjourned court until 9:30 Saturday morning, at which time he charged the jury. "You jurors have the facts," Simpson stated, "and it is up to you to return the verdicts regardless of whom may be injured or benefitted thereby. Remember that even if you find that bribes were paid and bribes were accepted, there can be no verdict of guilty unless you believe that a conspiracy to influence the votes of the legislators existed. Remember, also, that any person had the right to offer suggestions and to seek to influence lawmakers by lawful means. Remember that there is nothing unlawful in buying legislators food and drink and otherwise entertaining them if there is no attempt made to buy their votes by such means, even if the furnishing of food and drink to legislators is a practice which does not meet with your personal approval. You must not wander into other fields. You are not concerned with the acts of men not named in the warrant. Their acts are of not concern to the Court or you at this time. It is your duty to find that: 1) a conspiracy existed between January 1 and July 1, 1939; 2) the conspiracy was reached in Ingham County or that overt acts of furtherance of the conspiracy were committed in Ingham County; and 3) the defendants wilfully and intentionally entered into the conspiracy. You must fearlessly and courageously seek and follow the truth."[145]

XI At 5:25 Saturday afternoon, after deliberating four hours and fifty-two minutes, jury forewoman Mrs. Florence Wilcox rose and read the verdict. "We find defendants Mark S. Young and Samuel Hopkins not guilty. We find the remaining twenty defendants all guilty as charged."[146] Immediately, Simpson ordered all those convicted to rise. "I sentence you and each of you to the State Prison of Southern Michigan for a period of not less than three years nor more than five years."[147] Stays were granted, pending appeals to the Supreme Court, and all of the defendants, except previously convicted Stanley Dombrowski, were released on $4,000 bond.[148]

After court was adjourned, newsmen crushed around the jurors seeking accounts of the deliberation. "I was shocked by Major Hemans' story," stated Mrs. Wilcox. "Nevertheless, I believed him implicitly. His testimony was not marred by the cross examination. He conveyed the

71

impression of a man who was telling the truth about his associates with reluctance, and certainly not relishing his part in the case. I hold great admiration for Judge Carr's investigation, for it must have been a terrific job to unearth all the evidence presented by the State. The grand jury certainly has been justified and must be continued for the sake of the taxpayers until the slate at Lansing has been wiped clean."[149]

Mrs. Alice Haynes said that the jury had little difficulty in arriving at its verdict. "I believed Hemans implicitly and also Joe Roosevelt, his handyman and bartender. The bribery revealed by the trial was a brazen and outrageous thing and must be stopped before people lose their faith in our form of government. I'm in favor of more grand jury investigations. What kind of laws can we expect if conditions exist which permit the buying of votes for a few hundred dollars? Hemans had a very unpleasant job before him, but he did it like a soldier."[150]

"If Hemans had wanted to lie," said Cleyo Sanders, "he would have implicated others in his testimony. Why should he fasten bribes on a relatively few men and exonerate a great many others whose names were mentioned to him in direct examination? If he had lied, he would have become hopelessly involved during cross-examination. But defense attorneys couldn't scratch his story. Naturally he was vague about some things and made some misstatements in connection with dates, but who wouldn't after five years? Judge Carr can't be praised too much for his grand jury. It should be continued as long as the slightest suspicion of dishonesty clings to our legislative body."[151]

Mrs. Florence Hughes praised the work of Sigler. "The prosecution case all dove-tailed together," she said. "The story was very logical. Obviously the jury believed Hemans, for it would have decided otherwise had there been any doubt over the guilt of the defendants. Mr. Sigler conveyed the impression of complete fairness. He did not seem like a lawyer who would try to railroad a defendant to secure a prosecution record. The jury admired him tremendously."[152]

This sentiment was echoed by Mrs. Esther Jones, a rural school teacher. "Sigler was very fair throughout the case," she gushed, "and I hope that he and Judge Carr continue to expose the disgusting conditions at Lansing as long as they exist."[153]

Editorial comment followed the same line of thought expressed by the veniremen. The *Ingham County News* stated: "Our court and our jury have spoken out strongly against the corruption disclosed in the conspiracy case. The torch of legislative decency should be kept burning. It should be used to kindle fires throughout the state and nation. It should be used to rekindle the flames of patriotism, honesty, and fair-dealing which is our heritage. The Ingham jury has spoken fearlessly. Let us adopt their example and drive from the floor of the legislature and from the galleries and corridors of the Capitol, and even from hotels, the men who are lacking in proper conception of right and decency."[154] The *Hastings Banner*, basking in the triumph of their hometown lawyer, praised the grand jury: "Judge Carr and Special Prosecutor Kim Sigler make a great grand jury team. If they are allowed to continue, unhampered, their work is certain to have a wholesome effect on state government—not only in Michigan, but everywhere."[155]

Following the trial, Sigler did not gloat publicly over his victory. He quietly left the courtroom, saying only that he had much unfinished business which demanded his attention.[156] That evening, however, the Special Prosecutor had a champagne party with reporters Al Nieber of the *Detroit News* and Ken McCormick of the *Detroit Free Press*. They asked Al Kaufman of the *Detroit Times* to join them, but he declined, saying: "Hell, no. I'm not going to celebrate because you sent some dumb bastards to prison."[157]

This event, more than any other of the entire proceedings, showed something that the people of Michigan never truly were allowed to comprehend: the real Kim Sigler was not the courageous White Knight who appeared in public, but rather was a self-serving, self-promoting schemer who carefully masked his true goals except before a select cadre of friends. Yet, to all who witnessed him at Mason or read of his exploits there, he was a god who had their prayers as he prepared to drive corruption from their midst.

CHAPTER THREE

"I NEVER DREAMED OF MURDER"

I Following the finance company trial, Carr and Sigler lapsed into another period of apparent inactivity throughout September, October, and November. Only when William Henry Gallagher, who was a key member of Frank McKay's coterie of high-priced barristers, argued successfully before the State Supreme Court to have overturned Carr's sixty day contempt of court sentence against Francis Slattery for refusing to testify, was the grand jury involved in anything deemed newsworthy.[1] Because of this, rumors again surfaced that Wayne County Democrats in the legislature, in a desperate gamble to save themselves from further humiliation, would try to curtail funding in an effort to throttle the investigation before it could delve deeper into their misdeeds.[2]

Away from the prying eyes of the press, however, Sigler was feverishly gathering evidence which he confidently believed would make him the most influential man in the state, and which he dared to dream would launch him on a path identical to that of Thomas E. Dewey of New York, who used his crime-fighting record as district attorney to propel him to triumphant bids for both the governorship of the Empire State and the presidential nomination of the Republican Party in 1944. To make the initial giant stride toward his goal all that was needed was to do what the federal government had thrice failed to achieve—outfit Frank McKay with a suit of prison gray. While daunting in its magnitude, the Special Prosecutor beamed at the prospect of the endeavor because he felt he had the Grand Rapids financier's fate in the palm of his hand.

II The source of Sigler's confidence was Warren G. Hooper, former Republican state representative who had been elevated to the state senate in November 1944. The newly elected senator was an unlikely hero, as evidenced by his reluctance to testify against either his fellow lawmakers or lobbyists in his earlier appearance before the grand jury.

A native of Alhambra, California, forty year old Warren Green Hooper was a fourth generation descendant of William Hooper, a North Carolinian signer of the Declaration of Independence. He had attended the University of California and DePauw University but did not receive a degree. After leaving DePauw, he moved to Los Angeles, became a member of the California Stock exchange, and married a school teacher. In 1931, amidst the throes of the Great Depression, he lost his job and abandoned his wife, who subsequently gained a divorce on the grounds of desertion.[3]

Hooper then journeyed to Tacoma, Washington where he edited a weekly newspaper, the *Outlook*, for a year and a half. In the latter part of 1932, he left to become editor of the weekly *Herald* in Sequim, Washington. Another eighteen months found him in Chicago working at the copy desk of the *Herald-Examiner*.[4]

In 1935, Hooper took his journalistic talents to Albion, Michigan, where he became advertising manager for the *Evening Examiner*. While there, he enrolled at Albion College, taking courses primarily in the humanities. It was in college that he met, and married, a tall, attractive, musically-inclined brunette coed named Callienetta Cobb. His new wife worked as a music teacher, took in college students as boarders to raise additional household money, and helped finance a trip for Warren to Berlin, where he covered the 1936 Olympics as a free-lance writer.[5]

Upon his return, Hooper found that he had been replaced at the *Evening Recorder*, and so he purchased a service station, which he operated for eleven months. Capitalizing on acquaintances he had made in his business endeavors, he ran for the state legislature in 1938 and was elected to represent the First District of Calhoun County.[6] Critics quickly noted that his triumph at the polls was a fluke because many voters mistakenly thought he was the son of highly regarded Joseph Hooper, the late congressman from Battle Creek. Therefore, it was predicted that the new state representative would be seeking yet another line of employment in two years.[7] They were mistaken, however, as Hooper proved remarkably popular and was re-elected twice before running successfully for the state senate.

Life in public service seemed to suit Hooper, even though he was labelled as a "loner" by his colleagues. He had the appearance of a conscientious lawmaker and had earned the grudging respect of his constituents. However, in keeping with his unfailing bad luck, Hooper's career took a downward spiral with the creation of the grand jury probe into legislative corruption.

He managed to come away from his initial encounter with the investigation relatively unscathed, as his testimony against lobbyist William Burns left him on the side of honest government. Unfortunately, in his next appearance he would not fare nearly so well.

The source of Hooper's downfall was that of so many of his colleagues—his association with Frank D. McKay. Soon after his election, Hooper had gone to Grand Rapids to see McKay and offered the G.O.P. boss his services in any capacity that would be useful. Later Hooper arranged jobs for seven or eight Calhoun County people with McKay. McKay would call Hooper and give him errands to run or other odd jobs; in return, McKay would pay him a little "pocket money." By 1943 the Albion representative was well-known in Lansing as "one of McKay's boys."[8]

After collapsing before relentless questioning by Sigler and consenting to testify against William Burns, Hooper was deemed by the Special Prosecutor as a "neat little package of dynamite" which could explode the G.O.P. kingmaker's mantle of invincibility.[9] Thus, in October, 1944, Sigler called the Albion lawmaker to the grand jury headquarters once again and spent two days uncovering details about his relationship with Frank McKay.

Hooper related that in 1943, when House Bill 13 to regulate horse racing was before the State Affairs Committee, of which he was a member, he received a telephone call from Ivan Hull, a Grand Rapids associate of McKay and a former member of the Michigan Public Service Commission, to say that the Republican national committeeman was at the Olds Hotel and wanted to see him. Upon entering the hotel he found the financier and his wife in the dining room. McKay then invited him to meet with him privately in his suite. There, Hooper testified, McKay asked if he had seen State Representative Green or Benton Harbor sports promoter Floyd Fitzsimmons, and Hooper said no.[10]

McKay then said, Hooper recalled, "Well, we don't want that race bill out of committee. You get busy on it. Bill or Fitz were supposed to see you and take care of you on it. They have some money for you. You keep the bill in committee and don't worry about the money. You'll get it when the bill is killed." Later, Green telephoned Hooper and instructed him to come to his room in the Olds Hotel, saying: "I have something for you from Frank." Hooper said that he went to see Green and received $500 with the comment that "this is the money McKay had promised you."[11]

Barely three weeks later, shortly after 4 o'clock on the afternoon of November 14, 1944, Hooper walked hesitatingly into Judge Carr's courtroom in the Lansing City Hall to answer a summons from the grand juror and Ingham County Prosecutor Victor C. Anderson to discuss further any knowledge he might possess regarding the alleged attempt by Fitzsimmons, Green, and McKay to influence legislative action on House Bill 13. At 4:25, Anderson, after having consumed several minutes conferring privately with the senator-elect, formally opened the inquisition.

"Mr. Hooper, you and I have discussed a few moments ago a conversation you had in your Lansing office around 10:30 in the morning with Floyd Fitzsimmons a week or so ago, on the first or second of November, is that so?"

"Yes, he said he was calling from a pay phone at Haas's Drug Store in Albion."

"Just tell us what the conversation was," Anderson commanded the fidgety witness.

"He said, 'You know who this is?' and I said, recognizing his voice, 'Yes, I believe I do.' He said, 'Would you like to come down and have a cup of coffee with me. There are some things I want to talk with you about.' I said, 'No, Floyd. I don't think that that would be a good thing to do. Aren't you afraid to be seen talking with me?' And he says, 'Well, why should I? I have got a right to see you. You are a member of the legislature, and I want to give you some literature.' I said, 'Well, Floyd, I don't want to get you in any trouble,' and he says, 'Well, you can't get me into any trouble. I want to talk with you. Can't you come down?' I said, 'No, I don't want to come down, Floyd. If you want to come over to my office I'll see you here.'"[12]

"Then I told my stenographer that I was having a visitor—Mr. Fitzsimmons—who was, in my own words, a leg man of Mr. McKay," Hooper recounted, gaining a bit more self-assurance. "And I told her to keep her ears open, but not to pretend that she was listening, and to try to catch as much of the conversation as she could."

"When Mr. Fitzsimmons came in, he greeted me and said he wanted to talk with me abut the dog-racing bill that he proposed to re-introduce in the next session of the legislature. He says, 'If anybody asks you or sees me—I don't give a darned if all the State Police in Michigan see me here because I have got a right to talk with you about this bill, and I want to do it.' Then he handed me a pamphlet on dog racing, which I examined closely because I was suspicious that there might be some money contained in it, but there wasn't any."

"After we talked for about three-quarters of an hour in favor of legalized dog racing," Hooper went on, "he warned me, 'If anybody asks you, that is all I ever talked to you about while I was here.' Then asked me how I was doing up in Lansing before the grand jury last October.'"[13]

"Now, wait a minute," burst in Anderson. "Do you mean to say that out of a clear sky he asked you about your appearance before the grand jury?"

"Yes," Hooper said, trying to steady himself by lighting a cigarette with a shaky hand. "I said, 'Oh, I guess I was all right.' He said, 'Well, we are getting kind of worried, getting a little bit nervous, about you, Hooper. You were up there for quite a while this last time.'"

Startled by the opening of the courtroom door, Hooper stopped his oration long enough to permit Sigler to take a seat next to Anderson. "I knew then that he knew I had been here and kept over to testify again the next morning."[14]

"He wasn't asking you if you had been here," insisted Anderson, his expression showing concern.

"No," the witness insisted, "he was telling me that I had been here. Anyway, I smiled it off and said, 'Well they are questioning me about a lot of different bills, you know.' Then he said, 'Bill Green is solid. He is not telling them a thing. He would cut off his arms before he would tell them a darned thing.'"[15]

Noting a pause, Anderson looked up from his whispered conversation with Sigler and curtly instructed Hooper to go on. Lighting another cigarette, the lawmaker continued his tale.

"He got up out of his chair and moved toward the side of my desk and started fumbling in the pockets of his trenchcoat. I figured he was about to give me something, but he didn't. He just said, 'Oh, hell, I guess I can trust you Hooper. If there is anything you need, any money or any attorney, just get in touch with me in Benton Harbor. If I'm not there, why I'll get the word and we'll immediately take care of anything you need.'"[16]

"Then what took place," Anderson goaded the witness.

"Well, I said, 'I don't anticipate the need for either, Floyd, but thanks just the same, though.' As he left, he turned and said, right in front of Agnes Wickens, my stenographer, 'Now, remember if anybody asks you I was only here to discuss the dog racing bill.'"[17]

Staring at Sigler, who was sitting leisurely in his chair, Hooper grew pensive. "In thinking and reflecting on it afterward, I felt that there must have been a leak somewhere that he knew that I was here as long as I was. He didn't mention Mr. McKay's name in his reference to 'we' at all, and I didn't question him about it. But I do know that Frank McKay saw me here and stopped me out in the hall before I testified, and that surely must have told him. But how he knew that I was here overnight I never could figure out, except that McKay must be keeping pretty close track of me."[18]

"Now, you are expressing apprehension, Mr. Hooper," Anderson inquired rather inanely, "that through our inquiry someone may know that you have again been questioned about this situation?"

"Yes," Hooper responded, wiping perspiration from his forehead into an already damp handkerchief. "I felt that Fitzsimmons was setting a trap by coming to see me at that time and telling me these other things, so that if they were nervous about me, they would find out that I had come back here and told this again and would have me pegged. I am very fearful of that and fearful of any consequences, because I know that crowd would probably stop at nothing to gain their own ends in this matter."

"In other words," Anderson asked to clarify an already crystal-clear point, "should Fitzsimmons be recalled before us and inquiry made of the substance of what you told us, he would then know that you reported to us the conversation?"

"That's right."

"And you would be worried for your own safety as to what might happen to you?"

"That's right," Hooper said plaintively. "I couldn't help but feel that way."

The Ingham County Prosecutor nodded, and, seemingly oblivious to the importance of Hooper's plea, turned to ask if Sigler had any questions. Sigler shook his head, and Warren Hooper, his quivering legs barely able to support him, was ushered out of the courtroom, without even a promise of protection, into the hallway where on previous occasions he had been observed by McKay's henchmen.[19] It was almost as though Sigler, in his desire to get McKay, had designated Hooper as his martyr-in-waiting.

IV The following day at 5:20 in the afternoon, Hooper met with Sigler and Anderson, this time at the Special Prosecutor's office at 120 West Ottawa Street in Lansing, to rehash details of his relationship with William Burns.[20] Later that evening, shortly after 9 o'clock, the weary representative returned for another grilling, this time before only Sigler, regarding Fitzsimmons and horse racing legislation in 1941.

"Did Representative George Higgins introduce House Bill 22, which would have regulated pari-mutuel betting under the auspices of a state racing commissioner, during the 1941 legislative session?" snapped Sigler, immediately setting a more hostile tone for the one-on-one night session.

"Yes."

"And isn't it true that in various talks that you had with Frank Fitzsimmons he told you that Frank McKay was interested in the racing bill?"

"Yes," Hooper said, quickly adding, "interested from a negative standpoint. He didn't want the bill passed."

"Then there came a time, did there not, on House Bill 22 when Floyd Fitzsimmons offered you a certain sum of money to kill the bill in the State Affairs Committee?" Sigler asked, his voice still harsh.

"Well," Hooper replied, hesitating momentarily, "I think he said, 'There is a grand—'"

"— in it for you," interposed Sigler, finishing the answer.

"— in it for you," echoed the witness.

"To kill the bill," shouted Sigler.

"To kill the bill," came the parroted reply.

"And he meant a thousand dollars to each member of the committee?" Sigler demanded, knowing that it would be McKay, not Fitzsimmons, who could afford to put up such an amount.

"Yes," Hooper said, fingering his ever-present cigarette. "I had to catch my breath a couple of times to realize what he was talking about."

"That conversation took place near the doorway that leads into the House cloakroom, did it not?"

"Yes, it was."[21]

Thumbing through a sheaf of notes, the Special Prosecutor said sharply: "Fine, let us now go to the 1943 session. During that session Bill 13, which was the bill that Frank McKay was interested in and the one about which you talked with him and the one Bill Green paid you $500, you had talked with Floyd Fitzsimmons about that bill, too, had you not?"

"Yes," murmured the witness, "Floyd had mentioned to me that the bill was with us again and hoped that I would take the same position on it that I had taken in the previous session."

"In other words," Sigler stated with evident disdain, "he wanted it killed in committee."

"That's right. He insisted that it was Frank's wish that it be killed," Hooper replied, blowing smoke in the direction of his legal tormentor.

"Frank McKay's wish that it be killed?" Sigler sneered.

"Yes," Hooper reiterated, "Frank McKay's wish. Floyd said that I should go along, and that those that did, after the bill was killed, would receive the same consideration that he had offered in the previous session."

"Can you remember the name of any other legislator who may have been with you on any occasion when you talked with him?"

"No," came the rapid answer. "I don't recall that there ever was any-one with us when we talked. He would always motion with his hand over to one side and want to talk with me against the wall or in the corner somewhere."

"Fine. You may leave now," Sigler dictated, sending Hooper home to consider his future.[22]

V On the evening of November 29, Hooper again appeared at the grand jury conference room purportedly for yet another meeting with Sigler and Victor C. Anderson. Upon his arrival, he was told to take a seat next to the Ingham County Prosecutor while Sigler left the room. The Special Prosecutor returned momentarily with State Representative William Green in tow.

"I presume you gentlemen know each other," Sigler said sarcastically. Hooper, stunned by this unexpected confrontation, grew flushed and nearly dropped his cigarette as he stared into the eyes of his colleague. Extending a shaking hand, he whispered, "Hello, Bill."

"Did this man ever pay you money, Mr. Hooper?" Sigler asked softly, thrusting an index finger in the direction of Green, who promptly lowered his head, as if in shame.

"Yes, sir."

"How much?"

"$500 to kill the 1941 horse racing bill," Hooper replied.

"Did the money come from Frank McKay?"

"Yes, sir."

The Special Prosecutor wheeled abruptly and faced Green. "You see what we've got on you," he barked. "You might as well confess."[23]

After Green left the room, the same scene was recreated with both Fitzsimmons and McKay. Whatever trepidation Hooper felt before had to be magnified when his eyes met the steely glare of the Republican boss.

Having established that Hooper believed the bribe money came from the Grand Rapids politician, Sigler then sealed Hooper's doom by ask-ing one last question. "Mr. Hooper, did this man, Frank McKay, and Charles Bohn of Detroit, ever offer you money to vote against the anti-chain banking bill?" Almost in a state of nervous prostration, the wit-ness sobbed "Yes."[24] For whatever diabolical motive, Sigler had now cast aside what had remained of Hooper's cloak of secrecy, and the pitiable witness was now dangling helplessly as the bait on Sigler's hook.

VI Hooper arrived home late on November 29, having been detained at grand jury headquarters until past 11 o'clock, and found his wife waiting for him. Wearily he gave her his usual perfunctory passionless greeting and went to the kitchen for his customary bedtime snack of warm milk and cookies.[25]

Tagging after him, "Callie" grew remorseful at their plight. "Warren," she pleaded, "remember what I told you after you took that money from Bill Green?"

Virtually ignoring both her presence and words, Hooper grunted, and tried to leave the room, but was stopped by her firm grip on his arm. "Remember I told you that after that your life wasn't worth a penny, not a penny. From that time on I've been dreadfully afraid. I haven't let the children play in the yard. When I've gone out at night, I've gone in taxis. I've only been out once. Why, Warren, why didn't you stay out of it?"

His expression downcast, her husband gazed blankly at nothing in particular for several seconds before mustering the courage to reply. "Oh, Callie," he said ruefully. "I wish I could ask Sigler for protection because after tonight I think I'll need it. Sigler brought Bill Green in the room and asked me if he had given me money, and I said yes. Then he did the same with Fitzsimmons and McKay. You're right. My life isn't worth a penny now."

Turning ghastly pale, Hooper grasped his stomach. "I don't know about this now. I just thought it would be better to be a state witness and be for the right and have the protection of the state than to be a little man outside of McKay's pie." Racing from the room, his nerves having gotten the best of him, he vomited repeatedly.[26]

VII Based on Warren Hooper's testimony before the grand jury, on December 2, 1944 arrest warrants were issued by Judge Carr against Fitzsimmons, Green, and McKay on charges they had conspired in 1943 to influence the vote on House Bill 13, and a pre-trial examination date of January 15, 1945 was set. Without question, the bull's eye in this target was McKay, whose name the *Detroit Free Press* editorialized had become "a byword and a hissing among the people of Michigan in connection with every suspected racket, whether it was roads, liquor, utilities, bonds, or insurance."[27]

Upon hearing of the indictment, McKay cried to reporters that he was once again a victim of political persecution. "The grand jury went over that old liquor stuff on which I was acquitted by a federal jury and got nowhere. So they turned to this in a last resort. I never paid a legislator

83

in my life," he proclaimed with indignation, "and I never asked anyone else to pay a legislator either. I've never been interested in horse racing."[28] Regarding Fitzsimmons, McKay was solicitous. "I don't think Floyd was ever interested in a horse race bill. He was interested only in dog racing. I know Floyd very well, and I don't think he would pay any legislator for his vote. Floyd is an old friend, and I've seen him frequently. When he comes to the office to see me and I'm not in, he visits with the employees. He once asked me if I would finance a dog race track. I told him no because I would never put money in a business that a commissioner could put you out of with a nod of his head."[29]

A gaggle of newsmen easily cornered a beaming Sigler, who was waiting for their arrival, and asked if the newly-appointed prosecutor realized that by tackling McKay he was moving into the "big league." The smile faded as Sigler shook a warning finger and replied piously: "I don't care what league they're in if the evidence points to their guilt."[30] Mercurially becoming light-hearted again, he promised the reporters more indictments. "It has been a long grind in the grand jury chambers, but we are on our way again, brothers!" Sigler laughed. "Don't let your pencils get dull, boys!"[31]

VIII

Six days later Lansing insiders were stunned when Carr issued another warrant, this time naming only Fitzsimmons, charging the nationally-known promoter with having attempted to bribe Republican State Representative Gail Handy of Eau Claire in 1941 in an effort to prevent House Bill 22, which would have regulated horse racing through the creation of pari-mutuel betting under the auspices of a state racing commissioner, from being sent to the floor by the House State Affairs Committee. After a one day examination, in which Handy was the sole witness, Fitzsimmons was bound over for trial in Ingham County Circuit Court.[32]

The latest allegation against Fitzsimmons was viewed by savvy politicians and lobbyists as nothing more than a calculated and cruel plot by Sigler to strengthen his case against McKay. To those who knew the Special Prosecutor well, the tactic was not unexpected. Fitzsimmons, who had been closely associated with gambling, racing, and boxing, was an easy target. He was a trusting, decent man who was not blessed with great intellect. Sigler likely expected that a conviction of Fitzsimmons would set perfectly the stage for the major horse racing trial involving McKay. With a previously convicted co-defendant at McKay's side, Sigler could anticipate that a jury would receive visually a subliminal presumption of guilt for McKay and Green as well.

Speculation as to the grand jury motives heightened when it was revealed that in July 1941 Handy had informed Herbert J. Rushton about what he perceived as an offer of a bribe, but the attorney general, after conferring with Governor Murray D. VanWagoner, dismissed the charge, telling the lawmaker: "If there is no other witness than yourself, then there is not evidence to convict nor upon which to base an arrest."[33] Prominent legal experts concurred with the attorney general's opinion and questioned the validity of the grand jury's case since state statute required a minimum of two witnesses to any alleged bribery attempt.[34] However, the game stakes were now higher than before, and the ambitious Sigler, with the power of Judge Carr behind him, could bluff a weak hand with the best.

To many Capitol veterans, Sigler's apparent use of Fitzsimmons as a fall-guy assumed an even more callous ruthlessness because they knew that Fitzsimmons had been the person responsible for getting Sigler involved in the grand jury probe. When Bill Green, who had served sixteen years in the legislature, had been indicted by the Ingham County grand jury in August 1943, he had no counsel. While relating his dilemma to his friend Fitzsimmons, the latter suggested that Green retain Kim Sigler. Fitzsimmons, a renowned fight promoter, was a close acquaintance of Sigler, himself an ex-pugilist, and the two had spent many hours making small talk about the "manly art of self-defense" and the glory days when "Fitz" was the chief promoter for Heavyweight Champion of the World Jack Dempsey.

As a favor to Fitzsimmons, Sigler took Green's case for less than his normal fee and promised an easy acquittal. Within weeks, however, Sigler betrayed his client by resigning as defense counsel and joining the grand jury prosecutional staff. Green was outraged, as he had confided specific details to his attorney concerning grafting legislators. In turn, unknown to Green, Sigler violated the rule of confidentiality and used the information to impress Judge Carr with his deep insight into legislative criminal deeds and convinced he grand juror that he would be an indispensable addition to the staff.[35]

Fitzsimmons likewise fumed that his old "sparring partner" had set Green and himself up to "take a dive," but it was to no avail. Inadvertently Fitzsimmons, through Green, had made Sigler the grand jury's "White Knight" and had given the special prosecutor a second chance to use "Fitz" for his own selfish goals.[36]

IX While the grand jury cauldron was bubbling in Lansing, sinister figures were gathering to plot the fate of Sigler's key witness against Frank McKay. A vivid portrayal of the sordid details of the preparations was set forth by Louis Brown, an inmate at Southern Michigan Prison at Jackson who was a participant in the events, and whose story was accepted as true by both Sigler and the State Police.[37]

According to Brown, in early December, within the walls of Southern Michigan Prison at Jackson, a select group of inmates headed by Ray Bernstein and Harry Keywell, leaders of Detroit's notorious Purple Gang who were serving life sentences for murder as a result of their involvement in the Collingwood Massacre, received an offer of $15,000 from another convict, who was acting as an emissary, to kill an unnamed prominent politician. Without asking for details, Keywell said that the figure was at least $10,000 too light, and Bernstein concurred.[38]

About a week later, Brown testified, the prison's deputy warden, D. C. Pettit, and Inspector Robert Wilson reassembled the clique and suggested that the ante would be raised by the amount requested. A few days passed, and then Pettit introduced a man from Flint, who called himself "Mr. Wake," to the would-be conspirators. The visitor showed the convicts a photograph of Hooper and promised to pay $25,000 for the murder. Pettit promised Bernstein and Keywell guns, a state car, a bogus set of license plates, and passage from the prison if they would accept the offer. Three days later, another gathering was called at which Wake took $10,000 from a valise and stacked it on a table. Also making a brief appearance as a show of good faith for payment of the balance, Brown claimed, were Warden Harry Jackson and a man introduced by the warden as Frank McKay. After the guests departed, Pettit placed the money in a large envelope and entrusted it to Joe Poirier, the treasurer for inmate funds.[39]

Brown contended that Wake stated that he would ascertain the day the intended victim was to leave Lansing and would notify Pettit. He stressed McKay's wealth and influence and added that the Grand Rapids financier was relying on them to protect his gambling interests by silencing the Albion senator.[40]

Acting on his own initiative, Bernstein instructed his chief lieutenant in Detroit, Harry Fleisher, to hire a triggerman for $5,000. On December 26, 1945, Fleisher, his partner Myron "Mike" Selik, and two small-time petty crooks, Henry Luks and Sammy Abramowitz, who consented to split the fee for an opportunity to break into the big time, drove to Albion to case the job. According to Luks, they arrived approximately at 8 o'clock in the morning and parked about a block from the intended victim's house in hopes that he would soon depart.[41]

Not having been informed who the target was, Luks spoke for his partner in seeking information. "They [Fleisher and Selik] never said what the victim's business was in Lansing, but they did mention that he had some testimony to give there. But they never said to who," Luks later told Sigler. "I asked if Frank McKay had anything to do with it, and Mike Selik told me never to mind about that. He said, 'The money is up for this case and that's all you have to worry about.' I mentioned, 'Does this fellow have something to do with the grand jury?' and Mike told me not to worry."[42]

When Hooper did not appear, Luks said the four drove around the house twice and discussed how to bump off the would-be victim. "Harry said the guy was a doctor of some kind, so it was suggested that Sammy, who had a bad arm at the time, go into his office and show the doctor his arm. While he was looking at it, I was supposed to come from behind and hit him over the head with a blackjack or blunt instrument. Sammy also suggested just walking in and shooting him. We also discussed strangling him, using his necktie or belt or rope."[43] The four then returned to Detroit having failed to accomplish their mission.

Luks felt that the job was "too hot" and dropped out, so, on December 29 Abramowitz was picked up by Sammy Fleisher, like his older brother Harry an oft-convicted felon, and the two drove to Albion in hopes of having better luck. According to Abramowitz, they drove by the house twelve or fifteen times, but it appeared no-one was home. During this period, Fleisher told Abramowitz that the target was named Hooper and that he had to be "silenced real quick before he could talk to the grand jury."[44]

Once again failing in their objective, the would-be murderers met with Harry Fleisher at the mob's Detroit headquarters, O'Larry's Bar. When told of the abortive mission, the dark-haired mobster shook his head and mumbled: "Jesus, he's a tough guy to get. We'll have to try again."[45]

Daunted, but determined, Sam Fleisher and Abramowitz made their next trek to Albion on January 2, 1945. This time, Hooper was home, but no attempt was made on his life because his wife and two children were with him. When informed of their decision not to wipe out the Senator in front of his family, Harry Fleisher concurred that they had done the right thing.[46]

The elder Fleisher then visited Bernstein in Warden Jackson's prison office and related what had transpired. The Purple Gang leader, doubtless disgusted at his aide's inability to accomplish a task so simple as murder, realized that if the killing was to be done before the January 14 deadline, he would have to do it himself.

The Purple Gang chieftain was aware that D. C. Pettit previously had sent inmate Harold Johnson, driving the deputy warden's maroon coupe, to receive a .38 calibre pistol from the arsenal at O'Larry's Bar. Consequently, on January 8 he dispatched Ernest Henry, another member of his inside gang, to Jackson to purchase a pair of work gloves. Brown, who as one of Pettit's houseboys had many liberties, delivered the gloves to the deputy warden as Bernstein had instructed, and they were placed beside the revolver. Bernstein also arranged for Pettit to learn, and relay to him, the exact day and time of Hooper's departure from Lansing.

Early in the afternoon of January 11, Warden Jackson, in Pettit's absence, summoned Bernstein and Harry Keywell over the loudspeaker to his office. Jackson ordered Louis Brown to go over to the prison "dress out shop" and check out civilian clothing for the two convicts. Bernstein and Keywell then went to Pettit's house, picked up the revolver and gloves, and shortly after the 3:30 afternoon dinner bugle blared, drove away from the prison yard in the deputy warden's maroon automobile. Close behind in a red car, possibly that of Pettit's wife, came at least two other accomplices.

XMeanwhile, in Lansing, Warren Hooper was being closely monitored. Both his wife and secretary, as well as several legislative colleagues and personal acquaintances, were aware that he was planning to avoid the Republican state convention at Grand Rapids and the inevitable confrontation with McKay that would occur there. Instead, he planned to return to Albion on the afternoon of January 11. He ate a light lunch, packed his travel kit, drove from the Capitol parking lot to a local hotel to conclude some osteopathic business, and then embarked on what he expected to be a leisurely ride home.

Somewhere south of Lansing along M-99, the accomplices' red car pulled in behind the senator's green Mercury and proceeded to follow at a safe distance. Keywell and Bernstein had parked on a side road, north of the intersection of M-99 and M-50. After bolting on a phony license plate, they pulled onto the shoulder of M-99 and waited.

As Hooper neared the assassin's rendezvous point, the red car passed that of Hooper. Approaching the maroon automobile driven by Keywell, the driver flashed his headlights as a signal that the senator was in the car immediately following.

Suddenly, the maroon vehicle lurched into the Mercury's path, forcing it into a long skid across the highway. Keywell then cut in front of the stopped car to prevent an escape. Bernstein leapt from the passenger seat, raced to the senator's car, opened the left door, and seized the terrified driver by the overcoat. His hat jerked down over eyes, gangland fashion, Hooper was shoved to the right side of the seat. Gruffly yanking his prey back toward him, Bernstein pressed his gloved index finger against the trigger of the .38, placing the first of three bullets into Hooper's skull.

In the meantime, the occupants of the lookout car had re-entered the penitentiary, changed clothes, destroyed the license plate, and occupied themselves with odd jobs while awaiting the return of their comrades. Soon afterward, Bernstein and Keywell drove in, still in a state of excitement. At the deputy warden's house, they donned their prison garb and prepared to slip quietly into their daily routine. Before leaving, they handed the weapon, gloves and license plate to their accomplices to destroy.[47]

The murderous bargain had been fulfilled. Warren Hooper would never repeat in open court the testimony he had given before the grand jury, and, as he was the sole witness, Sigler's case against McKay, Green, and Fitzsimmons was as dead as their accuser.

X I Receiving news of the assassination, Sigler raced to the scene to take charge. Immediately knowing that his case against McKay was gone, the Special Prosecutor deftly, almost as though it was premeditated, decided to use the brutal elimination of his key witness to his advantage. He planned subtly to plant the seed in the minds of the state's citizenry that the probe into corruption obviously was on the verge of major revelations which placed the reputations of prominent people in grave jeopardy, and that the person who had the most to gain by Hooper's death was Frank McKay. Sigler knew that if he played his cards shrewdly, this tragedy would not only perpetuate the grand jury probe into legislative malfeasance, as well as his $100 a day salary, for years, but also would enable him to pin an accessory to murder charge on the Grand Rapids financier. To Sigler, the silver lining around the dark cloud of a lawmaker slain just four days before he was scheduled to perform his greatest public service grew larger by the minute.

Shortly after 10 a.m. on January 12, Sigler, having met with Judge Carr, called a press conference and publicly revealed, for the first time, that the slain senator was to have been a state witness in the horse racing conspiracy trial.[48] "Hooper made a complete confession involving McKay, Fitzsimmons, and Green before the grand jury," the Special Prosecutor intoned solemnly, "and was granted immunity to testify against them. His death is a serious blow to our case against McKay and the others. Because of this, I have received from Judge Carr a thirty-day postponement of the pre-trial examination."[49]

In private, Sigler did his best to maintain his posture of shock, even though his prior action in confronting McKay with Hooper had made the senator a marked man. To his *Detroit News* confidante Al Nieber, the Special Prosecutor poured forth an apparently remorseful tale, but one which, when published, would not only clear him of any wrong-doing, but also tighten the noose around McKay's neck. "After the confrontation, I suggested to Hooper that he ought to have protection, but he refused, saying it would be obvious and would be embarrassing," Sigler related, adroitly shifting the blame for the murder to the victim's shoulders. "We should have had the examination sooner, but Hooper pleaded for a delay, and I consented. Hooper wanted the honor of sitting in the Senate for a few days or weeks. He was elected to the Senate last November and was impressed by the honor. He wanted to be a senator as long as he could. Of course, the minute he took the witness stand and admitted bribe-taking his career as a senator would be over."[50]

Slowly walking from one side of the room to the other, Sigler turned his attention to McKay, tarring his adversary with a not-so-subtle inference that the G.O.P. boss should not be considered above suspicion when authorities investigated the assassination. "I never dreamed of murder. Maybe I should have, but I didn't," Sigler shrugged.[51]

Having cleared his conscience, the Special Prosecutor launched a series of stinging jabs at McKay. "Of course, McKay, Fitz, and Green knew we had them hooked, and that McKay knew if Hooper could be out of the picture somehow, he could get off the hook. But I just didn't think of murder. That didn't even occur to me when I learned that McKay and Fitzsimmons went to Chicago for some kind of a mysterious meeting—a meeting we have not straightened out yet," he sneered insinuatingly. "Incidentally, Hooper also linked McKay in the bribery on the bank bill and was also an accuser of [millionaire industrialist and Michigan National Bank Board Chairman] Charlie Bohn in Detroit. I hear Bohn is running up and down Griswold Street protesting he doesn't know a thing about the murder."[52]

XII Frank McKay, tanned and smiling, had arrived in Grand Rapids from his Miami estate on Thursday, January 11. Friday morning he was sitting, still clad in bright paisley pajamas, in his suite in the Morton Hotel, swapping stories with political cronies attending the Republican state convention, when a *Detroit Times* reporter entered and broke the news about Hooper's murder. McKay took it calmly, but leaped to his feet in shock when the newsman added that Sigler had publicly identified the Albion lawmaker as "the fingerman" against McKay in the upcoming graft conspiracy examination.[53]

Pacing the floor, an obviously troubled McKay offered his informant a scoop. He said that the slaying was "a terrible thing" and urged that "all law enforcement agencies should be relentless in their search for those responsible." Then he related his version of his dealings with Hooper. "The first time I saw him," he began, "was about two years ago when he came to my office and said the osteopaths in Michigan wanted to open a hospital in Grand Rapids. He asked me for $2,000 as a contribution toward buying the home of the late Bishop Plagens. I told him I had a lot of physician friends and couldn't contribute because of my friendship with physicians who opposed the project. The second time was about a year ago at the Book-Cadillac Hotel in Detroit. I had just come back from Florida and had just checked in my room. There was a knock at my door and it was Mr. Hooper. He apparently had been in the lobby and had followed me to my room. I said to him: 'Mr. Hooper, how is your hospital in Grand Rapids?' Hooper said it was coming all right, but he needed money to equip it. Hooper said: 'If you would give me $500 it would be very helpful.' But I again told him I could not do it, and he did not press the issue as he had done the first time in Grand Rapids. Then we made a little casual conversation about Republican politics, and he left. The last time was when I shook hands and exchanged greetings with him in the waiting room of the Lansing grand jury headquarters where we both had been called to appear. Hooper was a total stranger to me before that first visit."[54]

McKay instinctively sensed that Sigler was plotting to link him to the murder and that he would have to employ all his considerable skills to squelch that scheme. Given his lengthy background as a wheeler-dealer and his gangster connections through his Purple Gang bodyguards, that would be no easy task.[55] However, giving this interview, filled with half-truths and total fabrications, seemed to be a promising beginning.

Meanwhile, his co-defendants, after hasty consultations with their lawyers, also came out on the side of justice. Fitzsimmons, with Green at his shoulder, told reporters: "This is once that we are rooting for Kim Sigler and the Carr grand jury, and hoping that they will clear this thing up quick. We know what a lot of people are probably saying or thinking. Nobody who knows any of us would think such an awful thing for even a minute, but the other people are different. It's an awful thing, and the sooner the killer is found, the quicker this silly talk about us will stop.

On this one, we're in Sigler's corner." Green concurred, adding: "We are both family men, and it's tough on our families, too."[56]

Fitzsimmons' support for Sigler might have been tempered had the slow-witted fight promoter realized that he was to be Sigler's next "patsy." Although the main event against McKay had to be postponed because of death, the preliminary bout against poor "Fitz" would go on as scheduled.

CHAPTER FOUR

"FITZ" TAKES THE FALL

For Floyd Fitzsimmons, the brutal slaying of Warren Hooper merely meant that his already bad luck had taken a turn for the worse. Following the murder, Fitzsimmons' chief defense attorney, Fred R. Walker of Detroit, spent the rest of January in a futile attempt to postpone his client's trial on the grounds that newspaper coverage of the Hooper murder had prejudiced the case against Fitzsimmons. This claim rested on Sigler's repeated statements to the press that Hooper was to have been the state's star witness in the other horse racing trial.

Appearing before Judge Carr on January 17, Walker dramatically pointed to a stack of newspapers. "I insist that a fair trial is impossible at this time in view of the many newspaper stories linking Fitzsimmons' name in the Hooper murder," the barrister argued. "Senator Hooper was killed by someone with a motive. The public is bound to assume that Fitzsimmons is a person who would have an interest in what happened to Senator Hooper. There is a cloud of suspicion and no court could free that from any juror."[1]

Sigler opposed the motion, claiming that his "learned brother" was impugning the integrity of Ingham County residents by implying that they would not fulfill their oaths as jurors to listen without partiality to the evidence. Carr, as usual, sided with his protege and denied the request.[2]

Walker then notified the Court, in compliance with Michigan statutes, that Fitzsimmons would utilize an alibi defense and prove that the defendant was not in Lansing on February 20, 1941, the date of the alleged bribery attempt, but was in Grand Rapids attending the Democratic State Convention. To substantiate this claim, Walker sought permission to inspect the Olds Hotel registration records, which had been impounded by the grand jury. Once Again, Sigler objected and Carr favored the prosecution.[3]

93

Frustrated, but undaunted, by the apparent collusion between the Court and the Special Prosecutor, on January 19 Walker filed his client's alibi with the Ingham County Circuit Court. He contended that through the testimony of a minimum of six witnesses, including a former Deputy Michigan Secretary of State, he would show Fitzsimmons could not have committed the alleged crime.[4] Accepting the petition without comment, Carr denied another motion for delay and reaffirmed January 29, 1945 as the date for the trial to be held in the Mason Court House with Circuit Judge John Simpson of Jackson presiding.[5]

II With chill winds howling and whipping snow flurries around the picturesque Court House, Judge Simpson gaveled the proceedings into session on schedule. Walker, as expected, asked for a delay, making on an emotional presentation in which he pleaded with the Court to examine an intangible fact carefully. "When you read or hear, Your Honor," he begged, "that Judge Leland W. Carr said that Fitzsimmons stands to gain by Hooper's death, and that the writer or commentator fails to add that Hooper did not figure in this particular case, I say that it creates a cloud of suspicion that makes it impossible for my client to have a fair trial."[6]

Simpson, like Carr, was unmoved by the "cloud of suspicion" speech and denied the motion with the terse observation that he did not think people took seriously what they read in newspapers.[7] Referring to the finance conspiracy case, the jurist added contemptuously: "We managed to get a jury and conduct a fair trial last time, and I see no reason why we can't repeat now. Under your theory, Fitzsimmons could never be brought to trial if the murderers of Senator Hooper are not found."[8]

Sensing a tone of predestination in the judge's remark, Walker decided against emphasizing the obvious difference in circumstances—the murder of a witness—and retreated to the defense table. Within two hours a jury consisting of five farmers and nine housewives was impaneled and in mid-afternoon the trial began.

In his opening argument, Sigler exploded his initial bombshell by telling jurors that former representative Handy had erred in his pre-trial examination testimony by establishing February 20, 1941 as the date of the attempted bribery. Sigler stated, with what he hoped was enough conviction so that the jury would not wonder if the mistake had been remembered only after the alibi defense had been entered, that upon reflection the former state representative recalled that the $500 had been tendered to him on a day that the House State Affairs Committee, of which Handy was a member, held an afternoon session—and since that had taken place only once that week—the bribe had to have been offered on February 18. Thus, Sigler said with a shrug of his shoulders, Fitzsimmons' alibi was useless.[9]

Having removed the only sure stumbling block to his case, Sigler strode toward the jury. "The People will prove," he stated with assurance, "that the defendant met Gail Handy around noon in the House chambers; that Fitzsimmons and Handy walked together to the window and talked about the bill; that the defendant told Handy that he was interested in the bill and offered to put $500 in Handy's mailbox to keep the bill in committee. The People will further prove that Handy indignantly rejected the offer and promptly reported the matter to the State Affairs Committee."[10]

Speaking for the defense, assistant counsel Charles W. Gore of Benton Harbor traced Fitzsimmons' life as a sports promoter and upstanding citizen. He concluded by stating that the defense would definitively prove that Handy bore personal animus against the defendant and had threatened in public "to get Floyd Fitzsimmons if it is the last thing I ever do."[11] As Gore took his seat, Simpson adjourned court until the following morning.

With an air of supreme confidence, Sigler summoned his lone witness, Gail Handy, to the stand. With the jury sitting in rapt attention, the jut-jawed, wavy-haired forty-seven year old farmer and former lightweight boxer, speaking in a calm, steady voice, recounted the scene on February 18, 1941. "While I was standing at my desk in the House reading my mail, Floyd Fitzsimmons, whom I had known casually for some twenty years, stepped up to the rail behind me and said: 'Gail, I'd like to speak with you for a minute,'" the witness stated. "I walked behind the rail and he put his arm around my shoulder and we started to walk casually toward the back window on the eastern wall. He said, 'Gail, where do you stand on this racing bill?' I told him I didn't know what amendments had been offered and that I couldn't tell him where I stood on it. Well, he said, 'If you go along with me on it I've got $500 for you. I'll have the bill under control then, and I'll put the money in your mailbox.'"[12]

Pausing to follow Sigler as he subtly moved toward the jury so that the witness would have to speak in their direction, Handy continued his tale. "I told him I wasn't interested in that kind of money."

"What do you mean by 'that kind of money?'" Sigler interjected.

"I mean bribe money," came the quick reply. "I told him that if the bill had any merit it would come out. If it didn't, it would stay in."

"What was the effect of this upon you?" asked the Special Prosecutor, skillfully leading the witness to the next crucial revelation.

Anticipating what Sigler was trying to do, Walker rose and objected to the question as immaterial and possibly prejudicial. Simpson thought for a moment before instructing the witness to answer.

"Well, Handy said, "it made me a little mad and disgusted. So my wife and I went down to the attorney general's office."

"Did anything ever happen about it?" pressed Sigler.

"I object to that, as to what happened?" shouted Walker.

"All right," smiled Sigler, "if you object to that, I'll leave it right there."[13]

Herbert J. Rushton then was summoned to the stand by defense counsel. Known for his dislike of both Judge Carr and Sigler, as well as for his association with Frank D. McKay, the heavy set, brash, tough-talking former attorney general from Escanaba in the upper peninsula admitted that he had not acted on Handy's information, but that part of the blame had to rest with the grand juror.

"Carr was in his office when I talked with him," Rushton said gruffly, leaning forward to scowl at Sigler. "I told him we had thoroughly investigated it at a conference and decided there wasn't sufficient evidence to issue a warrant. I told him we had taken Handy's statement. He didn't ask for it, so I didn't show it to him. This matter was not presented to the grand jury because we were presenting other matters. Besides I didn't believe Handy because he had told me three different stories. One minute he said $2,000. One minute, $1,500. Another minute, $500. I told Judge Carr the story and the facts in his office or in the courtroom sometime between September and November of 1943. Two investigators, Jim Shepard and Loomis Preston, both recommended that a warrant not be issued because there were so many conflicting stories. I also discussed the matter informally with Floyd."[14]

"So you sat down and had a little friendly chat with Fitzsimmons and some others," Sigler said incredulously, "and that is all you did about this matter?"

"The conversation was not so friendly," was the curt reply.

"By the way, did you send a copy of Handy's statement of 1941 to Fitzsimmons after Judge Carr had issued the arrest warrant?" Sigler asked nonchalantly.

"Yes," blurted Rushton, his face flushed with rage, "it was my right."[15]

Sigler then called Judge Carr to the stand. Under questioning by the Special Prosecutor, the scholarly, gray-haired jurist, attired in his customary three-piece black suit, coldly denied the veracity of Rushton's contentions.

"Judge," Sigler said in an almost reverential tone, "Mr. Rushton has testified under oath that he told you about the Gail Handy matter sometime during the months of September, October, or November of 1943. Will you state whether or not that is true?"

"No. That is not correct," Carr declared. "Mr. Rushton at no time discussed with me or mentioned to me the Gail Handy occurrence."

"He further states, Judge Carr, that he talked with you either in your office or the courtroom in Lansing, Michigan concerning the fact that he had taken a statement from Gail Handy, is that true?"

"No, that is not a fact. It was not discussed with me at all. The first time I learned that Handy had made a statement to Rushton was when Handy told me so. That was when Handy was brought before the grand jury last September. The matter was then investigated."

"Just one further question upon the matter, Judge Carr," Sigler said solicitously. "The witness further testified that he took the statement of State Representative Loomis Preston and that Preston had stated something to the effect that Gail Handy had said something about $2,000 and that he told you about that statement. State whether or not that is true."

"No, that is not correct," Carr said sternly. "The matter of Representative Preston making a statement to Mr. Rushton was not at any time called to my attention."

Unable to contain himself any longer, Gore rose slowly to his feet. "I wish to move, Your Honor," he said in a loud voice, "that the testimony of Judge Carr—all of it—be stricken from the record on the ground that it has sought to impeach the testimony of another witness on a collateral matter, and that Judge Carr's presence in this courtroom is highly prejudicial to the defendant."

"Motion denied," snapped Simpson, his eyes blazing with scorn.[16]

With his index finger aimed at the jury, Sigler got in the last word of the day's session. "Floyd Fitzsimmons tried to corrupt this farmer from Eau Claire and he knows it and Herb Rushton knows it if he has a brain in his head," Sigler assured the panel, adding sarcastically, "and Herb Rushton has brains!"[17]

On the morning of February 1, Fitzsimmons, whose testimony barely had begun the previous day before being interrupted to interject the remarks of Rushton and Carr, resumed his own defense. Knowing that Fitzsimmons' fate had been sealed by Judge Carr's damning revelations against the defendant's chief witness, Sigler launched a relentless attempt to link Fitzsimmons to Hooper and McKay, neither of whom had any connection whatsoever with the case being tried. The tiny courtroom was crowded to capacity as the state's most colorful trial lawyer began his inquisition.

"Floyd," Sigler said in a friendly way, "you have worked for Herb Rushton in political campaigns, have you not?"

"Yes," the gaunt, graying witness replied.

"You knew Rushton well enough to call him 'Herb,' didn't you?"

"Well, I call him 'the general,'" Fitzsimmons said seriously,

"Oh, you give him a good title," Sigler said with a smile.

"I give him a title to which he is entitled, that's all," was the reply in a cracking voice.

"And Rushton is interested in racing, too?"

"Everyone knows Rushton owns trotting horses," Fitzsimmons said, quickly adding, "I'm interested only in dog racing."[18]

Picking up on the aside, Sigler immediately used it to his advantage. "Yes," he began methodically, "immediately after you were served with a subpoena last summer by the grand jury, you went to see McKay, didn't you?"

"Yes," admitted Fitzsimmons innocently, "but I didn't go to see him in connection with the grand jury. I went to see him about dog racing, but he wasn't interested."

"So who did you expect to get to finance dog racing tracks if you were successful in legalizing dog racing?"

"Well, I was going to incorporate with Jack Dempsey and sell stock."

Like a vulture pecking on the carcass of its dying prey, once again Sigler used the witness' statement to open another wound. "Tell us, Floyd," he said thoughtfully, "during the past ten years by what means have you made your money?"

"During the last seven years I have actually been retired," Fitzsimmons stated. "As a fight promoter and booking agent for Jack Dempsey between 1919 and 1932, I made about $100,000. Don't think I failed to lay away a little money."

"You never saw a hundred thousand dollars in your life," Sigler shot back.

"That's not so," Fitzsimmons responded sharply. "I am not in the poor house. I've been making a living."

"Really," Sigler said incredulously. "So who paid your expenses while you were promoting a dog race bill in Lansing?"

"I paid my own."

"Sure, you did, but who furnished the money?" Sigler asked, striking the rail of the witness box with the palm of his hand.

"I got it from Jack Dempsey," Fitzsimmons confessed, lowering his head.[19]

Refusing to ease the pressure on the witness, whose shoulders seemed to become more stooped and the dark circles around his eyes more pronounced as the minutes passed, Sigler asked in a voice louder than necessary: "During the past seven years have you made any money in politics?"

"Yes, " Fitzsimmons readily agreed, "I made some in the campaigns of Frank Fitzgerald for Governor, but I can't recall how much. I handled Governor Fitzgerald's campaign in the fourth congressional district."

"Frank McKay was also working for Fitzgerald, wasn't he?"

"Yes."

"Well, Floyd, who paid you?" Sigler inquired sharply.

"Mr. Fitzgerald paid me."

"Did Frank McKay pay you anything?"

"He never gave me a nickel," Fitzsimmons snapped, regaining a bit of vigor in his speech.

"How much money did you make on that campaign?" demanded Sigler, moving menacingly toward the witness.

"I don't know."

"That political campaign in which Frank McKay was involved?"

"I don't know," reiterated the shaken Fitzsimmons, leaving unchallenged Sigler's damning remark associating him with McKay.

"Tell the jury how much!" screamed Sigler, his face almost touching that of the witness.

"I don't know," pleaded Fitzsimmons, almost in tears. "I don't remember."

Unable to stand the badgering of his client any longer, Gore rose to object, saying "I submit the question has been asked and answered."

"It hasn't been answered," insisted Sigler, and the Court ruled in his favor.

"Can't you even give us an idea?" chided the inquisitor.

"No," came the whispered response, "I can't give any idea."

"Couldn't you tell us whether it was $1 or $100 or $5,000?" sneered Sigler in mock disbelief. "Can't you give us any help?"

His nerves frayed nearly to breaking, Fitzsimmons yelled back: "No! No! I didn't go out looking for money—chiseling. I worked for four months once for you in your campaign for state senator ..."

Waving frantically, Sigler tried to stop the witness, but Fitzsimmons continued, "... and didn't get anything."

Judge Simpson loudly banged his gavel and sternly cautioned the witness to make direct answers to questions. "Well," Fitzsimmons said in explanation, "he wanted to know something, so I told him."

"Are you in a contemptuous mood toward me?" Simpson barked. "You pay attention to the questions asked you and don't talk back like that to me or you will find yourself in contempt of court."

"Yes, Your Honor," Fitzsimmons muttered meekly.[20]

Knowing that he had completely exhausted his old friend, Sigler moved on to his main area of interest—linking McKay to the murder of Senator Hooper. Even though McKay was involved in no way in the trial being conducted, Sigler forged ahead, confident that all objections to his line of questioning would be overruled. The ruin of Floyd Fitzsimmons was now close at hand.

"All right, Floyd," Sigler said, almost purring at the emaciated figure before him, "how many times were you over to see Frank McKay after you were before the grand jury on the 31st of October, 1944?"

Bounding from his chair, Gore sputtered: "I make an objection on the grounds that the question is incompetent, irrelevant, and immaterial."

Raising a hand to silence a prosecution rebuttal, Judge Simpson ruled against the defense. "Well, I can't tell yet what the purpose of it is. Go ahead, Mr. Sigler," he stated, adding cryptically, "we'll take care of it."

"I often went over to Grand Rapids," Fitzsimmons said, his breathing now labored, "because I have relatives there, and I dropped into McKay's office because he was a friend of mine to find out what was going on politically. I do not run errands for McKay. I carted his lawyer—Gene Garey, who is a friend of mine from New York—down to Detroit once. I got acquainted with him because he was connected with Madison Square Gardens. I believe McKay asked me to drive him."

"Do you know Bill McKeighan, the former mayor over at Flint?" asked Sigler.

"Sure I do. I don't know how many times I've seen him. I did see him the night I took Gene Garey in. I was in Detroit and went up to his room at the Book-Cadillac."

"Why did you see Bill McKeighan?" prodded Sigler.

Flustered, Fitzsimmons blurted: "I wanted to ask him if he knew where I could get some nylon hose for my wife for her wedding anniversary."

"You drove all that way about some nylon hose," replied Sigler with a smirk.

"And other purposes as well," volunteered the woeful Fitzsimmons.

Lunging forward, his fist clenched, Sigler shouted: "Like you do whenever Frank McKay or Bill McKeighan want you to!"

"No! No!" screamed the trembling sportsman. "That isn't true!"

Abruptly altering both his demeanor and voice, Sigler calmly inquired of Fitzsimmons, who was wiping his perspiring forehead with a handkerchief: "Who signed your bond in this case, Floyd?"

"Frank McKay."[21]

To cement Fitzsimmons' guilt by association, Sigler casually inquired: "Oh, Floyd, did you also visit Bill Green, like McKay your co-defendant in another horse racing case, in Hillman after the grand jury warrant was served?"

"Yes," Fitzsimmons said, "but I went there to go pheasant hunting."

"Well, did you go hunting?"

"No," came the innocent admission, "because it was off-season. I got mixed up. Those things can happen to anyone."

"But you are a hunter, right?"

"Yes, sir."

"So when was the last time you owned a gun?"

"Fifteen years ago," sighed Fitzsimmons, realizing that his motive for seeing Green was now highly suspect.[22]

Like a master carpenter, the Special Prosecutor drove the final nail into Fitzsimmons' elaborately constructed coffin. "Did you see the late Senator Warren Hooper after the issuance of the warrant, too?" Sigler asked.

"Yes, twice," was the halting response. "Once in Albion and once at the House of Representatives."

"Didn't you go to Hooper after the warrant was issued and say to him: 'We're getting a little afraid of you. Bill Green is going along with us.'"

"No, I did not."

"When did you see him in Albion?"

"I was going to Detroit and was low on gas coupons so I stopped and asked Warren if he could help me out with a couple of tickets."

"So you knew Warren Hooper well enough so you could ask him to give you some of his gas tickets," Sigler repeated while gazing intently at the jurors.

Suddenly sensing the impact of the statement, Fitzsimmons spat out "No." The damage had been done, however, and Fitzsimmons was firmly ensconced in the jurors' minds as an intimate of McKay and his chief henchman Bill McKeighan, as well as Warren Hooper. His fate was sealed, and the prosecution rested its case.[23]

In an attempt to minimize the sensationalism of the prosecution's presentation, defense counsel set forth a two-prong response. First, a deposition was submitted from Thomas DeRosa, a twenty-seven year old sailor and former Berrien County deputy sheriff, who was at the time of the trial stationed at the Great Lakes Naval Training Base. DeRosa swore that he had heard Handy at a political rally at Eau Claire in August 1940, after learning that Fitzsimmons had withdrawn his support for the state representative, tell Fitzsimmons that "I'll get even with you if it's the last thing I do." DeRosa's allegation was corroborated by Walter Gillice who testified that he, also, was present when Handy's threat was uttered.[24] Second,

Gore moved for a mistrial claiming Sigler's references to Hooper and McKay had been prejudicial against his client, but to no-one's surprise the motion was denied.[25]

Following Simpson's ruling, Sigler, looking dapper in a three-piece gray pinstripe suit and burgundy tie, began his summation to the jury. Pacing slowly and carefully weighing his remarks, the Special Prosecutor paused to lean on the jury box rail. "There are things in this case I cannot understand," he said, shaking his head gravely, "and one of these is that the former Attorney General of Michigan had the nerve and temerity to come into this court and glibly testify that he had talked to Judge Carr about this bribe matter. We were compelled to summon Judge Carr to prove this was not true. If a man is going to hold high office he ought to perform his duty, and it shouldn't make any difference if it hurts his friends. Herb Rushton knew enough to issue a warrant, but he was not interested. He was interested in just one thing—to whitewash the situation. I'm not going to mince words. It would have disturbed Herb Rushton if anyone was brought to justice for graft."[26]

Having slandered his grand jury predecessor, Sigler moved on to discuss the defendant. "Fitzsimmons was in Lansing in 1941 as a lobbyist and thought he had the members of the State Affairs Committee in the palm of his hand. This committee was studying the horse race bill which was detrimental to Fitzsimmons' interests. When he found out he did not, he did the thing which may sound the death knell of all democracies—he offered graft. He offered a bribe to a man to violate his constitutional oath," he said caustically. "It is a sad state of affairs when a man in a position Handy occupied is approached for the purpose of getting him to violate his trust. Unfortunately, this is just another sordid story pertaining to the state legislature—a story of a certain interest seeking to get its end by means of bribery. Fitzsimmons is guilty of this terrible crime. I am confident you jurors have not been deceived."[27]

After Sigler concluded, Gore started what proved to be a ninety minute discourse in which he implored the veniremen to use their good sense and realize that his client had not received a "fair and impartial trial." He also again condemned the prosecution's tactic of changing the date of the alleged bribe after learning the defense had an unassailable alibi."[28]

Following Gore's statement, Simpson charged the jury, telling them there were three essential aspects to consider: first, whether a bribe offer had been made; second, whether Handy was a legislator at the time of the offer; and third, whether the offer had been made to influence Handy's actions as a legislator. In a pointed reference to defense counsel's claim, Simpson noted, in an interesting interpretation of jurisprudence, that the date of the alleged bribe was "not a material element" and that it would be sufficient "if you find the defendant offered a bribe sometime on or about the date specified." The jury then was led out of the courtroom by the bailiff.[29]

While the panel was deliberating, Sigler, in a jovial mood, grabbed Fitzsimmons by the arm. "Well, Fitz," he joked, "we went the full fifteen rounds, eh?" Pulling away, Fitzsimmons' only response was a stony glare.[30] Still smiling, the Special Prosecutor strode into the hallway to banter with reporters. Incredibly, he told the newsmen, who had not witnessed Fitzsimmons' snub in the courtroom, that when he made his congenial comment the defendant had responded warmly, telling the Special Prosecutor: "It was a fair trial, Kim. I haven't any kick coming. I'm still your friend. If there's ever a time you need help, come to me."[31]

At 5:05 p.m., after deliberating only ninety minutes, the jury reached a decision and found the fifty-nine year old defendant guilty as charged. Visibly nervous, his complexion more sallow than normal, Fitzsimmons stood, with head bowed, as Judge Simpson pronounced a three year prison sentence to be served at Southern Michigan Prison in Jackson.[32]

While Fitzsimmons' lawyers were announcing an impending appeal and the downcast defendant, after hugging his wife, was posting $4,000 of his own money as a cash bond, the boastful Special Prosecutor was informing his cadre of press followers that his next target would be lobbyists for medical professions. With another easy victory under his belt, Sigler pompously pledged that he would never let grafters have even a moment's rest.[33]

CHAPTER FIVE

AN AYE FOR A TOOTH

Following the conviction of Fitzsimmons, Sigler was eager to pounce upon more small-time grafters. His opportunity was not long in coming, as on February 10, 1945 Judge Carr swore out warrants charging that seven men, including four former members of the Michigan legislature, "did unlawfully and wickedly agree, combine, conspire, confederate, and engage, with and among themselves, to willfully and corruptly influence" the vote on House Bill 199 to regulate the practice of dentistry and dental surgery.[1]

Having arranged a press conference to coincide with Carr's action, Sigler promised his eager listeners that he would prove that in 1939 Drs. Clarence J. Wright of Lansing, M. S. DeViliers of Detroit, and Edwin J. Chamberlain of Grand Rapids, all officials of the Michigan State Dental Society, raised "several thousand dollars" for the purpose of purchasing the support of State Senator Stephen Benzie and State Representatives Ernest G. Nagel, Francis J. Nowak, and Earl C. Gallagher. The Special Prosecutor quickly noted that all the lawmakers named had been convicted previously on grand jury charges of accepting bribes to influence finance company legislation.[2]

Sigler contended that the State would prove that the Dental Society officers conspired with the legislative defendants to pass the controversial dental advertising bill. This measure, which was subsequently approved by a statewide referendum and upheld by the State Supreme Court, Sigler explained, banned cut-rate advertising by "chain dentists" who operated in large metropolitan centers. The bill was opposed by these urban practitioners as well as by virtually every newspaper publisher in Michigan because of an anticipated loss of advertising revenue.[3] Then, lowering his head, the Special Prosecutor invoked the name of the martyred Warren G. Hooper, whom he revealed had been a

105

co-sponsor of House Bill 199 and would have testified had he not been brutally assassinated.[4]

This blatantly contrived sentimentality on the part of Sigler was injected because the Special Prosecutor was convinced that the guilty verdict against Fitzsimmons resulted, at least in part, from his ability to link the sports promoter with the slain Albion lawmaker and Frank D. McKay. This "Hooper-McKay" strategy received an unexpected, and unintended boost, when Edwin Goodwin, a close friend and political supporter of McKay, ridiculed the prosecution's case in the *Michigan State Digest*. "The highlight is that officials of the Dental Society allegedly felt it incumbent upon them to commit a felony in order to prevent others from acting undignifiedly," Goodwin wrote sarcastically. "Such reasoning has impressive bobby-sox aspects."[5]

II The hearing began as scheduled on February 16, 1945 in Judge Carr's Lansing City Hall courtroom with the jurist reading a statement that Dr. Wright, Chairman of the Dental Society's legislative committee in 1939, and Dr. DeViliers had changed their pleas to guilty and had been released on $2,500 bond each while awaiting sentencing. Each also consented, Carr stated in his usual somber tone, to give testimony on behalf of the State.[6] Guilt had now been established for two of the defendants and was implied for the others. Recognizing the familiar pattern, Lansing lawmakers shuddered as they again prepared to watch justice being meted out in the unique style of the Carr-Sigler grand jury.

The first witness was Henry C. Gerber Jr., executive secretary of the Michigan State Dental Society. The Lansing resident who, along with former State Senators Chester M. Howell and Henry F. Shea and Dr. J. P. Jaxtimer, had been granted immunity in return for testimony, reluctantly described how on February 5, 1939 the Society organized a legislative committee to promote passage of a bill prohibiting all dental advertising except by business card. An identical bill had been defeated in the 1935 and 1937 sessions, Gerber related, largely through lobbying and bribery on the part of "advertising dentists."[7]

"Did dentists who were members of the Society discuss the probability that money had been paid by the advertising dentists in 1935 and 1937 to legislators, among them Senator James Burns of Detroit?" asked Sigler seeking clarification.

"Yes, sir," replied the witness softly.

"Then you decided to fight fire with fire, or dollars with dollars?"

"That is right," agreed Gerber.[8]

Under intense probing by Sigler, Gerber explained that the Society members had been advised on procedure by Henry Hunt, a Saginaw lobbyist for the Michigan Petroleum Industries. After listening to his speech, Gerber recalled, the Society dentists agreed to embark upon an elaborate campaign, utilizing fifteen dental district societies to contact lawmakers and persuade them, by any means necessary, that the ban on advertising was "required for public health."[9]

"There came a time when you paid the late Senator Warren G. Hooper, who was at that time Chairman of the House Public Health Committee, to jointly sponsor your bill in the House of Representatives with ex-Representative Frederick Gartner of Wyandot, former House minority leader, did there not?" Sigler demanded.

"Yes, I paid him $50."

"Didn't the Society give Gartner a gold watch and a 'blow out' dinner?"

"Yes, after the session was over he received a $35 dinner at the Grosse Ile Country Club and a $45 gold watch," Gerber admitted.[10]

Referring to May 10, 1939, the date the Senate voted on the dental bill, Sigler, holding his pince-nez glasses by their black ribbon, paced before the witness while interrogating him. "After the bill was voted on, Mr. Gerber, were you over at the Senate and were there a number of dentists also present?"

"Yes, sir."

"Bill Bradley didn't vote, did he? Wasn't Senator Bradley out in the men's toilet drunk?" Sigler inquired.

"Seems to me I heard that report, sir," Gerber replied sheepishly.

"Wasn't it true that there was a little plan worked out whereby Bill Bradley was to be kept 'tight' because he was sort of lined up with the advertising dentists?"

"I believe he was, sir," Gerber said, adding quickly, "but I don't know that for a fact."[11]

"After the session had adjourned, Chet Howell was the hero, wasn't he? The boys picked him up on their shoulders, didn't they, and carried him to Dr. Jaxtimer's room in the Olds Hotel for a victory party?" Sigler asked in a series of leading questions.

"Yes, sir."

"And Henry Shea got so drunk someone had to put him to bed, isn't that so?"

"Yes, sir," concurred the witness.

"Now, at that party there was a little discussion about the fact that there had been a payoff, wasn't there?"

"I did not hear it," Gerber said with an air of innocence.

107

"Didn't Dr. Wright tell you he had fixed some teeth for one of the distinguished members of the Senate and didn't charge him anything, and therefore he would keep the normal charge out of this bribe money?" persisted Sigler.

"Well, he may have," came the timid reply.

"To refresh your memory," hounded Sigler, "don't you remember that Senator Benzie had some kind of bad bridge and he wasn't getting along very good and he wanted to see Dr. Wright, and Dr. Wright fixed him up to the tune of about $75 or $80 worth and didn't charge him anything. And Wright filed a bill that was—"

"I recall he did some dental work for Senator Benzie," Gerber blurted.

"—$750 to Senator Howell, a watch and a party for Gartner, fixing Benzie's teeth, and the money that he turned back took care of the thousand he had taken from the legislative committee as money to bribe legislators?" finished the unflappable Special Prosecutor.

"Yes, sir," was the mumbled response.[12]

"Now, Henry," Sigler said amicably, "how else did the dentists influence legislators?"

"Well," Gerber replied, "a set of teeth were made for State Representative Ernest Nagel by Dr. J. P. Jaxtimer of Detroit. Later Dr. Jaxtimer was reimbursed by the Dental Society for the actual laboratory cost, which was $29.41."[13]

No sooner were the words out of the dentist's mouth than Nagel, who was acting as his own counsel, jumped to his feet, shouting: "That's a lie. I didn't get a bill for those teeth." Exhibiting a rare display of public emotion, the usually restrained Carr smiled broadly and said with a low chuckle, "Objection overruled."[14]

"I guess that's all," said Sigler with a wave of his hand. "At least for now."[15]

Lanky Chester Howell, the pug-faced editor of the *Chesaning Argus* who had recently ended two decades of legislative office-holding after pleading guilty to accepting a bribe in connection with a naturopathy bill in 1941, was the next witness. Dressed in a rumpled gray suit and holding a blotter which he nervously folded and unfolded, the former automobile racing promoter and creator of the popular "Chesaning Showboat" described himself as the key figure in the struggle between advertising dentists and the Dental Society because he was Chairman of the Senate Public Health Committee, which controlled the fate of House Bill 199. Before going on with his testimony, the man known in Lansing political circles as "Chiseling Chet" piously insisted that "in justice to members of that committee" the record should show that he [Howell] was not bribed to release the bill from committee and that "nothing was said about money until after the committee had approved the measure."[16]

Howell then proceeded to relate that after the bill was reported out of committee the State Senate voted 14-13 to adopt his motion that consideration of the bill be postponed for five days. During that span, Howell said he met several times with Gerber and Dr. Wright in his Lansing residence, Room 811 of the Olds Hotel.[17]

"Do you remember the attorney of the advertising dentists being present around the Olds Hotel," Sigler inquired in an off-handed manner which seemed to puzzle the witness.

"Who was their attorney," Howell said, folding the blotter.

"Edward N. Barnard," answered Sigler, pleased to know that the transcript now contained a reference to a known Republican boss and political crony of Frank D. McKay.

"Oh, yes," responded Howell with an air of new-found certainty, "I saw him around the hotel."[18]

Finally turning his attention to the actual bribery, Sigler launched into a vigorous interrogation of the visibly shaken ex-Senator. "When you told Gerber that he would have to fight fire with fire and he better get $1,000 to pay the boys, what did Henry say?"

"He said he would see Doc Wright to see what he could do," Howell recalled after a brief pause.

"Now, Steve Benzie, the defendant who sits here in this courtroom, do I understand that he came to see you upon the subject of money?"

"Well," Howell hesitated, "I talked with everybody in the Senate about this bill."

"Yes, I know you did, but specifically didn't both Senator Shea and Senator Benzie want to know what there was in it for them," Sigler reiterated, placing both hands on the rail and staring at Howell.

"Yes," was the ready reply, "but I told them I didn't know. I told them that if I got any money I'd see that they were taken care of. No amounts were agreed upon at this time."[19]

"Did Dr. Wright and Mr. Gerber also meet with you?"

"Oh, yes, in my hotel room. Dr. Wright said that he had some money. He said he didn't get the $1,000 I thought might be necessary, but he handed me an envelope with $700 cash in it. Then we discussed strategy. I don't think they were there over five or ten minutes."

"On May 9, 1939 did you see Senator Benzie," Sigler pressed.

"Yes, both he and Senator Shea came to my room at the Olds Hotel. I told them I had received the money and that I could help them. I gave them each $100 in cash."

"Now, when the bill passed the next day, May 10," Sigler continued methodically, "the Dental Society sort of made a hero out of you, didn't they?"

"Well, this legislation was the culmination of a dream on the part of the Michigan State Dental Society." Howell explained. "Naturally their emotions gave way, and they did feel in a celebrating mood. But I don't like to be placed in the role of a hero. It was like the conclusion of a Michigan-Ohio State football game. There was a lot of pent-up enthusiasm let loose."

"They picked you up on their shoulders and carried you about, didn't they? They then paraded you to the Olds Hotel, right?"

Embarrassed, Howell sorrowfully asked Carr if he had to answer, and when so instructed, he gave a hushed "yes" to the straining ears of the Special Prosecutor and court reporter.

"Then the gentlemen really had a celebration, didn't they?"

"They put on a party. There's no question about it," agreed Howell, adding with a grin: "If they didn't have a good time, it was their own fault."[20]

Howell then underwent a brief, rambling cross-examination by Senator Benzie. "Mr. Howell," shouted the graying former solon, his dark eyebrows arching even more than normal, "you know that you have never talked about any piece of legislation during the two terms you and I were in the Senate. Isn't that true?"

"No, Steve," came the quiet reply, "I wouldn't say that was true."

"You know that I have never been in your room in my life," Benzie insisted. "Mr. Howell, have I ever been in your room?"

"Yes," Howell said with a nod, "before the dental bill was passed and I paid you the $100."

"But it is a fact that you never talked to me about a bill in your life," pleaded Benzie, his face flushed.

"Oh, we talked about it several times, Steve," Howell said in apparent disbelief. "I don't know how many, but you wanted to know what was in it for you, and I told you I'd find out and if there was anything, I'd do what I could."[21]

After Benzie stormed back to his seat in the spectator section behind the tables for counsel, Sigler called Dr. J. P. Jaxtimer to the stand. Following the routine preliminary questions regarding the witness' background, Sigler began to elicit information regarding the role of the Dental Society with reference to the advertising bill. "Did you know, Doctor," he inquired, "that $50 was paid by Dr. F. G. McGuigan of Dearborn to Senator Stanley Nowak of Detroit prior to his vote on the dental bill?"

"Yes, Dr. McGuigan was assigned to contact Senator Nowak on the dental bill," Jaxtimer stated. "Senator Nowak's wife was about to be confined and he had no money. He consulted Dr. McGuigan. I understood that Dr. McGuigan took care of the matter."[22]

Sigler then introduced as evidence two letters, the first being from McGuigan to Dr. Wright. In it the Dearborn dentist reported with self-pride worthy of a successful secret agent: "My task has been completed without witnesses."[23] The second was from Jaxtimer to Gerber and concluded with an incriminating paragraph: "Here's the bug under the rug. How much money can the legislative committee of the Society allocate to Wayne County? The boys seem to be somewhat shy of dough. We have spent considerable here and need some more. See if you can get it."[24]

Jaxtimer admitted to seeing the former letter and writing the latter. In fact, he added, Dr. Wright expressed concern that the correspondence to Gerber "might get us into trouble because it was handwritten."[25]

"You had direct relations with other defendants in this case, didn't you, Doctor?" Sigler inquired, rushing his questions in a rather haphazard manner.

"Yes, I did," Jaxtimer responded. "I did dental work for Representative Ernest Nagel. Mr. Nagel came to me and said he would need some dental work done. I said, 'If you support the bill, I will help you out on the dental work.' He later came to my office with Representative Earl Gallagher. I told them both that if they would help us along, I would fix their teeth."

"Nagel then came sometime later to your office—December 5, 1940, I believe," Sigler continued. "Tell us about his condition when he came to your office."

"Well, sir," Jaxtimer began, with an expression of disgust, "when I was trying to get the impression for the upper and lower dentures that I made, he was somewhat—or considerably—intoxicated. I had considerable trouble with him, and he vomited very badly all over my place."

"All right," Sigler went on, vainly trying to suppress a grin. "Did you ever send Ernest Nagel or Earl Gallagher a bill or did you ever expect to get paid?"

"No, sir," the witness snapped.

"Neither one of them ever came to your office and said, 'Here, Doc, I owe you a little money on some dental work you did?'"

"No, sir," was the echoing reply.[26]

Nagel, a gruff, stocky, fifty-two year old former prize fighter who was long on nerve but short on intelligence, lumbered forward to cross-examine his accuser. "You remember," he bellowed in a hoarse voice, "that

111

after you completed the job on my teeth, I asked you, 'How about the bill, Doctor?' and you says, 'That can wait.'"

"No, I don't recall ever having been asked about a bill at all," came the polite response.

"You know you told me the bill could wait because the teeth were no good," Nagel shouted so loudly that Jaxtimer involuntarily pulled back in his chair. "I had to pay Dr. Poole of Detroit $20 to get them fixed. My lowers I could never use. You never sent me a bill, and that is true as I am standing here."

"No, sir," the dentist disagreed calmly.

"Your Honor," Nagel pleaded, "I never took a bribe in my life, so help me God."[27]

Turning to retake his seat, the ex-lawmaker suddenly clutched at his chest, crossed himself, and slumped to the floor having suffered what proved to be a mild heart attack. Judge Carr instantly recessed court, and Nagel, conscious but writhing in pain, was carried by State Police troopers to the press room to await the arrival of an ambulance.[28] After Nagel had been rushed to Sparrow Hospital, Carr decreed that the hearing would not resume until after the weekend recess and the Washington's Birthday holiday. At that time, Dr. Jaxtimer would be asked to retake the stand.

While the proceedings were in recess, Edwin Goodwin wrote an editorial in his *Michigan State Digest* which addressed the issue haunting most of the state's residents. He spoke of Howell's appearance and how "Michigan hangs its head in conscious and unmitigated shame as grand jury testimony candidly discloses past session corruption in the State Senate scarcely rivaled in any public parliamentary body in recorded statehood archives." Then he broached the most troubling aspect of the grand jury disclosures: "It forever amazes thoughtful citizens that with the Senate thus made into a bribe chamber and hoodlumed by raucous corruptionists celebrating the effects of their felonies, that during the remainder of the years 1939 and 1940 there was no publicity, no scandal, no charges, no retributive justice. Nobody talked! The Senators ... appeared as completely noncognizant of the prevailing corruption as unborn babes. And yet, among them, necessarily, it was a case of 'iz you iz or iz you ain't a felon.'"[29]

Sadly, the grand jury prosecutors never inquired of witnesses why they had retained a "code of silence" regarding their peers. Perhaps the answer was painfully evident in the mere fact that no witness who served in the legislature ever testified without first receiving immunity. Diogenes would have been disappointed in the Michigan legislature during those years.

Upon resuming his testimony, Jaxtimer related how the Dental Society officers had become "frantic when their records were seized by the grand jury." They held a hurriedly convened meeting, Jaxtimer stated, at the Statler Hotel in Detroit to establish uniform alibis. At that time, the witness continued, Dr. Wright took him aside and assured him that the only thing to fear was the check for $1,000 made out to him [Wright] on May 8, 1939. Wright said that the cancelled check was in the possession of the grand jury and that, if asked, Jaxtimer should tell the prosecutor "the money was used for office expenses."[30]

"Did you tell the grand jury that the $1,000 was needed for legitimate office expenses and was not paid out in bribes?"

"I did, sir," admitted Jaxtimer.

"Was that statement false?"

"It was."

"Then," Sigler went on, "you followed instructions from Dr. Wright and tried to cover up for the State Dental Society?"

"Yes, sir. That is right."

"But you later repudiated your original grand jury testimony?"

"I did," said the witness, without adding that he had done so only after being offered immunity from prosecution.[31]

Having been summoned by Sigler, Henry Gerber ambled back to the stand for the purpose of substantiating the testimony of Dr. Jaxtimer. Gerber spoke of this encounter with an edgy Dr. Wright in a Lansing restaurant in December 1944, recalling that the dentist told him that "it would be rather difficult to explain the purpose of the $1,000 check that had been paid to him [Wright] and that it might be plausible to state that the payment had been made to him to compensate him for his time away from the office and for his travel expense in connection with efforts to pass the dental bill."[32]

"Did he say he anticipated the calling of yourself before the grand jury?" Sigler asked absentmindedly.

With a rather perplexed expression, Gerber replied: "I didn't get that question, sir."

"Well," the Special Prosecutor admitted, "it wasn't a very well-worded question, anyway. Did you and he discuss the fact you expected to be called before the grand jury?"

"Yes, sir."

"So you knew when you were talking with him that there had been no such agreement made by which he was to receive compensation, did you not?" snapped Sigler.

"Yes, sir," murmured Gerber.

The witness was then asked if he had known that Wright was requesting that he lie to the grand jury, whether he did so lie, and whether he had entered into a conspiracy with Dr. Wright to request other dentists to become accomplices to the lie. To each query, Gerber whispered, "Yes, sir."[33] Gerber closed his account by stating that of the dentists he had agreed to contact only Dr. J. O. Goodsell of Saginaw, President of the Dental Society in 1939, refused to perjure himself before the grand jury.[34]

Sigler briefly interrogated Senator Henry Shea regarding the $100 he accepted from Howell and then called Dr. M. S. "Duke" DeViliers to the witness stand. DeViliers, who had his head bowed so low that his soft voice was barely audible, stated that Francis Nowak, a baby-faced young state representative with curly receding hair, had gone to the dentist's Detroit office in February 1939 and told him that he wanted $150. DeViliers said he gave Nowak the sum requested in cash, and, in return, the lawmaker signed a note.[35]

"What did he do then?" inquired Sigler.

"He left."

"And did he return?" the Special Prosecutor led the witness.

"He walked down the hall and then he came back again and put his head in the door and said, 'Doctor, I think Senator [Leo] Wilkowski is going to vote for that bill, too.'"[36]

"Now, then," Sigler asked, abruptly changing his line of inquiry, "sometime after that—in fact, the following year, in November, 1940— did you have a talk with Mr. Gerber in the Olds Hotel about the State Society paying you this money?"

"Yes. I told Mr. Gerber that in November, 1939, Mr. Nowak came to my office and borrowed from me $150 for which he gave me a note, but that he had never paid this note and that I felt that during this referendum I had collected through my own fingers about half the money that Detroit had contributed towards the fund for the referendum," a suddenly animated DeViliers said in a rambling, non-stop oration, "and seeing that there was some money left that was not used, I asked Mr. Gerber if I could send in a statement to him for the payment of this amount on the note which was incurred—that I didn't believe Mr. Nowak would ever have come to see for—to ask me for the money—if it wasn't for the fact that I was out in front in the profession and he got to know me through being out leading in the profession. I felt that if this was the reason that gave him the nerve or whatever you call it to come to me for the money—it was a loss that I sustained—I felt that since there had been money left from this referendum that was not used, I thought he could reimburse me for $150."

"Did Francis Nowak ever offer to pay that money to you?"

114

"No, sir," was the almost breathless reply, "but I think in the beginning of 1941 he said something about 'I still owe you that money.'"

"You never expected to send him a statement for it, did you, Doctor?" Sigler said, his eyes boring into those of the still gasping witness.

"Well," came the evasive response, "I expected that if the man didn't pay his note that it was useless to go after him."

"You knew at the time he came there and asked for the money," Sigler said, altering his tone to one of soothing amicability, "that it was in the nature of a bribe, didn't you?"

DeViliers hesitated momentarily, nodded his head, and in a hushed voice murmured, "Yes, sir."[37]

As DeViliers shuffled back to his seat he passed another self-admitted conspirator, Dr. Clarence J. Wright, who strode manfully toward the front of the court to assume his place. The dentist vainly attempted to lay part of the burden of the decision to engage in legislative bribery on Gerber, contending that the decision to pay off lawmakers was mutual.[38] Under gentle prodding by Sigler, Wright remembered that Representative Warren Hooper had insisted on receiving funds from Gerber before he would introduce the bill in the House and that Gerber later told the Chairman of the Dental Society's legislative committee that he had given Hooper $50.[38]

"Did you and Henry Gerber have any discussion prior to going to Senator Howell's room about whether you would give him the whole of the $1,000 or hold out on him a little?" Sigler inquired as he paced before the witness.

"Yes, sir. Mr. Gerber suggested that we give him $750," Wright asserted with an air of righteous indignation. "We thought he was chiseling and so we were going to cut him down as much as we could."

"In other words," chided Sigler, "You thought he was chiseling so you fellows were going to do a little chiseling, too. Is that it?"

"Yes," Wright agreed with evident disdain, "if you want to put it that way."[39]

After eliciting that Wright had performed $75 or $80 worth of free dental work for Senator Benzie and that he had never sent the lawmaker a bill because he "didn't want to incur his disfavor or ill-will," Sigler asked Wright if he had not become "a wee bit nervous" when the grand jury subpoenaed the books and records of the Dental Society.[40]

The witness confessed to an uneasiness about it and said that he had driven to Chesaning to visit Howell. The Senator, Wright recalled with certainty, met with him in his automobile and revealed that his stance was going to be that he "never had taken any money."[41]

"Let's call a spade a spade, Doctor, and not mince words about it," Sigler stated tersely, shaking a fist at the dentist. "You were not concerned about how he was going to testify nearly as much as you were concerned with the fact that he had not testified, or would not testify, that you had given him any money, isn't that true?"

"Well," Wright said in a matter-of fact tone, "naturally I didn't want him to testify that I had given him any money."[42]

The hearing concluded with Dr. John O. Goodsell's recollections. "Isn't it true, now, Doctor," Sigler inquired, "that when the $1,000 voucher came along to you, you knew there had been a payoff?"

"I must have," sighed the witness with a shrug.

"Isn't it true that you sat trying to figure out what should be done after the payoff had been made?"

"Yes, I undoubtedly did," admitted Goodsell. "I certainly—there wasn't anything in my mind that I could say—the thing came onto my desk. I'd seen these things lots of times before. What was I going to do with the darned thing? But it was all over. It was over the dam. There wasn't a darn thing I could do about it. I knew nothing about the payoff. That is, in time to prevent it. And, if I had been so inclined, and there is no use in being 'holier than thou' or anything, but I am sure I would not have been so inclined, because we had not planned the game that way, Mr. Sigler."

"Well, let's not get into that angle of the thing," quickly interjected the Special Prosecutor. "You just confine yourself here. You appeared before the grand jury here, and you told us you wanted to frankly set forth the whole situation, didn't you?"

"You're absolutely right, sir," replied Goodsell, nodding with evident pride.

"Isn't it also true that knowing the payoff had occurred, and having this voucher there, you concluded, 'Well, the best thing to do'—about the only thing you could do, in fact, in view of the fact that it had already been done—'is to go ahead and O.K. the voucher and let it go?'"

"That's right."

"Didn't it occur to you, Doctor, that if the payoff had already been made that the check must have been issued and that it had to come from Dr. Chamberlain?" Sigler continued.

"Oh, yes," Goodsell concurred enthusiastically. "The money had to come from someplace. That's the only place it could have come from for the Society."

"That's all, Your Honor," Sigler said smugly.[43]

III On February 23, Judge Carr, having patiently sat through eight days of testimony, ordered Dr. Edward J. Chamberlain, who had been excused from appearing because of his advanced years and illness, and the four legislative defendants bound over for trial in Circuit Court on charges of conspiracy to corrupt the legislature. In so doing, Carr denied a motion by defense counsel Ronald Dilley of Grand Rapids to dismiss all charges against Dr. Chamberlain on the grounds that there had been "not one word of testimony" given to indicate his client had known that the $1,000 check he had issued on orders from the Dental Society officers was to be used for illegal purposes.[44] The jurist claimed that the evidence showed "probable cause that each defendant was a party to a conspiracy."[45]

For some reason, Carr failed to set a trial date and the case became lost in the hustle and bustle of the grand jury probe into the Hooper murder conspiracy and other apparently more pressing matters. Perhaps Sigler convinced Carr that reconvicting four legislators and sending three dentists to prison was not worth the time, expense, or less than sensational press coverage the trial would attract. In any case, no trial was ever held.

On December 8, 1948, Circuit Judge Louis E. Coash, successor grand juror, sentenced Wright and DeViliers to pay $500 each or serve one year in the Ingham County Jail. The judge commented that in making his decision "the Court has taken into consideration the fact that this has been hanging over your head [since February 10, 1945], plus the fact that neither one of you gentlemen are public officials, plus the fact that I do not believe you will ever be involved in this sort of action again."[46] The sentence, in and of itself, is intriguing in light of the fact that they had plead guilty and were punished for a crime which had never been proven in a court of law as having occurred. In 1951 a memo from the Michigan Attorney General's office stated simply that "no final disposition appears to have been made, nor do the cases appear to have been closed" regarding those defendants ordered to stand trial by Judge Carr.[47] Once again, in the eyes of the grand jury all criminals were not created equal.

CHAPTER SIX

"THEM BONES, THEM BONES"

December 6, 1944 dawned as just another typical dreary, cold mid-Michigan late autumn day, but by early afternoon the temperature had soared in Lansing, at least figuratively, with the announcement that the Carr-Sigler grand jury had issued yet another warrant. Within minutes the news spread from the City Hall across the street to the State Capitol. Anxious lawmakers grabbed their comrades, whispered a few words, and consoled each other in hushed voices.

The cause of this near-panic in cloistered corridors and cloakrooms was the naming of Republican State Senators Chester M. Howell of Saginaw County and Carl F. DeLano of Kalamazoo, along with previously convicted Detroit State Representatives Francis J. Nowak, William G. Buckley, and Edward J. Walsh, as recipients of bribes from eight naturopathic physicians in 1939 to influence the vote on Senate Bill 269, which would have established a board of examiners to regulate the practice of naturopathic medicine.[1] When reached by the Associated Press at his family farm in Cooper, DeLano professed ignorance of the entire matter. "This is all news to me. Your telephone call is the first I ever heard about this," he said innocently. "I remember there was such a bill in 1939, but I don't recall anything particular about it. I didn't know any money was being spent on it."[2] To those familiar with the career of the Republican solon, this comment elicited gales of laughter, as DeLano was notorious for demanding money in return for his votes. Don Gardner, then a youthful member of the Capitol press corps, recalled that reporters used to ask legislators to explain the content of bills by saying, "What's in this bill." One night Gardner saw DeLano sitting at his desk in the Senate and said, "Carl, I see you've just introduced this bill. What's in it?" DeLano replied, with a broad grin, "About three grand for me."[3]

119

Howell, a dedicated family man and one of the best-liked members of the legislature, also initially denied participating in any illegal activity. "It was such a foolish bill," the Senator, puffing on his ever-present pipe, told newsmen who gathered at the office of the *Chesaning Argus.* "There was a lobbyist working for it who was the most lonesome individual you ever saw. We thought we'd have some fun with him. But if he had any money I never saw it, and I don't think he had done any lobbying before."[4]

At their arraignments, however, the accused Senators parted company. While DeLano stood mute before Judge Carr and was released on $2,500 bond, Howell, looking pathetic in an unpressed brown tweed suit, appeared before the magistrate and pulled out a yellow sheet of paper on which he had scribbled several sentences. Reading from the paper, the Senator confessed his guilt. "I realize that I have made mistakes as have others in the legislature, past and present. I know that the finest contribution I can make to a good government after all my legislative experience is to frankly admit my mistakes and help clean up graft in our government. I know I owe this to my family, of which three of our four children are in the service of their country. As a lifelong newspaperman and legislator over a span of twenty years, I hope my position may contribute in some small way to keeping this a great state and country."[5] In an exclusive interview later that afternoon, Howell told the *Detroit Free Press*, for which he had worked early in his journalistic career: "My part in the naturopathic bill to which I confessed this afternoon was a very minor one. As far as I am concerned, little money was involved, but my part did constitute a technical violation, and I decided to admit such a connection."[6]

Not everyone was touched by Howell's mea culpa, however. The *Michigan State Digest*, a McKay political sheet, ridiculed the "blessed reformers, Hemans and Howell," saying: "These two local Billy Sundays bought their friends into prospective prison. Princes of the double cross. American soldiers take Jap beatings, even death, while refusing to betray comrades. Not so with H and H. Their ethics remain ever the same. None at all. They claim they now live only to bless and safeguard their fellow men. Yet no-one has ever heard either of them making restitution, restoring to trustful owners the money which they took. Nor have they donated it to the Red Cross. Prayerfully, they hang on to it."[7]

Sigler, always avid in his pursuit of the limelight, called a press conference after the arraignments and intimated that the trial would provide surprises. "Hemans won't be there in person," the Special Prosecutor informed disappointed newshawks who hoped for an encore of the lobbyist's performance in the finance company trial, "but wait until you see who we put on the stand. He'll remind you of Hemans. There will be some very interesting developments. The grand jury is just getting well started. The nuts are back on our buggy, Mary Ann!"[8]

The spate of warrants in early December were calculated not only to bring felons to the bar of justice, but also to demonstrate to the taxpayers of Michigan that the grand jury was worth the cost. Grumbling had been heard that little had been accomplished, and claims by Sigler that elaborate preparation was required before going to trial did not quell the suspicions of critics that the only real conspiracy in the state was by Sigler trying to preserve his $100 per working day salary. Typical of this view was Edwin Goodwin's satirical editorial attacking the "witch hunt" led by Carr and Sigler. "Mr. Kim Sigler ... just isn't man enough, or even lawyer enough, to corral Michigan's entire list of bribe-givers and bribe-takers. Ten thousand sleuthing investigators couldn't get the evidential lowdown on them all. Michigan's population is a cigarette hunting and nylon grabbing maelstrom whom St. Peter in his palmiest days never would have dreamed could be so unethical," Goodwin stated, his cynical pen at its wicked best. "Any city of 100,000 population is believed to contain no less than 99,999 bribe-givers or bribe-takers. The other guy, unconscious, is in the hospital from wounds received when he tried to make a 'buy' without first offering a 'bonus.' Judge Leland W. Carr, if he were to work minus food and rest from now until Joseph Stalin has all the territory he wants, could not hope to catch up with any perceptible percent of these all-star bribers who now allegedly are in the business."[9]

With the names of McKay, Fitzsimmons, DeLano, and Howell surfacing, however, the lampooning ceased and calls arose for increased support of the probes. The *Ingham County News* spoke the sentiments of many citizens in an editorial entitled "Let's Follow It Through." In this the *News* rationalized why the grand jury had to be continued and set its views in the context of the war effort. "If the men named in the warrants are innocent, they will be freed. But if they are guilty, they should be sent to prison. They will have done more to weaken our representative form of government than all the communists, fascists, and Nazi propagandists who ever came to the United States or beamed a message in this direction," the column asserted with patriotic fervor. "Our way of life and our form of government are things our sons and brothers are fighting for in Europe and Asia. It is up to all of us to join the fight here at home, because there are dangers here, too. Judge Leland W. Carr, Special Prosecutor Kim Sigler, and the grand jury staff are serving their country with the same valor displayed by men on the war fronts. The members of the Circuit Court jury who knifed through the smoke screen of defense tactics at the trial in Mason upheld the American form of government with the same bravery and fortitude as displayed by Americans overseas. If the grand jury expense mounts up into high figures the investigation will be worth every cent provided the people are awakened to the fact that the structure of government must be protected from termites."[10]

I I I The grand jury investigation assumed a sinister overtone when witnesses suddenly began to die, some under highly suspicious circumstances. On August 22, 1944 seventy-eight year old former State Senator Miles M. Callaghan, a key state witness in the finance company trial, suffered a fatal stroke. Harry Bylenga, the forty-six year old vice president of the Star Transfer Company and a known associate of Frank D. McKay, was killed on December 5 of the same year when his stalled car was struck by a Detroit bound New York Central train. Bylenga's company was under scrutiny as part of a state liquor conspiracy probe. Kent County Prosecutor Menso R. Bolt ignored the obvious questions of whether the driver was already dead at the time of the crash or, if not, why he did not leap for safety, and ruled the death accidental.[11] Four days later, State Senator Earl Munshaw of Grand Rapids, chairman of both the powerful State Affairs and Judiciary Committees, was found dead, slumped over the wheel of his car, which had been left with the engine running in the closed garage of his home. The six-term Republican, who was a close friend of Chester Howell, had been called before the grand jury several times regarding "legal fees" he had taken from lobbyists for cosmetology schools and Consumers Power Company at the same time bills affecting these concerns were in his committees.[12] Despite the suspicious nature of the senator's demise, the Kent County coroner, Dr. Paul W. Bloxsom, declared that death was a result of "accidental carbon monoxide poisoning," and again Bolt, a political ally of McKay, refused to entertain any thoughts of foul play in the case.[13] Then on Christmas Day, former Democratic Lieutenant Governor Frank Murphy, still youthful at forty-six, succumbed to a heart ailment before he could stand trial on a liquor conspiracy charge.[14]

These mysterious passings were dismissed by most Lansing observers until the murder of Warren Hooper on January 11, 1945. Suddenly, questions arose as to whether the "death in many guises that dogged the men 'who knew too much' were, in fact, accidental."[15] While Sigler, for reasons never disclosed, chose not to pursue the deaths of any witness but Hooper, the potential impact of the grand jury disclosures were magnified by these "acts of fate." As the *Flint Journal* editorialized ruefully: "Until the murder of Senator Hooper little more than 'small change' was used to describe the transactions investigated by the legislative grand jury at Lansing, although moral considerations and good government were involved importantly. [The slaying] gives the grand jury a more serious tone and arouses the suspicion that the stakes may have been much greater than was thought."[16] Ironically, death had assured continuing life for the grand jury.

IV On December 16, 1944 Carr issued a second warrant involving naturopathic medicine. This time, in addition to the three previously cited Detroit state representatives, the grand jury charged State Senator Leo J. Wilkowski, a Detroit Democrat, former Republican State Senator William G. Birk of Baraga, and the oft-indicted William Green as having taken bribes in 1941 from two Detroit chiropractors, Paul Faulkner and Gunnar W. Wilkander.

Upon being notified of the warrant by his son, Faulkner returned voluntarily from his recently adopted home of Fulton, North Carolina to face arraignment before Judge Carr. After a brief consultation with Sigler, the fifty-two year old heavy-set physician pleaded guilty to both the 1939 and 1941 charges. With the Special Prosecutor standing at his side, Faulkner, in a soft voice pledged to do anything in his power to aid the grand jury. He then was released on $2,500 bond.[17] Soon afterward, two more naturopathic defendants in the 1939 case, Harry E. McKinney and his brother Clayton, pleaded guilty and agreed to give state's evidence.[18]

Assuming a different posture was ex-Senator Birk who demanded an examination before Judge Carr. Defiantly, the ten-year veteran of legislative wars appeared without counsel. "In the first place," he brusquely told Sigler, "there is no reason for me to have counsel. In the second place, I can't afford it." Examination was set for December 28, and he was released on $2,500 surety bond.[19]

The surliest of those accused was DeLano. His thin-lips pursed tightly, the Senator listened while his attorney, Frank L. Blackman, read to Carr a petition which was to be filed with the Court. In this, DeLano contended he had been deprived of both his state and national constitutional rights by being compelled to testify against himself, and therefore the charges against him should be quashed. Carr denied the motion and reaffirmed Monday, February 26, 1945 as the trial date.[20]

V The trial at Mason, with Judge Simpson again on the bench, had an inauspicious beginning when one of the defendants, Dr. Mikhel Sherman, president of the American Naturopathic Association of Michigan in 1939, failed to appear because of what his attorney claimed was a chronic heart ailment. Simpson then ordered the sixty-three year old doctor's $2,500 bond forfeited and issued a bench warrant to have Sherman brought into court.[21]

The judge's seemingly callous behavior was explained when Sigler was granted permission to call Dr. Cecil Corley, a Jackson heart specialist, to the stand. Dr. Corley, who had examined Sherman the preceding Saturday at the request of the Special Prosecutor, stated a thorough cardiographic examination of Sherman disclosed "no heart abnormality," and that in his judgment "although Sherman was highly nervous and apprehensive there was no reason why this man should not be in court."[22]

Under questioning by Sigler, Dr. Corley related that during the examination the Detroit chiropractor had confessed that his nervousness coincided with the date the grand jury decided to begin its investigation of the Naturopathic Association's activities. He lost his appetite and suffered sleepless nights, he told the physician. When Sherman read of Ernest Nagel's dramatic collapse in the dental conspiracy trial, Corley continued, he came upon the idea of feigning a heart attack to avoid the mortification of a court appearance.[23]

Over the course of the following three days a jury of nine housewives and five farmers was impaneled and opening statements were made by the prosecution and defense counsel. Then, on Friday morning, March 2, Simpson stunned those assembled by announcing that court would adjourn until Monday because of a "mysterious illness" which had struck down the Special Prosecutor several hours earlier.

Reporters scurried frantically to Sigler's Olds Hotel suite, which was cordoned off by the State Police who said the Special Prosecutor was too ill to be disturbed.[24] Sigler's physician, Dr. C. B. Gardner, chief surgeon of Lansing's Sparrow Hospital, was more communicative. He said Sigler had attended a dinner Thursday night with a small party of friends and had slept soundly until 7 a.m. when he doubled over with severe abdominal pain and extreme nausea. Gardner said he arrived approximately three hours after Sigler became ill, having been summoned by Detective Sergeant Leo VanConant, head of Sigler's State Police detachment. The Special Prosecutor's blood pressure was very low and his complexion was blue, the doctor recalled, while newsmen eagerly took down the graphic details. "Mr. Sigler's condition is serious, but not urgent. He is resting comfortably. You could call it food poisoning—although no one else at the party became ill—but that might place some restaurant in a bad light," Gardner said. As he started to leave, the physician verbalized what everyone in the room was pondering: "Of course, someone might have slipped him something."[25]

Fate continued to play tricks on the proceedings when Sigler, having recovered from his intestinal malady, filed a motion with Judge Simpson to remove Dr. Paul Faulkner, a former president of the Naturopathic Association of Michigan, as a state witness. This was shocking because in the preliminary examination, Faulkner, who had pleaded guilty and turned state's evidence, had gone into great detail relating how the Association had determined to bribe legislators to secure passage of a 1939 bill to legalize the practice of naturopathy. Unfortunately, Sigler explained, the stress caused by his guilty plea resulted in Faulkner becoming deranged. "Dr. Faulkner is suffering from a delusion that his cigars have been poisoned," Sigler declared.[26]

In support of his motion, Sigler called Dr. R. Phillip Sheets to the stand. The head of the Traverse City State Mental Hospital testified that he had examined Faulkner the previous evening, March 5, and diagnosed him as suffering from "manic depressive psychosis" which manifested itself in religious fanaticism and delusions of extraordinary healing powers.[27]

In an effort to discredit the prosecution's assertion that Faulkner's insanity was of recent origin, defense counsel introduced evidence that in April 1943 the chiropractor had called on the White House, claiming he was God, and asked to speak with President Roosevelt. He was seized by the Secret Service and spent several days in a mental institution undergoing tests before being ushered out of the nation's capital. After this revelation, which elicited strenuous opposition from Sigler as it would seriously undermine the credibility of Faulkner's earlier testimony, Simpson sustained both the objection and the motion for removal.[28]

After disposing of the Faulkner matter, Sigler called his primary witness, fifty-four year old Harry R. Williams, to the stand. As the bespectacled, obese self-proclaimed lobbyist and payoff man for the Naturopathic Association waddled forward, Sigler notified the Court that the witness would have to be "handled carefully because he has heart trouble." Simpson then consented to brief recesses at least every hour so that Williams could rest.[29]

"Mr. Williams, you have received immunity from Judge Carr in return for your testimony, have you not?" Sigler inquired.

"Yes, sir."

"Tell us, Mr. Williams," Sigler began, "what did you do before becoming a lobbyist?"

"I was a technician at Dr. C. B. McDonald's sanitarium in Benton Harbor," Williams stated, adjusting the knot of his paisley tie, which was virtually buried beneath his double chin. "I met a number of naturopaths there and in 1938 I helped them organize the American Naturopathic Association of Michigan, which was headquartered in the office of Mikhel Sherman in Detroit."

"Then you became a lobbyist for that organization?"

"Yes, sir. The officers—Mikhel Sherman, Gunnar W. Wilkander, Martin Hildebrand, Max Rosenfeld, and Ernest W. Alden—decided that money would be raised by collecting $10 yearly from each of the Association's 195 members, and that the funds would be used to bribe legislators. So I got this permanent suite at the Olds Hotel—it was one room away from that of Senator Shea—and I established a bar there to entertain legislators. It was really just a large table, but it was well stocked with liquor of all kinds," the witness boasted. "I was a neophyte at this sort of thing, but I soon learned my way around."

"Did legislators come to your room and patronize your bar?" Sigler asked, suavely leading the witness.

"Oh, yes. It was full every day. Senator Howell was there three or four times, Senator Shea and Edward Walsh practically every day."[30]

"Now, Mr. Williams, the bill to legalize naturopathic medicine was introduced on the 28th of March, 1939. Tell the Court what happened in your room during the week or so before that date."

"Well, Senator Shea and Senator Howell came to my room one afternoon. Senator Shea took me into the bathroom," the witness said softly, his round face becoming pink.

"For what purpose?" Sigler inquired, knowing full well what the answer would reveal.

"He wanted to talk to me about the price it would take to get this bill in and out of committee. He said it was the usual procedure to charge a fee for the introduction and getting the bill out on the floor. I said how much, and he said $500. I said I didn't have the money with me at the moment but that I would get it for him as soon as I possibly could."

"And where was Senator Howell while you were having this bathroom agreement with Senator Shea?"

"In my room."

"Did you pay any money that day?" Sigler queried, still leaning leisurely on the rail of the witness box.

"No, not that day," Williams stated emphatically. "I think it was two or three days later that I gave $250 to Senator Shea in my room for him to introduce the bill in the Senate."

"Why didn't you pay him the total amount?"

"I didn't have it at the time," the witness replied, again fidgeting with his tie.

"The boys all hadn't yet sent in their dues that Dr. Max Rosenfeld and Dr. Sherman ordered sent in, is that it?"

"That's correct."

"The brethren still had to pass forward and drop more nickels on the drum, eh?" Sigler asked cynically.

"Yes, sir. But I did pay the other $250 to Senator Shea just prior to the introduction of the bill," the witness proclaimed with pride, as though his personal integrity was verified by fulfillment of his corrupt bargain.[31]

Walking slowly from the witness, Sigler suddenly wheeled and inquired: "During the course of the time this bill was in the Senate committee and in the Senate of the State of Michigan, did you also make certain payments to Senator Chester M. Howell?"

"Yes, sir," came the ready admission. "I paid him about $350 or $400 in cash installments. I gave it to him either in my room or his or in the hallway in the hotel."[32]

Holding a letter dated April 3, 1939 before the witness, Sigler asked: "After the bill was introduced did you send this to Dr. Clayton R. McKinney, one of the defendants in this case."

"Yes, sir. I did," Williams said after glancing at the correspondence.

"Will you please read the letter, Mr. Williams," Sigler directed.

"Yes, sir," the witness replied, cleaning his glasses with the handkerchief he had been twisting in his hands during much of his testimony. "It says: 'This is a personal letter and an appeal from myself only for funds with which to carry on the legislative work that has entered the stage from which there is no turning back. In order to successfully bring this bill of ours to the statutes of law in this state it is absolutely essential and necessary that we have in hand by this Wednesday [April 5] $1,350. The bill now rests in the Public Health Committee of the Senate and I have been assured by the chairman of this committee [Howell] that it will be out on Wednesday next if I so desire it. I feel, Clayton, that we are going to be successful and that nothing but the required amount of money is going to stop us. This may seem like an old story to you, but nevertheless it is my honest and sincere thought, and I hope that you will be able to send me a substantial sum with which to take care of certain things that have to be done by this date.'"[33]

"Who were the legislators in the House to whom you were continually paying money?" shot Sigler, rapidly altering the thrust of his queries.

"Mr. Walsh, Mr. Buckley, and Mr. Nowak, the defendants."

"How much would you say you paid Ed Walsh on this bill?" asked Sigler, extending his index finger toward the defendant.

"About $200, in dribs and drabs," recalled Williams, shifting his ample body in the chair.

"How much to William Buckley?"

"About $100, Mr. Sigler," came the polite reply.

"On any occasion did Francis Nowak come to you and make any comment about your paying legislators?" asked Sigler in a stern voice.

"Yes, sir," Williams responded, still squirming in an effort to find a comfortable position in the hard wooden armchair. "He came to my room, took me into the bathroom, and said: 'Doctor, you're cutting all these other fellows in, why not cut me in, too?' So I gave him $25 then and about another $25 or $50 later."[34]

Displaying another letter, this one written by Williams to Dr. Rosenfeld, Sigler asked the witness to read it into the record. "About 5:00 p.m. Senator Shea and the Ethiopian came into my room," Williams quoted the correspondence. "We ironed out the Eloise proposition. However, make your contacts as you intend with the rest of the tribe. Shea put the heat on plenty and he promised to be a good boy."[35]

"When you get down there toward the bottom of the letter and you say Senator Shea 'put the heat on plenty,' what does that mean?" Sigler asked with a quizzical expression.

"It simply means I had approached Charlie Diggs of Detroit and I asked him to vote for the bill, and he told me he had strict orders from some doctor at Eloise Hospital that he was not to vote for the bill," the witness stated. "Later, Shea told me he had spoken to his fellow Democratic Senator and if Diggs didn't vote for the bill he would not vote for one of Diggs' bills. It was a horse trade."[36] With this, Simpson adjourned court until 10 o'clock the next morning.

When Williams resumed the stand, Sigler sought information regarding the main target of the trial, Carl F. DeLano, one of the most outspoken critics of Carr's one-man grand jury. "You met with the defendant Carl DeLano, did you not?" was the initial query.

"Yes, in his room at the Olds Hotel. I had been told that he had powerful friends and could get the bill through the House. He told Dr. Fred Grabow, a Kalamazoo naturopath, that it would cost at least $2,500 though."

"Tell us, if you please, in your own words, what took place there in DeLano's room?"

"Well,—"

Raising a hand to silence the witness, Sigler interjected: "Before we start on that, how much money did you have with you at that time in cash?"

"I had $2,000 in my pocket."

"Fine," Sigler smiled, "now continue with your story."

"I told Senator DeLano that I had $2,000 which I would give him in order that he should take care of this bill, and he said that he would pre-arrange it. Then he put the money on his bed and he counted it out," Williams said, shaking his head at the recollection, "just as though he were fixing a deck of cards. That is, spades, diamonds, clubs, and hearts—in denominations, in which I had the money. Then he made a notation in a little black vest pocketbook."

Casting a glance toward DeLano, who sat at the defendants' table glowering with his fingers tightly interlaced, Sigler forged ahead. "What was the next thing that occurred?"

"Well, he said: 'We'll go and get busy on this thing. We haven't got much time, but we'll get together on it.' As he left, I said: 'Senator, I'm broke. I have only six or seven dollars left on my person.' He said: 'Doc, do you need some money?' I said yes, and he returned $100 to me."

"Did you see him after that, from time to time?"

"I saw him every day either at his desk or in the Senate when passing through," Williams said with more than a hint of bitterness. "And he always told me: 'I'm working hard on this thing, Doc, and I think we'll have some action. It certainly looks all right.'"[37]

The Special Prosecutor then presented the Court with an encapsulated history of the legislation in question, including correspondence from naturopaths to Governor Kelly shortly after the grand jury was created in 1943. He related how the naturopathy bill had been reported favorably out of Howell's committee on May 3, 1939 and passed the Senate 22-7 on May 29, but had been killed in the House State Affairs Committee, despite a promise to Williams of sixty-six sure votes if the measure got to the floor. Naturopaths blamed the downfall of the bill on "dishonest tactics" of William Burns, the lobbyist for the medical doctors.[38]

Returning his attention to the witness, who had been sitting downcast throughout the recitation, Sigler resumed his interrogation. "Later, after the bill's defeat, you drove out to defendant DeLano's farm, didn't you?"

"Yes, sir. He took me into his house, and we had a general conversation. He said, 'Doc, I've been looking through my little book here and find that you still owe me some money. I'm trying to collect all these amounts that are outstanding. I want to go away.'"

129

"Did you try to raise more money for him?"

"No, sir, I did not," was the indignant reply. "I felt I'd been sold down the river. I paid these fellows through the nose all through the session. Bought their liquor, had liquor stolen from me, and given it away by the bottles. I was pretty sore about the whole thing."[39]

Seeing that Williams was breathing heavily and perspiring profusely, Sigler requested a recess. Instead, Simpson adjourned court until the following morning in an effort to have the witness in physical shape to undergo the rigors of cross-examination.[40]

At 10:00 a.m. Williams, attired in an expensive navy suit, wedged himself again into the witness chair and prepared to endure having his testimony challenged by the battery of defense counsel. Walter North, attorney for Martin W. Hildebrand, led off the attack, asking: "What was your first bribe?"

"I can't remember that," Williams shot back. "As I've said before there were so many, and they came so thick and fast, I couldn't keep track of them. It was every day. It was $10 here, $25 here, $50 here, whatever the case may be. They would hammer on the door of my room wanting money almost every night of my life while I was in the Olds Hotel."

"Can you tell how much money you paid in bribes?"

"Approximately $4,000, and plenty of that was spent on liquor."

"Was this your first legislative experience," queried North.

"Absolutely," said Williams, who added with a broad grin, "and my last."

"Are you a licensed practitioner, Mr. Williams? Do you have a degree?"

Coughing and swabbing his scarlet features with his ever-present handkerchief, Williams hesitatingly confessed: "No, I faked the Bachelor of Science degree I used in signing my name to certificates. I call myself a Doctor of Naturopathy, but I have no training in that field."[41]

Confident that he had planted a fertile seed of doubt regarding the truthfulness of the witness, North turned the questioning over to Paul Watzel, court appointed attorney for Buckley and Nowak, who began to delve extensively into the distribution of liquor by the witness. "I assume you had some scotch there?" he inquired.

"Yes."

"And probably some of the products of Kentucky and Tennessee known as bourbon?"

"Yes."

"And possibly some rye?"

"Yes," reiterated the witness, who, in an effort to hasten the liquor litany, volunteered, "and some gin."

Sigler, bored by the irrelevancy of the questions, buried his head in his hands and sneered, "Don't forget the chasers."

Watzel smiled and said: "I'm coming to the chasers now, Mr. Sigler. I suppose, Mr. Williams, that you had soda and ginger ale sent up by the hotel?"

"Not always," shrugged the witness. "I bought it mostly at the drug store."

"How did you get your ice up there?"

Unable to contain himself any longer, Sigler bounded to his feet. "Wait a minute. What difference does it make how he got his ice? Whether they had napkins and served doughnuts? I object to it."

"I just wanted to get a picture of what the bar looked like," Watzel said with a sly grin.

"If you want a picture, we'll give it to you. Answer the question."

"Bellhops," was the curt reply.[42]

Following another adjournment, Dr. Sherman took the stand and tried to discredit Williams' account. Sigler than entered into a brutal cross-examination.

"You didn't trust Harry Williams, did you, Doctor?" Sigler snapped.

"I didn't trust Williams and Williams didn't trust me. I wished he would have quit," Sherman retorted angrily.

"Do you trust anybody, Doctor?"

"Oh, yes," Sherman cooed, "I even trust you, Mr. Sigler."

Taken aback, the Special Prosecutor nodded his head slightly. "You do? Well, you're very kind. I appreciate that. Now, isn't it true, Doctor, that you have quite a bad temper?"

"No, no, not that I know of," the witness said calmly.

"Didn't you become angry a number of times because you didn't have control?"

"No, not that I know of," was the slightly less serene response.

"Did you get up and become so excited on occasions that you couldn't even talk?" hammered Sigler.

"No, no. I am sure about that. I can't even—I—I control myself quite well because I've practiced that," stammered the chiropractor.

"My," posed Sigler thoughtfully, "why would you have to practice self-control unless you knew you were quick-tempered?"

"No! No!," screamed Sherman, leaning forward.

"No more questions, Your Honor," Sigler said with a smirk.[43]

The highlight of the proceedings for the spectators in the gallery came on Friday afternoon, March 9, when William G. Buckley and Francis J. Nowak, both of whom were serving three to five years as a result of being convicted in the finance conspiracy case, testified on their own behalf. On direct examination by Watzel each denied accepting bribes from Williams during the 1939 session. They claimed not to have met the lobbyist until 1940 and insisted that they had no opportunity to vote on the 1939 naturopathy legislation because it was never sent to the floor of the House and neither were members of any committee to which the bill was referred.[44]

On cross-examination, Sigler stood in front of the baby-faced Nowak, paused for several seconds, and shook his head in disbelief. "You sat there on that same stand, as did Buckley, last summer," the Special Prosecutor recalled vividly, "and denied that you took money from Charles Hemans."

"Yes," fired back the hot-headed youthful convict, "I denied it and still deny it. You also threatened me—"

"Be quiet," yelled Sigler, a fierce scowl contorting his features. "I told you that until you told the truth I would keep on indicting you. I told you you were guilty then, and you were. I know you are guilty now."[45]

The thirty-seven year old Buckley, still classically handsome with his wavy black hair perfectly coiffured despite his incarceration, refused to give an inch when confronted by Sigler. "I was not sick during the session of the legislature in 1939. I was never in Harry Williams' room and I had no drinks there during the legislative session," Buckley asserted.

"You sat there on the same witness stand and denied you'd ever received money from Major Charles Hemans, didn't you?"

"That's right," sneered the witness.

"And you are also indicted on the second naturopathy case?"

"Yes."

"Well, Mr. Buckley," Sigler stated, matching the hostile stare, "you know you've met Harry Williams, don't you?"

"You know, Mr. Sigler," Buckley said with controlled fury, "I just don't believe you think I met Harry Williams in 1939. I don't believe you think I'm guilty in this case. I tried to impress upon you as much as I could at the arraignment in this case that I was not guilty."

"You've always done that, haven't you, Mr. Buckley?"

"Mr. Sigler, I came over and talked to Vic Anderson and said there was a mistake made and he sent me to you—" Buckley attempted to explain.

"Now, listen—" Sigler interrupted, only to be drowned out by the unstoppable witness.

"—and you told me to come into court and confess because it would be the best thing for me."

"Yes, I told you that because you are guilty," replied Sigler in disdain.

"Well, you can belittle me all you want to. That's the reason you're in the saddle, but, believe me, I will never confess to anything that I'm innocent of," bellowed the defendant. "And I am innocent of this one and you know it."

"All through now? Anything else to say?" asked Sigler sarcastically. "You could make those same flowery speeches over in the House of Representatives here, couldn't you? Is that the reason Harry Williams paid you, Mr. Buckley, because you could make those flowery speeches?"

"You hypocrite," Buckley hissed.[46]

Following the weekend recess, the summations were presented. Defense counsel harped on the common theme that Harry Williams, a self-confessed dispenser of bribes and liar, was not a credible witness. The possibility was raised that Williams even put some of the money he was alleged to have distributed into his own pockets.[47]

In his ninety minute closing argument, Sigler resorted to flag-waving and an overt appeal to emotionalism. "What good is it," he asked rhetorically, "to send men to fight in the four corners of the earth when lawmakers have their hands out for graft to introduce a measure in the legislature? This is a vicious evil which threatens to destroy the nation's democracy. It is a great tragedy when the highest men in the legislature become grafters, striking at the very foundations of our government. Think of it. Here is Senator Howell who is head of the Senate Public Health Committee, which is supposed to look after the health of the people of Michigan and the school kids—here he is taking graft. It is not something that happened in Russia or in chaotic Germany, but under the Stars and Stripes. These men entered into an unholy conspiracy to corrupt the legislature. It must be stopped, and it can only be stopped by bringing these chiselers to justice."

Pausing and striking a pose with his pince-nez glasses held high, Sigler spoke of the defendants individually. "Despite the fact that Dr. Hildebrand is a gentleman and we like him personally, he contributed to the naturopaths' bribe fund," he began, never taking his eyes from the jury box. "Dr. Sherman was very ill, but he got better each day he was in court. He was active in raising money to get their bill passed, and he knew that the money was spent for legislative votes. Dr. Alden served in the British navy and is a suave and polished gentleman, but too many Americans are suckers for a British accent. Carl DeLano was simply the arch-chiseler of the whole gang. Edward Walsh, the minority leader of the House, took $200 for his vote. Williams was just building fences when he bribed Buckley with two hundred smackers. He figured Buckley would

133

help him when the measure got on the floor of the House. Williams entertained Nowak and gave him $75. He would have used Nowak later on. If there ever was, ladies and gentlemen of the jury, a stinking condition where men should be brought to justice, this is it."[48]

Shortly before noon on Wednesday, March 14, after charging the jury to arrive at separate verdicts for each defendant, Judge Simpson ordered the panel to begin their deliberations. When no decision had been reached by 10 p.m., the judge ordered the jurors to go home and resume their task at 9:30 the following morning.[49]

Members of the jury were obviously agitated when they returned to the courtroom at 1:15 p.m. Thursday. Speaking for his worn and tired comrades, jury foreman O. E. Ames informed Simpson that they were hopelessly deadlocked. "Have you reached a verdict on any of the defendants?" Simpson asked. When Ames nodded in assent, Simpson instructed them to "go back in your jury room and we will take the verdicts on those you have agreed upon."[50]

Five minutes later Ames made the announcement before a crowded, hushed gallery. "We find Carl F. DeLano and Mikhel Sherman guilty as charged. We find Ernest W. Alden and Martin W. Hildebrand not guilty. No decision was reached on William G. Buckley, Francis J. Nowak, and Edward J. Walsh."[51]

Simpson polled the jurors, thanked them for their service, and stated that he would accept their verdicts and hold no new trials for those not convicted. He then sentenced DeLano and Sherman to three to five years at Southern Michigan Prison.[52]

VII n the maelstrom of jostling, shouting questions and congratulations, and posing for photographers which followed the adjournment, Sigler displayed no apparent dismay that the jurors found his case against only two of the defendants worthy of a guilty verdict, although his disappointment was keenly felt by his uncharacteristically terse post-trial comment: "A great credit is due the good people on this jury who had the courage to stand up for good government. I'll see you all at the next naturopathy trial." A teary-eyed Dr. Hildebrand sought out each juror and expressed his appreciation for "a just verdict," while DeLano and Sherman were busy posting $4,000 bonds to permit them to remain free pending appeals. Ames, in the midst of a crush of reporters, said that the jury had split 8-4 on the guilt of the three legislators and took nine ballots before concluding DeLano's guilt.[53]

Sigler bustled from the scene, buttoning his Chesterfield as he strode away. Doubtless his mind was reeling with the implications of this trial. No matter how convincing his oratory might be, jurors seemed to be hesitant to reconvict men already serving prison sentences. If the mantle of crime-fighter was to rest easy on his shoulders, Sigler knew he would have to seek out more important targets, such as Frank D. McKay, and use his connections with the press to fan the flames of public interest.

VII Before the second naturopathy trial, which, upon recommendation of Sigler, was set by Judge Carr for April 16, 1945, the Associated Press ran a series of articles praising the work of Carr and Sigler. With titles such as "Grand Jury Not Half Way Through Its Work" and "Where Will Grand Jury Strike Next?" the citizens of Michigan were not only reminded of past convictions, but were promised that the scope of the probe would widen to include highway department malfeasance, illegal gambling and slot machines, milk marketing, insurance frauds, and other illicit acts committed by state agencies. The articles, penned by G. Milton Kelly, revealed yet another previously undisclosed form of graft. Lobbyists, it was rumored, when business was slow, would bribe lawmakers to introduce controversial legislation and then hire themselves out to opponents of the bill so that they could bribe other lawmakers to vote against it.[54]

Perhaps the timing of these stories was coincidental, but no one associated with Sigler thought so. As one critic cynically wrote: "Lawmakers may come and lawmakers may go, but Kim Sigler's $100 per day goes on forever."[55]

VIII Naturopathy trial number two had a déjà vu quality. Judge Simpson again presided in the Mason courthouse; Harry F. Williams was the star witness for the prosecution; and many of the old familiar faces—Buckley, Walsh, Nowak—sat at the defendants' table, along with chiropractors Paul Faulkner and Gunnar Wilkander. For variety, they were joined this time by State Senator Leo J. Wilkowski, and former lawmakers William G. Birk and William Green.

Once a jury of nine women and five men was selected, Sigler set the stage for Williams' testimony by calling Chester B. McDonald and Hubert K. Ellison to the stand on Wednesday, April 18. Dr. McDonald, a Benton Harbor chiropractor and naturopath, was American Naturopathic Association of Michigan president in 1940. He admitted that the

Association had given Williams a free hand to pass out bribes in 1941 because similar legislation had failed two year's earlier. When asked why graft was used, after it had failed to secure the desired results previously, McDonald shrugged his shoulders and said it "was customary practice to bribe legislators."[56] Ellison, the auditor for the Olds Hotel, produced records showing that Williams paid $503 in personal hotel bills for Wilkowski and Birk during the five month 1941 session of the legislature.[57]

The next day Williams, who again had been granted immunity in return for his testimony, wheezed to the stand and assumed his familiar uncomfortable position in the wooden chair. Williams testified that he had distributed approximately $1,200 to the six legislative defendants in a futile effort to get the bill legalizing naturopathy out of the House Public Health Committee, but when the Association refused his request for an additional $5,000 he ceased his bribery activity.[58]

Referring to the earlier trial, Williams described how he duplicated his practice of establishing a bar in his room at the Olds Hotel and distributed cash in small amounts to the defendants. Breathing noisily, the witness recalled that he gave Green $250 for introducing the bill, either $200 or $250 to Walsh because he was the Democratic floor leader, $100 or $150 to Buckley because he was "Walsh's lieutenant," and $100 to Nowak simply because "he came around and asked for the money."[59] Covering the hotel bills of Birk and Wilkowski was just "building fences for the time when I might be lucky enough to get the bill out of the House and into the Senate," Williams explained.[60] "You know," Williams solemnly intoned. "I came to Lansing with the intention of getting the bill passed on its merits and resorted to bribery after other lobbyists told me it couldn't be done."[61]

Ex-Representative Walsh, acting as his own counsel, bitterly objected in vain to what he considered to be the prejudicial practice of the prosecution by its repeated reference to the prior naturopathy trial. "We tried that case in Mason for five weeks," Walsh reminded Simpson. "Why must we sit here and go through it again?"[62]

Williams also confessed that he had burned his documents detailing the Association's "slush fund" in 1941. "You knew they contained records of bribery of legislators, didn't you?" Sigler demanded.

"Yes, I did," Williams concurred.

"You burned the records because you considered them dynamite?"

"That's right," the witness said with a nod.[63]

Defense attorney George Fitzgerald inquired of Williams on cross-examination whether he had told the Association Board members that the money to be paid into the trust account was to be used for bribery. "Certainly, not," Williams replied incredulously. "You don't think I'd be that foolish do you?"[64]

Fitzgerald then tried to get Williams to admit that the letters he wrote to naturopaths requesting money were really "shakedowns." Before the flustered witness could speak, Sigler hotly objected. "My learned brother," the Special Prosecutor thundered, "is trying to kick up a smoke screen to blind the jury. It's an old trick, but it won't work this time."[65] Simpson concurred, and the objection was sustained.

On Friday afternoon, April 20, the defense began calling its witnesses. William G. Buckley admitted that he had visited Williams' hotel room "for a drink or two," but denied that he had ever taken any money from his genial host. "I was opposed to the bill," the defendant stated, "because it would have permitted naturopaths to use N.D. after their names, and I thought that was too much like M.D."[66]

Demonstrating his contempt for the proceedings, Birk swaggered to the stand and audaciously swore that the only gift he took from Williams was a "little bottle of liver pills" which he sneered "could hardly be considered a bribe," and that he never knew Williams was a lobbyist for naturopaths. When asked about having his room paid for, Birk brought forth laughter from the gallery by glibly stating: "I come from upper peninsula where we are hospitable people. I thought it was just big-hearted hospitality to pay my hotel bill."[67]

On Monday, Nowak and Wilkowski proclaimed their innocence from the witness stand. Wilkowski, his ample jowls draping over his collar, earnestly related that he had always been in favor of the naturopathic bill and had informed Williams that he did not have to receive favors for his vote. As to the hotel room, the Detroit Democrat said Williams had done it without the Senator's knowledge or consent. "He moved all my belongings into a room next to his," Wilkowski said innocently, "and he asked me to use it. I occupied it about sixty days, vacating the room on weekends. He paid the rent, and I paid the telephone charges and luncheon checks."[68]

Closing arguments were another rehash of the prior trial. Sigler characterized the former legislators as men "who sold their lousy souls after raising their hands on high to swear to support the constitution" and who had turned the "Capitol into a trading post rather than a citadel of government."[69] Defense attorneys, on the other hand, portrayed Williams as a lying thief, who destroyed his records and fabricated tales of bribery as an elaborate scheme to mask his own embezzlement of Association funds.[70]

To the delight of Sigler, it took the jury less than forty minutes to bring in guilty verdicts against all six legislative defendants. Simpson sentenced Green and Birk, as first-time offenders, to three to five year prison terms, while the others received four to five years. The judge said that in the cases of those previously convicted the first three years would run concurrent with their prior sentence, thus adding only one year to their imprisonment. Green was released on $4,000 bond, but Simpson repaid Birk for his insolence by refusing to set bail and ordering the former lawmaker to begin serving his sentence at once.[71]

As reporters shoved bystanders aside to get a "scoop," jury foreman George McElmurray said the decision had been easily derived. "There was no doubt in any juror's mind," he stated. "We believed Williams implicitly when he said he maintained a suite of rooms in the Hotel Olds, plentifully supplied with whiskey, which he used as a headquarters for entertaining and bribing legislators. We believed that Wilkowski and Birk received their free rooms in the suite in return for their promise to help him pass his legislation."[72]

"This was a very important verdict," Sigler beamed, accepting congratulations from admirers. "I commend the common sense and courage of the jury. The verdict proves that an attack upon the integrity of the state's witnesses is futile."[73] Members of the grand jury staff standing at Sigler's side hoped that this statement by their boss would prove prophetic, because the success of their next venture—their biggest to date—rested upon the testimony of men who made Williams look angelic. It would require all of the Special Prosecutor's famed courtroom abilities, plus unparalleled good fortune and the specter of the slain Warren Hooper, if Frank D. McKay was to be fitted for a suit of prison gray.

Murl DeFoe
15th District

Ivan Johnston
11th District

William Stenson
Ontonagon District

William Green
Presque Isle District

Joseph L. Kaminski
Wayne County 1st District

Earl W. Munshaw
16th District

Ernest G. Nagel
Wayne County 1st District

Henry F. Shea
32nd District

Walter N. Stockfish
Wayne County 3rd District

Edward J. Walsh
Wayne County 1st District

Isadore A. Weza
Ontonagon District

William M. Bradley
5th District

D. Hale Brake
25th District

William G. Buckley
Wayne County 1st District

James A. Burns
4th District

Miles M. Callaghan
28th District

Michael J. Clancy
Wayne County 1st District

Carl F. Delano
Kalamazoo County
2nd District

Charles C. Diggs
3rd District

Stanley J. Dombrowski
Wayne County 1st District

Earl C. Gallagher
Wayne County 1st District

George O. Harma
Houghton County
2nd District

Martin A. Kronk
Wayne County 1st District

D. Stephen Benzie
31st District

Jerry T. Logie
24th District

Chester M. Howell
22nd District

Harry F. Kelly Vernon J. Brown Luren D. Dickinson

John Simpson   Leland W. Carr

Leiter   Schwartz

McKay's business associates, former Purple Gang members Charles Leiter and
Isadore Schwartz.

Herbert J. Rushton   Frank Murphy   Charles F. Hemans

Murray D. VanWagoner

Governor VanWagoner signing legislation into law.

The many faces of the combative Kim Sigler.

A youthful Richard Foster vigorously asserts his point in the courtroom of Judge Louis Coash.

"Boss" Frank McKay gets a whispered message.

Purple Gang leaders Ray Bernstein (L) and Harry Keywell (R).

Warren G. Hooper

Senator Hooper's Automobile.

CHAPTER SEVEN

"WON'T SOMEBODY BET ON THE BAY?"

Late April and early May 1945 found Sigler preoccupied with the pre-trial examination of four Purple Gang members—Harry Fleisher, Mike Selik, Pete Mahoney, and Sam Fleisher—who were charged with conspiracy to murder State Senator Warren Hooper. After the hearing ended on May 15 and the defendants were ordered bound over for trial, the Special Prosecutor resumed his pursuit of grafters in the legislature, this time taking aim at two State Senators, Republican Jerry T. Logie of Bay City and Democrat Charles C. Diggs of Detroit, who were accused of taking bribes of $800 and $150 respectively from their Senate colleague Chester M. Howell to help kill in committee House Bill 22 to regulate pari-mutuel betting.

On Monday, June 4, at the Mason Court House, Judge John Simpson began selecting a jury. Within two hours, six men and six women were impaneled, and court was adjourned until 9:30 the following morning.

In his opening statement, Sigler promised to prove that the defendants conspired to defeat legislation regarding the Detroit Racing Association. "House Bill 22 was introduced by Republican Representative George Higgins of Ferndale at the 1941 session of the legislature to amend a racing law adopted in 1933," the Special Prosecutor said, outlining the case to the jurors. "The bill provided for the appointment of a three man racing commission, instead of one commissioner, the payment of a daily racing fee of 2.5 percent of the money bet for the privilege of operating at the state-owned track in Detroit, a minimum fee of $3,500 per day regardless of the percentage, and the installation of totalizers. The fee collected by the state at that time was $2,500 per day of racing, although the law provided that a fee up to $5,000 could have been imposed. The bill passed the House of Representatives on May 16, 1941 and was sent to the Senate where it was referred to the State Affairs Committee, of which

Chester M. Howell was vice chairman. The defendants, Senators Logie and Diggs, were also members of the nine man committee."[1]

"Former Senator Chester M. Howell will testify that he accepted $3,000 from the late Constantine Daniels, a Grand Rapids lobbyist," the Special Prosecutor went on. "He will tell how Daniels instructed him to give Logie $1,000 and Diggs $250. Howell will admit that he held out $200 on Logie and $100 on Diggs. He will testify that he bribed these defendants in the Olds Hotel in Lansing. The payments were made after the bill had died in the Senate State Affairs committee. The bill's death resulted in an enormous loss of state revenue—a minimum of $1,000 a day during the racing season. Teen Daniels represented a faction of 'smart boys' who wanted to keep control of the betting odds and the gambling racket at the Detroit Race Track and were violently interested in having that bill killed, and these defendants agreed to kill that bill for money."[2]

"Ladies and gentlemen of the Jury," Sigler continued, his voice taking on a confidential tone, "graft is a peculiar thing. Some people wink at its existence and do not appreciate the significance of it. Chester Howell was a grafter, but he realized when the jig was up. He offered to tell what he knew in order to help clean up the situation which prevailed in the legislature. There comes a time when every man wants to clean the slate, and Senator Howell should be respected for reaching such a decision."[3]

Not all the denizens of the Capitol shared the Special Prosecutor's view of the ex-solon. Edwin Goodwin, a close friend of Teen Daniels, assailed the prosecution's key witness as being unworthy of trust or credibility. "Ex-Senator Chet Howell, the 'Brother Rat' of this sordid bribe drama, says that the late Constantine Daniels gave him $3,000 to bribe legislators," Goodwin began his scathing editorial. "But Daniels is dead. He cannot speak. The worthiness of Howell's charge against the dead man rests upon Howell's reputation. Howell, upon oath, has contended that he, Howell, a Senator, lied, cheated, thieved, gave bribes, took bribes, was corrupt, and corrupted others. It's embarrassing to try to praise a man who insists that he, himself, is a no-good jerk, the arch-poltroon of craven senatorial iniquity. Now, too, he desecrates even the memory of a man of high ideals who lived in peace. Howell—the 'Lucifer of Law-making'; the 'Cheating Chet of Chesaning.'"[4]

Defense attorneys Albert W. Black and James R. Golden, representing Logie and Diggs respectively, responded by assuring the panel that their clients were not intimate with Howell, did not agree to kill House Bill 22 on promises of graft, and did not receive money from anyone to influence their votes.[5] After defense counsel concluded their statements, Sigler spent the remainder of the day examining Norman Phillio, clerk of the House of

140

Representatives, and Fred I. Chase, Secretary of the Senate, for the purpose of establishing the nature of House Bill 22, its passage through the House, and its arrival before the Senate State Affairs Committee.[6]

On Wednesday, June 6, the State's star witness, Chester M. Howell, assumed his now familiar seat in the witness box in the Ingham County Courthouse. Skillfully maneuvered by Sigler, the small-town editor initially told the jurors how ashamed he was of his past dishonest behavior and then began to elaborate on his role in the horse racing legislation.[7]

"After the race track bill had passed the House," Howell said, staring at the floor to avoid eye contact with his long-time friend Logie, "the late Constantine Daniels, whom I had known for eighteen or twenty years, approached me in the lobby of the Olds Hotel and offered me $3,000 to kill the bill in the Senate State Affairs Committee. Daniels said he wanted Senator Logie to have $1,000 and that $250 should go to Diggs. All three of us were members of the State Affairs Committee. I said, 'All right. I'll do what I can.' I told Logie he was to get $1,000 and I told Diggs he was to receive $250. They agreed to help."[8]

In a wavering voice, Howell related that when the bill reached the committee, he moved that it not be taken up or reported out. The motion prevailed unanimously, he added, thereby postponing indefinitely any action on the measure.[9] "On Monday, May 24, 1941 Daniels telephoned me saying that the money was ready," the witness continued. "I drove to Daniels' home in Grand Rapids and received an envelope containing $3,000 in denominations of ten and twenty dollar bills. I then drove to my home in Saginaw, where I stayed until the following Monday when I returned to Lansing."[10]

Shifting nervously in his seat and wringing his hands, the rumpled ex-lawmaker paused to take a sip of water. "Two days after I got back to Lansing, I saw both Logie and Diggs and invited them to my room at the Olds Hotel. They came at different times, and I gave Logie $500 and Diggs $150," Howell said softly.[11]

Instinctively sensing what the jurors were thinking, the trembling witness peered in their direction. "I cheated them. I just might as well admit it," he whined. "I'm tired of this whole business."[12]

"After the legislative session ended," Howell stated, having regained a semblance of composure, "I met Logie in mid-June at a meeting of the Eastern Michigan Tourist Association at the Green Bush Inn near Oscoda. I took him to my hotel room and paid him another $300."

"Is this the Green Bush Inn?" interrupted Sigler, handling Howell a brochure which included a photograph of Logie and others playing cards.

"Yes, sir, it is."

"Is that the defendant, Senator Logie, in the picture?"

"Yeah, that's him," the witness stated. "He's playing smear, I guess."[13]

"Where did Mr. Daniels get the $3,000 in payoff money, Mr. Howell?" asked Sigler in a sharp tone.

"I don't know," Howell said in a whisper. "He never told me why he wanted the bill killed either, and I didn't ask."[14]

"Did any money ever change hands between Senator Logie and yourself prior to this time, Mr. Howell?" the Special Prosecutor inquired, a knowing smile forming at the corners of his mouth.

"Yes, sir," came the murmured reply. "During the 1939 session, Mr. Logie paid me two bribes of $100 each in connection with medical legislation."

"Thank you, Senator," Sigler said with a wave of his hand toward the defense table. "Your witness."[15]

Albert Black, who had known Howell for many years, did not permit his friendship to interfere with his cross-examination. After eliciting that the witness and Logie had been social and business acquaintances for years, Black asked: "When did you first decide to come forward with your tale of accepting money for legislative influence?"

"Sigler convinced me he was shielding no-one, and I decided to tell him what I knew," Howell confessed, adding quickly: "I had some conscience left, and I wanted to do what I could to clean up matters. I'm not proud of the fact that I'm here in court."

"But you did not feel so compelled, did you, until the grand jury had granted you immunity?" Black shot back.

"No, I guess not," Howell replied, his head bowed to his chest.[16]

Following Howell's testimony, Sigler rested the State's case, and defense counsel called Senator Logie to the stand. The thin-lipped pharmacist stared relentlessly through his round, dark framed spectacles at Sigler as he related his legislative career and reputation for personal and professional integrity.

Sigler rose to begin his cross-examination and strode quickly toward the witness, barking out his initial remarks in midstride. "Let us get down to the ace in this deck," he commanded loudly. "The real reason bribes were paid to kill the racing bill in 1941 is because it would have forced the Detroit Racing Association to install a totalizer, isn't that true?"

"No bribes were paid to my knowledge," came the terse response.

"Isn't it the truth that the Detroit Racing Association had a homemade contrivance that would not accurately keep track of the bets?"

"Not to my knowledge," the witness said. "I have never seen a totalizer or any betting machine."

"Didn't you know if a totalizer was installed, a race track could not cheat the bettors?" Sigler pressed.

"I do not know that," Logie said with a shrug of his shoulders.[17]

Rapidly altering his line of inquiry, Sigler yelled at Logie: "Didn't you take money from both sides on the bank bill of 1941?"

"I did not take money from anyone," Logie answered indignantly.

"And you took money from both sides in connection with medical legislation in 1939, didn't you?"

"I did not," Logie snapped.[18]

"Well, you certainly don't deny taking money from Senator Howell on this racing bill, do you?"

"Yes, sir, I do," Logie said defiantly. "I never paid bribe money to Howell or to any other person. I did not receive money from Howell or even discuss the racing bill with him. I was never in Howell's room during the time he set forth, and I was never in Howell's room at the Green Bush Inn. My wife, who was with me all day, will testify that I never even talked with Howell while at the Green Bush Inn."

"But you did vote against the racing bill, did you not?" Sigler continued, with a smirk distorting his handsome features.

"Yes," admitted the lawmaker, "but it was because I didn't like the provision to set up a three-man commission."[19]

After Senator Diggs categorically denied any involvement with Howell, Black called Michigan Secretary of State Herman Dignan to the stand on Logie's behalf to offer expert testimony on the mechanics of horse race betting. Upon cross-examination, Dignan was asked by Sigler: "The odds board at the Detroit track is one that makes conniving possible, isn't it?"

"I don't know about that," Dignan responded. "When a lot of money is bet on one horse, you don't get much odds. I can say though that I was never aware of any effort being made to kill House Bill 22."[20]

On Thursday, the defense rested its case, and Sigler then started a one hour impassioned summation. "As I said earlier," Sigler, looking cool and refreshed in a light brown suit with matching shoes and tie, implored the jurors, "somehow people are inclined to wink at graft. But when a Senator sells his vote for money, he is selling his right to represent the people in a democracy. These two Senators sneaked around hotel rooms and took money to defeat a bill which was of the utmost importance to the people of this state. The bill provided for the installation of a device to protect the people who gambled at the race track by informing them of what the honest odds would be. It was a foolproof gadget which could not be tinkered with. Bettors would have been given an honest count. At present the track has a contraption that crooks in the basement can fiddle with if they want to fix things. It would have meant the loss of thousands of dollars to those who conducted races. Somebody wanted to keep that contraption crooked. So, these statesmen conspired to kill that bill. They dished out, and took, money in hotel rooms after making their filthy deal beneath the Capitol dome."[21]

"I charge you ladies and gentlemen of the jury," Sigler concluded, "that whether Senator Howell paid to the defendants the full amount that it is claimed they were to receive is not material. If you find that the defendants entered into an unlawful agreement with Senator Howell, as claimed by the People, then your verdict would be guilty as charged."[22]

In his closing remarks, Black made an emotional appeal, urging the jurors to compare the character of his client with that of his accuser, Senator Howell, who told his incriminating story only after being granted immunity. "I charge that you consider testimony that has been given in this case as to the good character and reputation of the accused Jerry T. Logie and as to his being a law-abiding citizen. This testimony, or quality of testimony, in a criminal case is of great consequence and importance both to the people of the state and to the accused," Black pleaded, his voice rising and falling with his level of passion. "To the accused it is of the greatest value, and in cases of doubt growing out of conflict in testimony, when you are not satisfied beyond a reasonable doubt of his guilt, it is entitled to be weighed by the jury. This kind of evidence is admitted on the ground of improbability that one who has always before borne a good character in life could suddenly cast it away by the perpetration of great crimes. The law is not so foolish as to ignore the daily lessons of life, but recognizes the fact that character is much a temple of human art and labor. When a party is charged with a serious crime, which is endeavored to be fastened upon him by circumstantial evidence or by the testimony of doubtful witnesses, he may induce proof of his former good character for honesty and integrity to rebut the presumption of guilt arising from such evidence which it may be impossible for him to contradict or explain."[23]

Digg's attorney, James R. Golden, who had come to Battle Creek to practice law because few blacks were permitted to engage in criminal practice in his home state of Virginia, based his client's defense on similar grounds. "Good character is an important fact with every man, and never more so than when he is put on trial charged with an offense which is rendered improbable in the last degree by a uniform course of life wholly inconsistent with any such crime," Golden told the jurors, his soft, melodious voice filling the room. "Good character may not only raise a doubt of guilt which would not otherwise exist, but it may bring conviction of innocence. Remember, the presumption of innocence never shifts. It remains until it has been removed by testimony so positive in its character that the jury can say they are satisfied beyond a reasonable doubt that all of the elements necessary to make up the offense charged have been proven. I charge you, ladies and gentlemen, to decide whether there is reasonable doubt as to my client's guilt."[24]

After deliberating only two hours and forty-minutes Thursday afternoon, jury foreman Dewey Brown read the verdict which found both defendants guilty as charged. Logie and Diggs showed no emotion as Judge Simpson immediately sentenced each to four to five years in Jackson Prison. Mrs. Bessie Logie seemed dazed as she heard her husband sentenced to prison for the second time in a year. She walked to him and patted his shoulder. He looked up, and tears came to his eyes.[25]

Judge Simpson set bail at $4,000 for each defendant, and, after sentencing, they were freed under bond. A beaming Sigler triumphantly packed his briefcase and left the courtroom having successfully prosecuted his fifth consecutive grand jury case. Now, he could devote all his attention, at least for the next few weeks, to the trial charging the four Purple Gang members with conspiracy to murder Warren Hooper. With luck, he thought, one might crack and implicate Frank McKay. That, to the ambitious Special Prosecutor, was the "thing that dreams were made of." But this was not to be, and Sigler was left with the liquor conspiracy charge as his sole remaining hope to send his Grand Rapids nemesis to prison.

CHAPTER EIGHT

STRIKE THREE—MCKAY'S NOT OUT

As Michigan's snows melted and balmy breezes turned spring buds into summer's burst of colorful blossoms, one name kept echoing in the ears of the state's citizenry: Frank D. McKay. Scarcely a day passed without reference to the embattled financier by the Carr-Sigler investigative squad, who continuously linked McKay, by innuendo more than fact, to virtually every evil in the state's recent legislative history. Indeed, not even illness could bring a temporary cessation in the attack. On June 20, 1945, ten days after being served with a warrant charging him and several others with attempts to corrupt the state's liquor control commission, McKay underwent a sinus operation at Ann Arbor's St. Joseph Mercy Hospital to relieve intense pressure behind his right eye. Sigler called a hastily convened news conference and announced his belief, which was contrary to medical evidence in his possession, that the illness was nothing more than a "subterfuge" to postpone the trial which was scheduled to begin in a week. "As soon as the warrant was issued," Sigler sneered contemptuously, "McKay ran to the hospital, using pull to get in, and underwent this operation, not because he needed it, but as an excuse for not appearing."[1] Despite his ravings, the Special Prosecutor consented, albeit gracelessly, to Judge Carr's decision to move the trial to July 5.[2]

To Sigler's dismay, on July 5 defense counsel was granted yet another continuance, this time until September 5. One week before the September date, however, McKay's high-priced defense team of Eugene L. Garey of New York and William Henry Gallagher of Detroit dropped a bombshell by revealing that their client was presenting a petition requesting both a one year delay and a change of venue.

The petition submitted by McKay initially set forth a belief that because Judge Carr, who had issued the arrest warrant, was held "in such universal esteem in Ingham County" no jury could be impanelled in that county which would give him "his constitutional presumption of innocence."[3] He further charged that Carr bore animus against him because the jurist believed McKay had been instrumental in having the Republican party convention deny Carr a nomination to a seat on the Michigan Supreme Court.[4] For these reasons, and because Ingham County forbid the sale publicly of liquor by the glass, McKay begged for a change of venue.[5]

The remainder of the sixty page document, which was accompanied by scores of newspaper stories and editorials, was targeted at Sigler, whom McKay derided as an "unscrupulous prosecutor who was making a studied effort to sully and besmirch" McKay's reputation "to the end that no fair trial could be obtained."[6] Sigler's goal, it was asserted flatly, was "to get McKay at any price."[7] McKay alleged that his Hastings nemesis had used the recently completed murder conspiracy trial at Battle Creek as a forum to "convertly convey that there was some sinister connection between the Hooper murder and the fact that he was a star witness against me at a forthcoming examination."[8] The affidavit continued: "The impression was conveyed that I was guilty of the charge against me, and, therefore, I had Hooper killed to prevent this star witness from testifying against me. The fact is that I had no more to do with Hooper's murder than the court which is hearing this motion. If Sigler's inferences had any foundation, why was I not made a respondent in the murder case?"[9] The petition closed with a recitation of the effects of Sigler's "poisoning the minds of Michigan residents" against McKay: "I became a murderer . . . an employer of assassins . . . a grafter . . . a champion of criminals and desperadoes . . . a grand jury obstructionist . . . a noted corruptionist . . . a crooked politician who belonged in jail . . . a sinister political overlord who manipulated, and still manipulates, the affairs of state. I was pictured as a man who would stop at nothing, even to the hiring of ex-convicts to murder a man for a price to gain my ends."[10]

Upon hearing of McKay's legal tirade, Sigler smugly told newsmen: "The trouble with him is that his chickens are just coming home to roost. The strong arm of the law is catching up with him, and he is whining."[11] Turning serious, Sigler then spoke in a confidential tone to his eager listeners. "We are not surprised. We have been expecting it for more than a year," he disclosed, "ever since we caught a detective slinking around the grand jury. He confessed, telling who assigned him to 'get' something against Judge Carr and myself. Now it is being whispered that I am running for political office, a motive actually furthest from the truth. Apparently McKay thinks he is above the law and anybody who has the temerity to try to bring him to justice must have political ambition. If his campaign to discredit the integrity and the motives of the grand jury succeeds, McKay will have accomplished a clever defense. If he gets that idea into the mind of even one juror, it will have helped him."[12]

The whispering campaign to which Sigler alluded regarding his political ambitions sprang from a single sentence in Mark Beltaire's "Town Crier" gossip column in the *Detroit Free Press*: "Kim Sigler plans to run for Governor . . . on the Democratic ticket."[13] Beltaire subsequently retracted his report, admitting: "That information came from a source I had every reason to believe was sound . . . and without a political axe to grind. He was wrong, and so was I. Now the McKay forces are using my honest mistake in an attempt to persuade the potential jurors that the coming trial is a political persecution. Their work is making the going more difficult for Sigler, who says: 'I haven't the slightest ambition to run for Governor . . . and I am not a Democrat.'"[14]

Even prior to Beltaire's confession, editors friendly to the Special Prosecutor hastened to his defense. The *Ingham County News* said: " . . . Kim Sigler has never made any announcement or intimations; nor has he said or done anything which would lead to any such inference. The story was planted. It may have been planted to injure him personally, or it may have been planted to make someone believe he is using the grand jury as a stepping-stone to the nomination. . . . If Kim Sigler had any desire to be Governor, he would not be so foolish as to make the announcement on the eve of the start of the biggest conspiracy trial in the whole batch. He would not be so stupid as to jeopardize the outcome of the trial and his nomination in one fell swoop. . . . The man or men who planted that story about Sigler being a candidate for Governor did not plant it to compliment him. The story was planted to induce someone to believe that as a special prosecutor he also has one eye on political preferment."[15] The *Detroit News* said in similar tones: "The report bore all the earmarks of a plant, which Sigler believes it to have been. The trick is an old one. If Sigler could be convicted, out of court, of harboring political ambitions, that explanation of his motives might handicap materially his work in court. Said Sigler: 'I'm too damn busy to run for anything. It looks like some scared politicians are trying to inject politics into our trials. Judge Carr and I don't have to play politics. We've got something else to do.'"[16]

To the surprise of few, if any, Judge Carr denied the defense motions, rejecting in toto the claim that there was a need for a change of venue. "So far as allegations of prejudice are concerned," Carr intoned sternly, "they are wholly unfounded."[17] The Ingham County legal legend then proceeded to set forth his unbounded faith in the judicial process as his main motivating factor. "It is inconceivable to my mind," Carr said solemnly, "that any juror taking an oath to try to determine the truth on the basis of evidence received in open court would permit himself to be influenced by any such consideration as the motion for a change of venue suggests. Obviously the fact that publicity had been given to the case is not of material importance. It is to be expected that a case of this nature would receive discussion and comment in newspapers. The fact that respondent McKay had been prominent in public life in recent years doubtless had a tendency to increase the extent of comment."[18] On a personal level, Carr tartly noted that McKay's petition contained "exaggerated, improper, and possibly contemptuous remarks" against the grand juror.[19]

Following Carr's ruling, an outraged William Henry Gallagher spewed forth his venom to all within shouting range. "Never before has there been such a vitriolic or more extended campaign to discredit a defendant than in this case," he bellowed. As to the opportunity for a fair and impartial trial, the dapper Detroit barrister snorted that Carr should have disqualified himself from ruling on the defense motions because he had been the judge who issued the arrest warrant. "It is against common moral judgment," he continued, his face growing more flushed, "for a man to sit in judgment on his own case."[20]

Sigler chose to seize the occasion to land several well-placed body blows to his reeling Grand Rapids antagonist, whom he labelled as a "strange individual" possessing "a feeling of personal animosity and viciousness toward the Special Prosecutor."[21] Smiling benignly, he assured the assembled newshawks that he had conducted himself always "in a dignified manner and at no time had shown any different attitude toward Frank D. McKay from any other respondent."[22]

Compounding the defense's difficulties was the announcement that two of McKay's co-defendants, forty-nine year old Charles Leiter, a former Purple Gang gunman, and Isadore Schwartz, had changed their pleas to guilty and would testify against McKay. Looking business-like in a gray plaid suit, Leiter, McKay's swarthy former bodyguard, spoke pleasantly to reporters, explaining that he made his decision because he was "sick and tired of protecting McKay."[23]

The trial began in Mason on September 5, 1945, with Jackson County Circuit Judge John Simpson presiding. The thin-faced, bespectacled, soft-spoken jurist relished his reputation as "Jackson County's honest judge," but political insiders knew that he was a close friend of McKay.[24] Thus, defense counsel anticipated favorable

150

rulings as they again poised themselves to present the identical motions which had been denied by Carr.

The tiny courtroom was a beehive of activity, although only six spectators were present in the gallery to view the proceedings.[25] Sigler and his staff were positioned inside the railing immediately before the jury box, while Gallagher and Garey were at a table farthest from the jurors. The defendants sat behind their counsel, inside a cordoned section of the room. The seventy-five prospective jurors suffered inside an eighteen by twenty foot anteroom, which rapidly grew suffocating as a result of the sweltering late summer heat. To capture the day's events for visual posterity, at least a dozen photographers kept the room in a flashbulb popping glare.[26]

The trial began, as expected, with Garey, perspiration gleaming through his thinning black hair, renewing his call for a change of venue. The New York attorney pleaded: "Judge Leland W. Carr enjoys such confidence and respect in Ingham County that the mere fact he issued the warrant is enough to condemn a man in the eyes of the citizens of Ingham County. They do not know the teamwork between Special Prosecutor Kim Sigler and Judge Carr is actuated by personal political ambitions. Sigler wants to be Governor and Judge Carr has long aspired to the Supreme Court."[27] Interrupting, Sigler leapt to his feet and yelled: "I don't want McKay's scalp. I have no desire to be Governor and anyone who wants to be Governor in these unsettled times is crazier than I think William Henry Gallagher and Garey are!"[28]

Undaunted, Gallagher then rose and argued for a two month continuance, rather than a year, on the grounds that there had been "undue haste" in bringing the case against McKay and his four co-defendants— former Flint mayor William McKeighan, Fisher Layton, Earl Williams, and Charles Williams, all liquor company agents—to trial when other cases had been pending for more than a year.[29] Moreover, he added smugly, McKay and the other defendants had been acquitted by a federal court in 1942 on similar charges after a previous federal court jury had been unable to reach a verdict.[30]

Sigler shot out of his chair, shouting: "That was when former Attorney General Herbert C. Rushton was prosecutor, and Rushton happened to be one of your client's pals. That was a bum case Rushton started!"[31]

"If it was a bum case," Gallagher responded serenely, "you were derelict in your duty to keep my client under bond for a year."[32]

The suave attorney, sensing he had penetrated Sigler's previously unflappable confidence, bore in all the harder. "There has been no occasion in the history of a case, Your Honor," he stated in a voice filled with conviction of purpose, "where any litigant was called on to go to trial under conditions of such adverse publicity and such long sustained publicity. It is one thing for a prosecutor to be zealous in the prosecution of a crime and another to so mold public opinion of a man who is going to be prosecuted for a crime so as to prejudge him. Sigler has proclaimed to all the world that it is his personal conviction that McKay is guilty of obtaining the murder of Hooper as well as being guilty in the present case. When you have six months of testimony to review, with thousands of exhibits, it takes more than a few days or a few weeks to prepare for the case."[33]

Slowly rising to present his rebuttal, Sigler made no effort to conceal his contempt for the opposing counsel. "Your Honor, the defense says this is just a rehash of the old liquor conspiracy federal trial," he said sarcastically, "but in the next breath it asks for a sixty day delay to prepare just the same. The Great Gallagher and Broadway Garey and the rest of them were engaged in that federal case for nearly two years. If it is only a rehash, why aren't they prepared to come into court?"[34]

Peering up at Judge Simpson, who was idly jotting down notes, the irate Special Prosecutor raged on. "The Great Gallagher is a past master at the art of creating smoke screens. This is just another. Frank D. McKay means no more to me than any other respondent," Sigler asserted to the disbelief to all who knew him and his motives. "He forgets that long before this grand jury started, Frank D. McKay was in the public eye in Michigan with the anti-McKay factions and the federal grand jury in Detroit. When Senator Hooper was murdered, and he was the principle witness—practically the only witness of importance—against McKay and his co-defendants in the horse racing bill trial, why was it improper for us to say so? Aren't the people of Michigan entitled to know the facts concerning the murder of a state senator? Is the prosecution to be condemned because we told the facts to the people of Michigan that the examination would have to be continued and the case eventually dropped?"[35]

After listening to another two hours of Garey and Gallagher alternately reading motions—a process so tedious and boring that it put not only two spectators, but also McKay and McKeighan, to sleep—Judge Simpson adjourned court.[36] The following day Simpson made a decision which brought smiles to the defense counsel. "In all fairness to myself and everyone concerned," the jurist said softly, "I must have time to review these motions. I have no ouija board or all the answers on an index card. I will take this case under advisement for thirty days."[37]

152

III During the continuance, an event occurred which altered not only the course of the Ingham County Grand Jury, but also the future of Kim Sigler. On September 16, Associate Justice Howard Wiest of the Michigan Supreme Court died and pressure was placed on Republican Governor Harry F. Kelly by party leaders to elevate Carr to the Supreme Court to fill the vacancy. The Governor, however, was reluctant to act because of uncertainty as to the impact of Carr's removal on the grand jury investigations.

After three days of uncharacteristic silence, Sigler called a press conference and removed the last barrier to his benefactor attaining his life-long dream. "The grand jury," Sigler told reporters in a voice hesitating and choking with emotion, "can conclude its work without Judge Carr—now. One or two years ago, I would have said no. But Judge Carr held the fort when the going was tough. He has set the pattern—laid the bricks—and from here on out it's a matter of following them. And I know Judge Carr wouldn't leave the job if there was any question about the grand jury not being able to be carried to completion by another judge."[38]

Sigler's new boss was forty-one year old former Lansing Municipal Judge Louis E. Coash, who had been on the Circuit Court only four months when Carr, as his last official act as presiding judge of the Ingham County Circuit Court, named him grand juror. The good-natured, dark-haired, moon-faced jurist, who relied more on instinct than knowledge of the law, professed enthusiasm about his latest challenge but admitted his weakness. "Since I am grass green about grand juries," he confessed, "I shall have to depend heavily upon Mr. Sigler and the members of his present staff for guidance."[39]

The Special Prosecutor's hope that he could manipulate Coash in the same manner he had done Carr was quickly dashed, however, when Coash instructed Sigler that henceforth only the grand juror would dictate policy and warned him against trying to "run the damn thing without consultation." In the future, the grand juror ordered, in a well aimed blow at Sigler's massive ego, all press releases would have Judge Coash's name listed first.[40]

IV Tanned and rested after a two week vacation in Florida, Sigler was prepared finally to satisfy his "magnificent obsession" by putting McKay behind bars on liquor conspiracy charges. Federal Justice Department officials, who twice before had been stymied in their efforts to convict McKay on similar charges, wished the Hastings attorney luck, but scoffed at the "johnny-come-lately's" ability to succeed.

"If we of the Justice Department could not find anything upon which a jury could convict McKay," one said pompously, "we have serious doubts if anyone else can turn the trick."[41] Upon hearing this, one of the Special Prosecutor's youthful, admiring legal aides boasted: "The Justice Department lawyers will find out before this thing ends that Sigler knows a few tricks in the prosecution game which Justice Department lawyers may not know!"[42]

Less than a week before the oft-delayed trial was set to begin on January 14, 1946, Ingham County Prosecutor Victor C. Anderson announced that prospective jurors had been tampered with, and, in response, Judge Coash issued bench warrants for the immediate arrest of several of McKay's private investigators, including former Michigan State Police Captain and head of the Detective Bureau Ira H. Marmon and John A. Wilson, as well as McKay's close friend Edwin A. Goodwin, editor and publisher of the *Michigan State Digest*.[43] Anderson alleged that Marmon had investigated prospective jurors' backgrounds and turned the information over to Wilson, who, while posing as an investigator for the Ingham County Circuit Court, threatened would-be veniremen. One of those victimized, Mrs. Edgar Morgan, testified in an affidavit that Wilson telephoned her and asked about her husband's business and social activities. When told the couple had no children, Wilson remarked with sinister implications, "Well, you are the only one he has to leave then."[44] Another, Mrs. W. R. Rauling, a Catholic, related in her affidavit that Wilson had told her that if there was a Catholic on the jury of a Catholic defendant, there might be an improper verdict.[45] Another woman, whose name was withheld, said in her sworn statement that Wilson told her that "if you don't want personal family connections exposed, don't serve on the McKay jury."[46] Similar statements were received from four other female prospective jurors.[47] Goodwin was alleged to have printed and distributed an extra one thousand copies of his January 2, 1946 newspaper which carried an editorial highly defamatory to Sigler and charged that the Special Prosecutor was engaged in a personal vendetta against McKay.[48]

When Judge Simpson gavelled court into session on January 14, Garey, heading McKay's team of seven attorneys, sought yet another continuance as well as a change of venue, this time basing his claim on prejudice against his client resulting from Anderson's allegations. As a supporting document, Garey submitted an affidavit from McKay in which the Republican boss set forth his response to Anderson's charges.

"I heard of Wilson's activities before the newspaper articles appeared, and I had requested my attorneys to see Circuit Judge Louis E. Coash to have him stop the telephoning. Yet it is clearly inferred, if not directly charged, that I procured Jack Wilson to make inquiries," McKay stated. "The charge that I did so is utterly without foundation. I hired Marmon to investigate prospective jurors only after I had been advised by counsel that I had a right to engage him, and I did so because of his long experience in investigating the qualifications of prospective jurors and because he had done such work recently for the prosecution. The charge that I hired him to tamper with the jury is a lie."[49]

Sigler, livid with fury, strenuously opposed the defense motions and the veracity of McKay's affidavit. "Your Honor," he pleaded, "nowhere does Anderson charge the defendants with doing these things. But it is a strange thing that copies of a weekly newspaper containing defamatory articles about me were circulated in this county to people who never before received it. The charge that I have been making political speeches in Ingham County is a bald-faced lie. I am not a candidate. I have not been a candidate. I will not be a candidate. I have a job to do, and I'm going to do it. The only person who has charged me with this is Frank McKay. The only reason the charge has been made is to inject politics into this trial."[50]

After listening to all the arguments, Judge Simpson ruled against a continuance, but he ordered the trial moved to Jackson, the seat of the county bearing the same name. The judge said he "regretted very much the unfortunate affair" which necessitated the change of venue. However, he explained, "the scandalous articles bode no good for anybody, either the defense or the prosecution, and, in my judgment, the only thing to do is move the trial."[51]

Because of anticipated public interest in the proceedings, Simpson decreed that the trial would not be held in the courthouse, but rather in the 1,800 seat Jackson County Building auditorium. As this locale was utilized primarily for festive civic functions, most recently a symphony, a high school production of "The Pirates of Penzance," and a gold glove boxing tournament, a hasty conversion was necessary. A temporary judge's bench was placed on the stage in front of the orchestra pit, and off to its side a jury box was constructed of wooden slats covered with green wrapping paper. Tables were brought in for the attorneys, clerks, and reporters, with a press area set up in a dressing room. Lighting was poor, with spotlights from the balcony casting an eerie yellow hue over the room. To facilitate hearing, a loudspeaker system was installed, with its amplifiers concealed behind a screen decorated by dancing girls in diaphanous gowns. Just outside the main entrance to the auditorium, a young female entrepreneur erected a booth from which to sell ginger ale.[52]

Expecting a lengthy trial, Simpson proclaimed that fourteen jurors would be selected, and at the trial's conclusion two would be eliminated by lot from participating in the deliberation.[53] Then, in a soft voice, the judge, peering intently through his round, shell-rimmed spectacles, methodically began calling forth individuals from the pool of 101 possible veniremen, asking each a series of questions: (1) "Do you have any idea that Frank McKay was connected with the murder of Warren G. Hooper?" (2) "Do you have any idea McKay was connected with, or mixed up in, the recent investigation of Southern Michigan Prison?" (3) "Have you formed any opinion as to the guilt or innocence of the defendants from reading newspapers or listening to the radio?" (4) "Have you been approached by anyone who wanted to discuss this case?" (5) "Are you prejudiced against McKay because he is a politician or because he has been in the liquor business?" and (6) "Have you ever been, or are you now, a member of a temperance organization?"[53]

For the prosecution, Sigler's challenges rested on three issues: (1) did the prospective juror know Frank Fitzsimmons, the Benton Harbor sports promoter and friend of Frank McKay, who was appealing his prison sentence following conviction in an earlier grand jury conspiracy case? (2) would the prospective juror be prejudiced against the Special Prosecutor because he previously had brought to trial and convicted several members of the state legislature? and (3) would the prospective juror be reluctant to convict the defendants because they were all Republicans?[54] Defense counsel's main concern was whether the would-be jurors knew any State Police officers or grand jury aides.[55]

After a surprisingly brief one and a half days of queries, eight housewives and six men were sworn in as jurors.[56] Judge Simpson informed the panel that although they would not be sequestered they should not talk to anyone involved with the trial. "Don't even accept a cigarette from a person connected with this case," he commanded. "Lawyers are very suspicious people, especially when they are on opposite sides of a law suit."[57]

Before calling for opening statements, Simpson granted a prosecution motion that all charges of accepting and receiving bribes be dismissed, thus making the state's case against the defendants one of "simple conspiracy to coerce the liquor commission by threat and intimidation."[58] William Henry Gallagher quickly presented a motion to quash all charges. "With the charge of bribery," defense counsel argued, "there is a criminal conspiracy case. As it stands this morning, we are not called upon to face a criminal charge, and there is nothing of a criminal nature to present to a jury. The only means of corrupting a law which comes to my mind is bribery. To charge defendants with a crime, the criminal means used must also be charged. Now there is only a polyglot statement of generalities charging nothing of a criminal nature."[59]

"The gist of the offense is the unlawful agreement," Sigler replied. "These defendants controlled the activities of the commission—if men can so control a board or a commission that directs activities of a state law, there is no question they have unlawfully conspired."[60]

"In 1933 the legislature passed a law for the control of alcoholic beverages," Sigler tutored the Court, using his most professorial manner. "It was the duty of the liquor commission and its employees to administer that law without favor. Frank D. McKay was the recognized boss of the Republican party. One could not even get a job in government without McKay's approval. McKay told the Governor what to do. He even elected the late Frank Fitzgerald governor, and he put up the money. He got at least some of that money back by his control of the liquor commission and its employees. Sales and distribution were the cores of the state's liquor business. If one controlled them, he controlled the liquor business. Frank D. McKay and Bill McKeighan had that control, and they unlawfully conspired to corrupt this law."[61]

Having listened patiently, if not attentively, to the Special Prosecutor's lecture, Simpson denied the defense motion. Court was then adjourned.

Finally, the long-awaited battle formally began. Sigler, his long wavy silver hair as immaculate as his tailored gray suit, paraded in anxious anticipation around the prosecution table. McKay, sporting a deep tan acquired during a recently completed Florida vacation, sat glowering at his legal antagonist, and occasionally whispered an aside to McKeighan, who was seated to his left. Behind her husband, Mrs. McKay, dressed in a black suit, sat stoically.[62]

"Ladies and gentlemen of the jury, the State will show that Frank D. McKay, William McKeighan, and the other defendants joined together to elect Frank Fitzgerald governor," Sigler promised solemnly. "After Fitzgerald was elected, this group moved in, so far as the administration was concerned in Lansing. The State will show that this group of men had such complete control over the destinies of the State of Michigan and one of its agencies—the liquor control commission—that they would determine how a certain law—the liquor control act—should be enforced. The State will show that they, having this influence and control, not only saw that the commission gave out larger orders to their clients, but also saw that their clients' products received preferred distribution. The State will show that in conversations between the defendants and liquor commission officials, a special code was used to designate the preferred liquor companies—Hiram Walker, Mohawk, and Arrow—as 'Republicans' and the ones to be discriminated against—Schenley and Calvert—as 'Democrats.' The State will further show that agreements between the preferred companies and the accused existed during 1935 and 1936. These were abandoned during the 1937 and 1938 regime of former Governor Frank Murphy, but they were resumed during the 1939 and 1940 administration of Frank Fitzgerald and Luren Dickinson, who replaced Fitzgerald upon his death in office."[63]

Garey waived his opportunity for an opening statement, and Sigler called Thomas H. Gibbons, Vice President of Hiram Walker and Sons Distillery, as the first of thirty-seven scheduled State witnesses. Led by the prosecutor's direct questions, Gibbons recounted that in 1935 his company's Michigan agent was Sol Sallin, a Detroit jeweler with powerful connections within the Republican party. Walker officials grew dissatisfied with Sallin, however, because only five of their twenty brands were listed in Michigan. Gibbons said that he went to McKay seeking more orders, but McKay told him to go to the liquor control commission. Later, Gibbons stated, he returned to McKay and repeated his request. This time McKay directed him to contact a "Mr. Woodbury," who subsequently was revealed to be G.O.P. boss and five-time mayor of Flint William McKeighan. Having obtained the Walker account, McKeighan assigned it to the Duo Sales, Engineering, and Service Company, which he controlled. In 1936 the Duo Company garnered $135,281.18 in fees, based on collection of 1.5 percent on Walker brand selling for less than $12.50 per case and 2.5 percent on those above that ceiling price.[64] After Murphy was sworn in as Governor in 1937, McKeighan's contract was cancelled and Democrat J. C. Whitliff was appointed Walker's agent. When the Republicans regained the governorship in 1939, McKeighan was reinstated, but this time, Gibbons recalled, his front organization was the Williams Sales Agency, owned by Charles and Earl Williams of Detroit.[65]

Under cross-examination by Gallagher, Gibbons admitted that he could not remember what, if anything, McKay had said about "Mr. Woodbury." Defense counsel also elicited from the witness that the Walker Distillery employed agents not only in Michigan, but also in all liquor monopoly states, and that the commissions paid were utilized to cover sales promotions and expenses.[66]

Following Gibbons on the stand was Richard Haynes of Detroit, who had the Schenley Distillery account. Haynes stated that in 1936, in his capacity as Schenley agent, he had hired Charles Leiter and paid him $12,956 in commissions.[67]

"When Leiter first approached me, he told me his name was Abe Brown," Haynes testified. "He said that he had a sales organization set up, that he knew saloon owners and bar tenders throughout Detroit, and that he could increase our sales. I asked him what other qualifications he had, and he said he knew the man in Grand Rapids."

"Did you know who he meant by 'the man in Grand Rapids?'" prodded Sigler, fully realizing that McKay's residence was in that city.

"I did not," was the terse reply.[68]

"Well, then," Sigler instructed the witness, "explain please your relationship, in a business sense, with Mr. Leiter."

"I paid him monthly in cash. I met him in hotel lobbies, taxi cabs, and once, perhaps, in a telephone booth. In each instance I would write a check for cash and withdraw the money myself," Haynes said.

"Why did you do that?" inquired Sigler.

"Because Leiter, who was using the name of Brown, told me he would have trouble cashing checks," the witness explained.[69]

After Sigler entered as exhibits eight checks, which were identified as having been written by the witness to get cash for Leiter and which ranged in amounts from $300 to $2,490, Garey rose and objected to the Special Prosecutor's method of examining Haynes.[70]

"Well," Sigler snapped, "I'm not from Broadway, so I guess I don't know how to act."

"Then spend a couple of days on Broadway and find out," Garey retorted sarcastically.[71]

During cross-examination, Haynes admitted that he might have used part of the money for himself as "pocket cash."[72] He concluded his testimony by saying that in the Spring of 1937 he fired Leiter because "the Democrats had taken over in Lansing, and I didn't see how he could continue the same work."[73]

The State's next two witnesses, Godfrey Hammel of Detroit and Deputy Wayne County Clerk Eugene W. Method, testified regarding McKeighan's role in the alleged conspiracy. The former asserted that the ex-Flint mayor, using the alias of William B. Gallagher, helped him acquire a liquor order from the Arrow Distilling Company. Of his $1,704 commission, Hammel stated, he gave $1,200 or $1,300 to McKeighan "for getting me the distribution."[74]

His features displaying obvious disdain, Garey approached the bench and again requested a mistrial. "This is a dirty business, Your Honor," he pleaded. "We listen and listen, but no conspiracy has been proven. Even Your Honor has intimated this fact by admitting all the testimony thus far submitted subject to eventual showing that a conspiracy existed."[75]

Storming forward, Sigler threw up his hands in disgust. "Your Honor," he complained bitterly, "Mr. Garey keeps repeating that statement in front of the jury in a most prejudicial way. A conspiracy of this nature must be developed step by step, and we'll prove it, have no fear."[76] This pledge was met by a staccato burst of applause by spectators in the balcony.[77]

The next of Sigler's key witnesses, Charles Layton, who was also known as Charles Lipsitz, walked timidly to the box and was sworn in. "I went to see Mr. McKeighan in the latter part of 1935," the swarthy, silver-haired former manager of the Mohawk Liqueur Corporation began in a muffled voice, "and asked him to see if he could do something for me in obtaining more business from the liquor control commission or help in selling more of our products."

"Please speak up," Judge Simpson interrupted.

"Yeah, put a little steam on it," Sigler urged.

"I went to him again," Layton continued, nervously clearing his throat and trying in vain to increase his volume, "and he said for me to go ahead the way I'd been going, seeing the liquor commission, and he'd see what could be done for me. A month or so later I saw him again. I told him I had received a few orders from the state, and McKeighan said: 'If you think I am helping you a little bit, you should help us, or help me, with the administration. That is, as far as politics is concerned, a donation.' From then until the end of 1936 I paid McKeighan between $15,000 and $20,000 for his assistance."[78]

"In 1939," the witness went on, "McKeighan suggested that I hire the Williams Sales Company, at a commission of $1 per case ordered, as an agent, and I did. The next year, also at McKeighan's suggestion, I fired the Williams Company and hired Fisher Layton of Flint to serve as agent. I met these men both in a Detroit hotel room rented by McKeighan."[79]

As Sigler was deftly leading Layton through his tale, he was interrupted again by cheers from the gallery. "You are having these people try to prejudice the jury," screamed Garey in protest. "You have been doing nothing else since the trial started."

"Oh, don't judge other people by yourself," Sigler replied with a smirk.

"Some sort of clique seems to have developed," Garey raged on, "and I object to this. This is not a theatre. This is a courtroom. I don't know whether Mr. Sigler has brought this clique in here or not, but I have a pretty good guess."

"I ask the Court to strike that smart-aleck remark," Sigler yelled.

Trying desperately to restore decorum, Judge Simpson banged his gavel repeatedly and instructed the jurors to "disregard all personalities." Then, sounding like a harassed school teacher, he implored the spectators, many of whom were teenagers, to remember that "anyone who does any demonstrating again can leave the courtroom."[80]

Emmanuel Rosenthal, President of the Mohawk Liqueur Corporation, was the next witness, and his testimony centered around Fisher Layton, whom he claimed had presented himself as "an all-round politician."[81] "He told me he had certain political connections in the territory up around Flint," Rosenthal stated. "He told me he knew a lot of clerks, that he went to school with them, and helped them get jobs. He emphasized that he belonged to all the different clubs and lodges. It was just the regular line a salesman gives you when he comes in. I fired Williams because we weren't satisfied with the amount of sales he was showing, and I hired Layton to make at least ten surveys of distribution patterns and to promote Mohawk brands."[82]

Tempers reheated shortly into the testimony of Republican State Senator Murl H. DeFoe, who had been a member of the liquor control commission in 1939 and 1940. The short, pudgy, bespectacled newspaper editor strode to the stand using his cane more as a sartorial accouterment than a medical necessity.[83]

"Did you speak with anyone regarding the operation of the liquor commission?" Sigler asked during the course of his examination.

"Yes, I did," was the reply.

"Did you and the secretary of the commission, Fred C. Ehrmann, have discussions, and did you and the Governors, Fitzgerald and Dickinson, have discussions over the control you people had over the liquor commission?" continued Sigler.[84]

Before DeFoe could respond, Gallagher objected on the grounds that any statement DeFoe made would be hearsay evidence and inadmissible.[85] Sigler responded angrily: "We contend, Your Honor, that the liquor commission under the administrations of Fitzgerald and Dickinson delegated its powers to Fred Ehrmann who, as secretary of the commission, ran its affairs. Fred Ehrmann was under the domination and control of McKay and the other defendants because he was afraid of losing his job. We expect to prove that through Senator DeFoe."[86] After sustaining the objection, Simpson adjourned court until the following morning.

Upon resumption of his testimony DeFoe stated that Ehrmann had prepared all liquor orders. "The commission was merely a rubber stamp," he charged. "Fred Ehrmann had complete control of whiskey purchases and distribution. He was a stooge of Frank McKay, and, indirectly, I was a stooge myself."[87]

Rising slowly from his chair, William Henry Gallagher launched into a vicious cross-examination. DeFoe, clearly shaken by the onslaught became alternatively evasive and defensive in his answers, which merely served to intensify Gallagher's assault.

"Will you withdraw your statement, Senator, that the commission was just a 'rubber stamp' and 'stooges' for Ehrmann?" thundered the defense counsel.

"I will not," insisted DeFoe defiantly. "The liquor commission when I was a member was a rubber stamp."

"Then you violated your oath of office and did not carry out your duty as a liquor commissioner, is that right?" sneered Gallagher.

DeFoe hesitated, his face becoming as crimson as the carnation in his lapel, before sheepishly whispering, "I guess that's right."[88]

"Did you treat, as a commissioner, large and small distillers differently?" inquired Gallagher.

"Yes," DeFoe replied slowly. "I favored giving smaller distillers larger orders because the big distillers have a way of looking after themselves. The big four distillers always had someone to look out for them in Lansing."

"Were you aggressive in that belief?" Gallagher asked loudly.

"Well, I was usually outvoted on the commission, but I did not maintain my attitude vigorously," he admitted, but added testily: "However, it looks to me that you're trying to make it appear that I was so much for the underdogs that I was offensive to the big ones."

"Well, were you?"

"No," DeFoe insisted. "But representatives of the big fellows never came to see me at all. They didn't need to. They always got their orders."

"So far as you know Orrin DeMass, the Chairman of the commission, had no part in determining the liquor the state would buy," queried Gallagher.

"Mr. Ehrmann, in that sense, was the commission," DeFoe responded.

"Do I need to repeat the question, Senator?" the barrister yelled. "Can you just answer yes or no?"

Shifting in his chair, the legislator replied curtly: "I say yes."

"Can you give us any occasion when you saw Mr. Ehrmann determine the liquor the state would buy?"

"I can't do that," stated DeFoe, glaring at the attorney.

"Well, if you can't cite a single occasion, how can you swear he always determined it?" asked Gallagher smugly.

"He did it twice a week," DeFoe shot back.

"My," said the counsel in mock horror, "weren't you shocked the first time you learned that Ehrmann determined purchases?"

Returning the sarcasm, DeFoe replied: "Well, it takes quite a lot to shock a person on the commission."

"Was Frank McKay, the defendant, a frequent visitor to the commission?"

"Mr. McKay visited the commission only twice while I was there," DeFoe recalled. "One was a purely social visit. The other had something to do with breweries in which McKay was interested. I'm inclined to think the commission favored his plan and adopted it one day, but nullified it the next."

"Well, what happened," snorted Gallagher. "After all, you were there, I wasn't."

"You know," DeFoe said ruefully, "sometimes I wonder if I was."

"So do I," huffed the counselor.[89]

Court then recessed, giving the beleaguered state senator an opportunity to regain his composure. The respite was short-lived, however, for when Court was gavelled into session, the Detroit barrister resumed his verbal barrage.

"Did you, Senator, have an open house at your Charlotte residence for former heavyweight boxing champion Gene Tunney, who was then Chairman of the Board of American Distilleries Incorporated?"

"I did," DeFoe said smiling. "It was attended by quite a reputable group of my own citizens and half a dozen or so from Lansing."

"Were any liquor salesmen present?" inquired Gallagher, his voice now suddenly soothing and reassuring.

"Yes," said the witness, adding quickly, "but there was no liquor served at my house—ever. I'm not trying to be a prude about it, but it is true that I'm a total abstainer. I was proud to have Mr. Tunney in my house. He told me more things about what brought this trial together than I had ever known."

"What things," prodded counsel, his voice growing harsher.

"Well, I cannot recall specifics," the Senator whispered.

"Do you mean to say—oh, never mind," sighed Gallagher. "Let's return to your Tunney party. Do you mean to say that the Schenley Distillery agent in Michigan attended this gathering, but he did not send you liquor for it?"

"He did not!" shouted DeFoe, his face florid.[90]

"Your Honor," pleaded Gallagher to Judge Simpson, whose expression was a reflection of his displeasure with the responses of the witness, "I have given this witness extended opportunities to furnish the facts upon which he based his allegations regarding Mr. Ehrmann and the operation of the liquor control commission because the jury is entitled to facts. But there are no facts. His testimony is merely a conclusion and is utterly incompetent. I move that all his statements regarding Mr. Ehrmann be stricken from the record."[91]

"I would say plenty if I had a chance and you would let me. You don't want me to tell the facts," burst DeFoe, who was immediately ordered to be silent by Judge Simpson.[92]

"Your Honor," Sigler implored in an effort to salvage DeFoe's testimony, "we will show that Mr. Ehrmann acted under the direction of McKay and McKeighan. Mr. Ehrmann will testify for the State under a grant of immunity. He will state that he would place orders for millions of dollars which were not signed by any of the three members of the commission, even though the law stipulates all orders must be signed by at least two of the members. Senator DeFoe has testified to situations which existed several years ago. His testimony was based on facts he could not now recall."[93] Simpson disagreed and granted the defense motion, ruling that "the testimony of this witness must be based on facts; that is required by law."[94]

At this point, Simpson had not only grown exceedingly provoked with the nature of the prosecutor's case, but also was doubting his own wisdom in moving the trial to such an informal setting. In an attempt to establish some vestige of judicial decorum, Simpson issued a new set of rules. No longer would attorneys and spectators be permitted to gather around the ginger ale stand while court was in session; henceforth refreshment could be purchased only during a recess. Likewise, autograph seekers now could pester attorneys and defendants only during a break and not while court was in session. Finally, to enforce the no smoking ordinance, which was being violated by attorneys on a regular basis, Simpson brought Jackson policemen into the courtroom.[95]

Sensing his prospects for victory were slipping away, Sigler nonetheless confidently expected his fortunes to turn with the testimony of his "star witness" Fred C. Ehrmann. Before Sigler could begin his examination, however, he once again had to endure the daily ritual of Garey, the short, broad-shouldered defense counsel, unceremoniously dragging his chair across the room, placing it directly in front of the prosecution table, and then sitting down with his back to his legal adversaries.[96] Smarting from this theatrical stunt, Sigler embarked on his quizzing of Ehrmann, especially his interactions with Frank McKay and Frank Fitzgerald.

"When did you first meet Frank Fitzgerald?"

"In 1934," Ehrmann stated calmly. "I went around the state setting up Fitzgerald for Governor clubs. He promised to take care of me if he won. A short time after he took office in 1935, I went to see him. He gave me a job with the Secretary of State, but it paid only $2,800 or $2,900, and I couldn't live on that in Lansing. So I went back to him. He sent me to

164

John S. McDonald, then Chairman of the liquor commission, who gave me the job of purchasing agent."

"Sometime after you became purchasing agent," Sigler pointedly inquired, "did you talk with the defendant Frank McKay?"

"Yes, on several occasions. He wrote the name of the Arrow, Mohawk, and Schenley Companies on a slip of paper and told me they had helped elect the administration and should have their regular orders. He said I should do my part or I wouldn't have a job. Well, I figured he was head of the Republican party, and if I didn't obey orders I wouldn't have a job. I was in frequent telephone communication with McKay in 1939 and 1940. I used a special line which I had installed in my office in Lansing. I called McKay in Grand Rapids, Flint, Lansing, and Florida."

"How many times did you talk with McKay during those years?" Sigler asked, feeling for the first time that he was truly on the offensive.

"About one hundred times in 1939 and about fifty in 1940."[97]

When Sigler had completed his interrogation, Gallagher started what proved to be an inquisition so lengthy that it had to be carried over to the next day. The cross-examination began with the defense counsel recalling that he had encountered Ehrmann several years earlier at McKay's federal trial in Detroit.

"We have been on friendly terms ever since then, haven't we, Fred?" Gallagher said with a broad grin.

"Yes."

"But when I wanted to talk with you this morning you were afraid to do so. I had no objection to talking with you for a couple of minutes in private," continued the attorney.

Casting a wary glance toward Sigler, the witness mumbled: "I thought that with the position I was in it was better not to talk with you alone."[98]

Having planted the fruitful seed in the minds of the jurors that the Special Prosecutor was dictating behavior to his witnesses, Gallagher adroitly switched to the issue of influence-peddling. "Did Frank McKay get you your job with the liquor commission, Fred?" he inquired.

"No, it came directly from Governor Fitzgerald," Ehrmann said softly. "Mr. Fitzgerald told me he thought he had a place for me on the utilities commission, but that didn't come through so he sent me to the liquor commission. I never asked Frank McKay for any kind of a job."

"Didn't McKay advise you not to take the liquor job?"

"No, but he told me he thought I should take the utility job if I could get it," Ehrmann admitted. Suddenly, for the first time the former liquor

165

commission secretary smiled and added with a chuckle: "He said I wouldn't have so many hounds after me."[99]

"When you got on the liquor commission, both McKay and Fitzgerald spoke with you regarding giving favors to companies who had supported the Governor's campaign, did they not?"

"Yes, especially the Governor," Ehrmann replied. "He told me that I should see that they got 'proper orders' from the commission."

"Was it something new that a political party should try to help those who placed it in office?" Gallagher queried with feigned innocence.

"No," Ehrmann responded quickly. "The rule in politics is to help those who help you. Every job I had open I gave to a Republican."

"What about Mr. McKay?" Gallagher demanded.

"Mr. McKay met with me in the lobby of the Olds Hotel in Lansing and gave me the names of distillers who had been instrumental in restoring Republicans to power in Michigan. He told me that if we wanted to stay in power and keep our jobs, we should help those who help the administration."

"Did Mr. McKay ever threaten you or ask you to do anything improper?" Gallagher asked, leaning over the witness until he almost touched him.

"No, he never threatened —"

"Speak up and stop mumbling," snapped Judge Simpson.

"No, he never threatened me or asked me to do anything irregular or improper," Ehrmann finished. "He just told me I should do my part or I would lose my job if the Republicans lost power. He never offered me a reward or brought pressure on me to obtain any improper action on my part."[100]

Judge Simpson, whose eyebrows had raised when he heard Ehrmann's statement, interrupted and asked: "Do I understand, Mr. Ehrmann, that you gave orders to these companies merely because they had supported the Republican campaign?"

"Yes, Your Honor," Ehrmann replied meekly.

"And that McKay told you to see that these companies had regular orders?"

"Yes."

"I see," said the jurist thoughtfully. "The defense may proceed."[101]

Fred R. Walker of Detroit, counsel for William McKeighan, then approached the witness. Like Gallagher, Walker began with a chatty observation that "we became acquainted, didn't we, Fred, in the federal trials?"

When Ehrmann's response was inaudible, Simpson said sharply, "Keep your voice up. Don't be so chummy the jury can't hear you."[102]

"Yes, sir, we did," was the barely louder response.

"Didn't you tell me at those federal trials that you never favored anyone or cheated anyone on liquor orders?"

"I never cheated anybody in my life," Ehrmann agreed.

"In fact, as we looked over the commission records together didn't we find that you had given Seagram's, a distillery identified as being a 'Democrat,' 90 percent of the liquor orders placed and Hiram Walker, a 'Republican distillery,' only 50 percent?"

"According to the records, yes."

"You never deprived anyone of an order that was justified?"

"I gave my best judgment," Ehrmann replied somberly.[103]

As Walker returned to the defense table, Gallagher requested a few more questions on cross-examination. "After you were granted immunity by Judge Carr in June of last year, you sought State Police protection, did you not?"

"I talked it over, and we thought it was the best thing to do," Ehrmann responded.

"As a result a detective was assigned to you and accompanies you wherever you go?"

"Yes, sir. Either that or they followed me."

Slowly getting to his feet, Sigler implored: "May this man be excused now, Your Honor?"

"From the custody of the Court or the State Police?" shot back Gallagher.

"He is going to have protection as long as he wants it, I hope, Mr. Gallagher," Sigler pompously replied.

"And no longer, I hope," sneered defense counsel sarcastically.[104]

"Oh, if I may, Your Honor," Sigler inquired nonchalantly, "I have one more question of this witness." Simpson offered silent consent with a wave of his hand.

"Who was your lawyer at the first federal trial, Mr. Ehrmann?"

"Jay Linsey of Grand Rapids."

"Was not Linsey also Frank McKay's attorney?" Sigler asked with a sly grin.

Garey and Gallagher bellowed in unison their objection, which was sustained. Only then did Ehrmann's ordeal come to a conclusion.[105]

Despite this momentary triumph, Sigler had been staggered by the potential impact of Ehrmann's testimony. However, he anticipated reviving his case with the next witness, Max Lee, a former liquor commission purchasing agent.

"When you first went in as purchasing director did you have a talk with Fred Ehrmann on following orders and instructions?" Sigler asked while strolling casually back and forth before the stand.

"Yes, He said I was responsible to him. At our meetings, out of courtesy, every member was given the opportunity to suggest purchases, but before I wrote them down I always looked at Ehrmann for his approval. The final decision was at his discretion," explained Lee. "Occasionally the commission might revise or suggest orders, but it generally just okayed Ehrmann's recommendations."[106]

Under cross-examination by Gallagher, Lee staunchly refused to budge from his contention that Ehrmann ran the commission. "Mr. Lee," Gallagher insisted, "tell this Court if Fred Ehrmann was subordinate to the commission."

"He should have been," Lee said in exasperation, "according to commission operations."

"But was he?" prodded an equally exasperated defense counsel.

"Well, he should have been," reiterated Lee.

"Let me put it to you another way," Gallagher tried gamely. "If a commission member said you should order 800 cases and Ehrmann said 700, you'd put down 700?"

"In such a case, yes."

"But did such a think ever happen?" grumbled Gallagher.

"I don't recall," Lee said serenely.[107]

After Lee stepped down, Sigler approached the bench and requested that, since former liquor commission distribution manager Charles Webber was deemed by his physician as being too ill to come from his Detroit home to testify, the prosecution be permitted to read into the record the thirty-two page text of Webber's statement made at the preliminary examination. Garey objected to the irregular procedure, saying that he had not bothered to cross-examine Webber at that time because he believed that the preliminary examination was "unfair and nothing the defense could do meant anything."[108] The jurist, citing the extenuating circumstances, overruled the objection, and Sigler, his pince-nez glasses perched near the tip of his nose, sat in the witness chair and began what would become a forty-five minute recitation.[109]

According to Webber's statement, he followed Ehrmann's orders to give preferential treatment to "good Republican" distillers. He recalled that he would notify the managers of the Detroit and Escanaba liquor warehouses of Ehrmann's instructions, using the code "green light" and "red light" to indicate respectively the favored and not-so-favored companies. Sigler read that Webber had been appointed distribution director of the

1935-1936 and 1939-1940 liquor commissions by Governor Fitzgerald, but that Webber stated that he "had to have the approval of Frank McKay first because he was the top man in the Republican party in Michigan." Webber's testimony further revealed that when he first approached Judge John S. McDonald, Chairman of the liquor commission in 1935, with McKay's recommendation, the crusty McDonald rebuffed him with a caustic: "Frank McKay does not run this commission." The deponent also confessed that he did Ehrmann's bidding because "I had a political job, and I wanted to keep it; I thought if I didn't follow orders I would be fired."[110]

After Sigler's reading was concluded, Judge Simpson exploded a bombshell under the prosecution's case. Earlier in the trial, Simpson had denied a defense motion to have the prosecution add five additional witnesses, but now he announced he was reversing himself. Sigler would have to call former liquor commission Chairman Orrin A. DeMass, former commission member Frank Gorman, former Escanaba warehouse manager John Bennett, George Ackers, director of the commission's statistical department, and Irene Pomella, former secretary to Charles Webber. The jurist explained his action to opposing counsel in a brief, matter-of-fact fashion. "When I ruled on this motion sometime ago," he stated, "there was a very vital point—bribery—included, but it has been deleted on the prosecutor's motion. The question now is what was the unlawful act? Under the situation and the way the case has developed, I am of the opinion we should have the then commissioners and other employees as witnesses. It must be determined whether the crime charged lay with the corruption of the 1939-1940 liquor commission or with the corruption of the Liquor Control Act."[111]

Sigler argued strenuously against the additional endorsements. "This case," he pleaded, "does not wholly depend on the corruption of the commission as a commission. This case may be maintained on the fact that they conspired to prevent the lawful operation of the law pertaining to liquor."[112]

"No," Simpson disagreed, extending an index finger toward the Special Prosecutor, "it is a question of whether it was a corruption of the commission or the acts of Fred Ehrmann and other employees. Commission members operated the liquor commission with the authority to act all the way through. They are the ones who saw how much liquor should be bought."[113]

Simpson also took under advisement a prosecution motion to allow telephone company employees to testify to records of telephone calls between various defendants to demonstrate "continuity of relationships."[114] Garey and Walker opposed the motion on the grounds that such testimony would be "based on inferences" and would therefore be merely another prosecution effort to prejudice the jury.[115] "I don't know how anyone, not even Solomon, could determine which telephone calls dealt with social business, politics, or liquor transactions," Garey said huffily.[116]

"I do not propose to show conversations," Sigler replied vehemently, "but only to show continuity and constant communication among them. Mr. Garey has indulged in some very interesting mental gymnastics, saying we could not rely on inferences supported by another inference supported by another. He overlooked the fact that the Supreme Court held that conspiracy cases may be established by circumstances and may be based on inferences."[117]

"I don't intend to engage in any contest of personal invective with Mr. Sigler, but if I did I don't think I'd come off second best," Garey thundered, his eyes sparkling with fury. "I didn't know I was an issue in this case, but I'm prepared to be one any time he wants it. The Federal Communications Commission ordered those slips destroyed long before Mr. Sigler learned he could use the federal government's brains and effort in an attempt to ride to fame on its coat-tails."[118]

"Your Honor," Sigler fumed, "I move that Mr. Garey's smart-aleck remark be stricken."[119] Simpson so ruled and then adjourned court.

The parade of witnesses resumed with seventy-two year old Frank Gorman. The former State Treasurer testified that he could recall not even a hint that McKay or Ehrmann exercised control over the liquor commission while he was a member in 1935 and 1936. He further assured the Court that Frank McKay had never asked him to grant any considerations or favors to a particular brand of liquor. In fact, Gorman said, to virtually everyone's disbelief, that he had never even discussed the subject of liquor with McKay.[120]

"Did you see McKay and McKeighan associate with one another?" Sigler inquired.

"I can't recall," Gorman replied with a shrug.

"If you could recall, would you admit it?" sneered the Special Prosecutor.

"Don't answer that!" commanded Garey. "That question is improper."

"Oh, never mind," said Sigler with a sly grin. "I'll withdraw it."[122]

Upon taking the oath, John Bennett quickly proved to be a hostile witness for the prosecution, both literally and figuratively, as he categorically refuted the statements set forth by Webber. "Webber never asked me to push brands or hold them back," Bennett assured the glowering Special Prosecutor. "Distribution was automatic. There was no way to discriminate. Distribution was based on sales and inventory. I never heard of 'good Republican' or 'green and red light' codes."[122]

"You like your job, don't you?" Sigler hissed.

"Yes."

"And you want to hold it?"

"Yes."

"So," Sigler shot back, "would you tell us if you had received such instructions from Webber?"

"Certainly I would," was the self-righteous reply.[123]

Sigler received yet another heavy blow when George C. Ackers, head of the statistical department of the liquor commission, testified that Webber had told him that he was proud of the distribution system and "thought he had achieved between 96 percent and 98 percent perfect distribution." Ackers steadfastly also maintained that he never saw any sign of discrimination or favor shown to distillers.[124]

When Judge Simpson ruled that Ackers' statements on the profits the state made from liquor sales were "immaterial," Garey protested. "The defendants," the barrister claimed, "are charged with doing something harmful to the state. We are trying to show that the state actually made a profit."[125]

"Had they not been engaged in a conspiracy, there is some question as to whether the profit might have been more," Sigler blurted.

"That interruption, Your Honor," Garey cried out, "was designed for the purpose of prejudicing the jury."

"Oh, you may be great in New York—" began Sigler, only to be drowned out by Garey's shrill warning: "You behave yourself and Mr. Garey will have no reason to make objections!"[126]

After what must have seemed like an eternity, Sigler finally received a boost from one of his witnesses when Mrs. Patricia Andre, commission secretary in 1939 and 1940, shocked the courtroom participants and spectators with the revelation that the supposedly accurate minutes of commission meetings were fabrications.[127] Responding to Sigler's probing into how records were kept, the chagrined witness confessed: "All information about commission action in 1939 was given to me by Fred C. Ehrmann. I did not go to any of the meetings. In 1940, the information was given me by Ehrmann or Orrin A. DeMass. Mr. Ehrmann usually told me which commissioners were present at the meeting, and I used my imagination when I wrote the minutes. I would put in that Mr. DeMass or Mr. DeFoe had made a motion to buy a certain lot of liquor. I would record the vote on the matter in the same way."[128]

Sigler, who had been trying throughout the trial to prove that Ehrmann had dictated purchases, pressed the witness: "Then you did not know who recommended the purchases of liquor, or whether any vote was actually taken?"

"No," she repeated, "I made those things up."[129]

The newly found silver lining on Sigler's cloud was soon to be dimmed, however, as Judge Simpson inquired: "Mr. Prosecutor, in questioning this witness, you referred to Mr. Ehrmann as a 'conspirator.' Do you claim him to be such?"

"Yes," said Sigler, somewhat taken aback by the query. "That is why he was granted immunity."

"But Ehrmann's name is not listed in the State's information as a conspirator," chided Simpson.

"That is not necessary under our laws," corrected Sigler.

"Shouldn't you have specified him in the information?" persisted the judge.

"I don't think so," parried the irate Special Prosecutor.

"Well, there is a question in my mind about it," countered Simpson.[130]

The prosecution rested its case after Mrs. Andre's testimony. Garey then announced his intention to ask for a directed verdict of acquittal because the prosecution had failed to prove "any crime known to the laws of Michigan," and that he required a two day continuance to prepare his twenty-five point motion.[131] Simpson concurred, saying wearily: "It will do us all good to get a little rest."[132]

Interviewed by a reporter from the *Battle Creek Enquirer*, Judge Simpson, in the confines of his chambers, sat at his desk twirling his glasses in his hand. "This is the toughest one yet," he confided. "In the other grand jury cases you had an out and out criminal act of bribery— here that charge has been dropped. The big question is now simply what was the unlawful act committed?"[133]

"There is no question that McKay had a right to take money from these men," Simpson went on, offering an insight as to the legal avenue he might choose. "He could establish a sales agency for the Hiram Walker Company, or any liquor firm, and go to the state as well as anyone else. He could hire salesmen to call on the state, and they could pay him a commission. After all, the state was in the liquor business. Now, the question is what did the defendants do? As I see it, the question is whether this was a criminal conspiracy to unlawfully corrupt the administration or the liquor laws. If not, what was the object? If the object was not illegal, or if they did not attempt to influence employees by threats and bribes or some such means, then the prosecution's case has got to fail."[134]

172

As promised, when court reconvened after its day and a half recess, defense counsel methodically began the tedious process of entering the twenty-five motions to delete huge segments of testimony from the record. Gallagher initiated the proceedings by moving to strike all references made by Thomas H. Gibbons to William McKeighan and the mysterious "Mr. Woodbury."

"The record is barren of any evidence," Gallagher intoned, "to show a conspiracy was participated in by anybody in 1935, and if there is any evidence of any conspiracy, it is not common to all the defendants. All the State does is to show that in a conversation between two men the name 'Woodbury' is mentioned, not whether it was in approbation or disapprobation, nor whether McKay knew McKeighan sometimes used the name of 'Woodbury.' There is a total lack of evidence that McKay had any knowledge that the defendants were engaged in the liquor business, and, even if he knew and encouraged it, it still does not make him responsible for their actions."[135]

"You cannot take the testimony of Gibbons out," implored Sigler, quickly advancing toward the bench, "considering everything else McKay did. It should be left in the record, and the record should not be emasculated. At the very time defendant McKeighan was sailing under the colors of 'Woodbury,' what was McKay doing? The innocent Mr. McKay was collecting thousands of dollars through Isadore Schwartz from one of the four companies McKay had written on a piece of paper and given to Mr. Ehrmann."[136]

Fred R. Walker, who was representing McKeighan, chimed in with a motion that all testimony relating to his client be stricken. "There is no testimony to establish the allegation that Mr. McKeighan promised vendors he controlled the liquor commission," the attorney stated bluntly. "The State's own exhibits show it was impossible to do that."[137]

As defense counsel assailed the statements, citing numerous specific cases and laws to support their contentions, many of the more than eight hundred spectators grew bored and a grumbling exodus ensued. Even the ginger ale concession shut down early, which prompted the court bailiff to remark with a knowing wink: "The gallery don't like this part. The lawyers do, though."[138]

Much to their delight, the two hundred or so remaining viewers were treated to one last verbal flurry which was prompted by Garey's contention that "McKay had a legal right to take commissions; he was not a state officer and committed no illegal act."

"The testimony shows he did commit an illegal act," rebutted Sigler. "If the time comes when a group of men can conspire to corrupt the

173

administration of the law, we are in a fine state of affairs. If they can corrupt one, they can corrupt ten or one hundred, and that could well lead to a revolution."

Simpson, whose legendary patience had reached it breaking point, leaned over the bench and spoke directly at the Special Prosecutor. "There is no revolution here. This is a simple conspiracy case. You are one hundred million miles off the track," he scolded. "Just take your case as a whole and connect it up."[139]

Momentarily taken aback by the severity of Simpson's reprimand, Sigler assumed a more subdued tone. "Your Honor," he said without much hint of contrition, "The People believe they have a strong conspiracy case, and we believe we have the duty of doing everything we can to help the Court make the proper determination. It is the theory of the People that the defendants unlawfully and feloniously combined and conspired to corrupt, impair, and defeat proper administration of the liquor control commission act. It isn't a question of whether the commission was corrupted. The gist of the offense is the unlawful conspiracy."[140]

"The Court thanks Mr. Sigler for his consideration," Simpson stated with obvious scorn. "Court will adjourn for the weekend."[141]

When Simpson rapped his gavel to open what he earnestly hoped would be the final day of arguments, William Henry Gallagher stood and again trumpeted his call for a directed verdict of acquittal. "Never in the history of the common law," he asserted, "was there an indictment or information charging as a crime the thwarting or interfering with or corrupting the administration of a law until this indictment was filed. This information is an innovation in law. If our alleged conspiracy was one to interfere with the sale of liquor, then all the churchmen in the state who are opposed to the sale of liquor are engaged in a criminal conspiracy."[142]

Pacing slowly before the jury, Gallagher continued to question the logic of the prosecution's case. "When McKay told Mr. Ehrmann that certain liquor firms should get their regular orders because they helped elect the administration, he was doing no more than telling him he should do his duty. When McKay told Ehrmann he had to 'do his part' or he 'wouldn't have his job,' there were no sinister implications. Was that a threat or a prediction? I say it was a prediction. All McKay was saying was that if those people didn't get the orders they should have they wouldn't be friends of the administration and the Republicans might not be re-elected. In that case, Ehrmann would probably lose his job. It was just an expression of the truth—if you don't do your duty, and no more than your duty, towards these men, you ought not to be there. If there were any irregularities in the liquor commission, they would have shown up in its records. Moreover, Your

Honor, it is fact that every bit of liquor purchased from these so-called favored distillers was promptly purchased by the public."[143]

Following his co-counsel, Garey made brief, but pointed, remarks. Standing before Sigler, Garey shook his head and said with mocking remorse: "We know the embarrassment in which you were placed when Judge Carr wrongfully, because of his inability to act fairly and impartially in the matter, passed on the motion and bound these defendants over for trial."[144] Ignoring the Special Prosecutor's sputtering objections, Garey pivoted briskly on his heel, and said to Judge Simpson: "Now that you have heard the prosecution and its attempt to show you what the unlawful act was, it is up to you to assume your true responsibility as a judge. How can the Court allow this case to go to a jury and allow it to draw inferences and thereby allow the prosecution to get what it has always sought, the conviction of Frank McKay?"[145]

"If the Court please," Sigler interjected. "Despite Mr. Garey's fine speech, I have not yet made my summation."[146]

"Proceed then, counselor," urged the judge.

"This is a strange set of facts which fit together so perfectly they must have been the result of a scheme of some sort," Sigler started. "These distillers didn't pay this money for nothing. They didn't pay it for fun. They paid it because they got results."[147]

Ignoring the jury, Sigler made an intimate appeal to Simpson, as though he were the only other person in the courtroom. "The uncontroverted facts," he asserted, "as disclosed by the record for this trial for the past five weeks, clearly indicate a set of circumstances from which a jury can reasonably find that a combination was formed for the sole and expressed purpose of corrupting, influencing, impairing, obstructing, interfering with, and defeating the lawful functions, operation, and the administration of the Michigan Liquor Control Act for the financial betterment and advancement of the defendants. The uncontroverted facts clearly indicate a plan or scheme on the defendants' part to corrupt the act by the utilization of their political influence with the distillers and their veiled threats to the employees of the commission, which were made with the intent to intimidate and coerce said employees into following the dictates and directions of the defendant Frank McKay."[148]

Putting emphasis on the testimony of Fred C. Ehrmann, Sigler told the Court: "It is uncontroverted that in the year 1935 the defendant Frank McKay told Ehrmann to see that certain companies got their regular orders. Ehrmann, without question, followed the directions of McKay both then and in 1939 and 1940. It is uncontroverted that McKay told Ehrmann that he had to do his part or he would lose his job."[149]

Turning abruptly toward defense counsel, Sigler replied to one of their contentions. "Were McKay's remarks innocent political propaganda or were they sinister?" he asked no one in particular. "Such an answer depends upon the state of mind of both persons. Sinister if so intended and acted upon, innocent if not. It is uncontroverted, however, that Ehrmann followed McKay's direction literally."[150]

"Your Honor," Sigler said with conviction, "there should be no directed verdict. Let the jury decide the merit of the State's case upon the evidence. To do otherwise would be a clear invasion of the province of the jury as a fact-finding arm of the Court."[151]

Having heard, and deliberated upon, the arguments presented, on February 13 Judge Simpson gave the assembled counsel, defendants, jury, and gallery a scholarly dissertation on the laws pertaining to criminal conspiracy. "The actual criminal or unlawful purpose must accompany the agreement, and if that is absent the crime of conspiracy has not been committed," he began. "Now, before this Court can let this case go to the jury it must be able to say what the defendants did was criminal. The Court must be satisfied that a crime has been committed from the evidence as given."[152]

"Now, what are the facts in this case?" he inquired. "As testified by Senator Murl H. DeFoe, who was commissioner during the years that this conspiracy is charged, the State of Michigan was in the liquor business. There is no question about that. The State of Michigan was in one of the largest businesses we have in the state—the operation, purchasing, and distribution of the liquor business. Likewise, it is not claimed by the prosecution that these defendants corrupted the liquor commission. Their records, minutes, and other evidence shows that they purchased liquor that was required for the needs of the state. Also, as testified by Senator DeFoe, there is no proof of any discrimination between the various companies that were selling liquor to the state and that he favored small companies."[153]

"It is significant," the judge noted, "that there are no records in this case to show any discrimination; nor are there any records to show the distribution was not properly made. Certainly had a discrimination been made, or stocks held in the warehouse, the records which came in to the company would readily have shown the same, but there is no proof of any such records in this case. Moreover, as testified by Fred C. Ehrmann, former commission secretary, and Senator DeFoe, all the liquor that was purchased was sold and the public was demanding more. Likewise, the state sold all the liquor at a very handsome profit."[154]

"At the time this Court ruled upon these motions for acquittal previously, the information had included in it the claim that these defendants

176

had bribed state officers and employees of the state. Clearly, bribery is a criminal offense, both in common law and under our statutes," he went on. "At the opening of this trial the prosecution struck out the claim of bribery, nor is there any proof of bribery. So now we have information that charges no criminal act on the part of any of these defendants other than the general charge that they conspired to do the act as set out in the information above. From the entire evidence in this case there is no testimony, direct or circumstantial, that they did a single criminal act, as we know that term."[155]

Turning his chair so that the jurors could see his dour expression, Simpson then reflected upon the validity of the State's allegations. "Now, what is it that the prosecution claims in this case? First, that Mr. McKay sent a 'Mr. Woodbury,' who turned out to be William McKeighan, to the Hiram Walker Company. Clearly this was not illegal. It claims that the Walker people made a contract with the Duo Sales Company, which Mr. McKeighan represented. Clearly this was not illegal. The prosecution claimed that Mr. McKeighan stated that he had friendly relations with the state administration. Clearly this was not illegal," the judge stated. "There is no claim by the Walker people that they did not get value for their money. There is no proof in the case that anything illegal was done by the Duo Sales Company or the Williams sales Company. It is no offense for a person to call upon the state liquor control commission to try to have it increase their listings. Certainly salesmanship isn't criminal or illegal. In fact, as the Court intimated during the hearing of the arguments, there is nothing to prevent Frank McKay from setting up his own sales agency and selling liquor to the state. This he had a right to do. There is no fraud or any other criminal act charged."[156]

"In the Court's opinion," Simpson continued in a grave tone, "Mr. Ehrmann's testimony clearly indicated that no threats were used against him. Mr. Ehrmann was under the control of the liquor commission, and the testimony shows that his report was submitted to the commission for the purchase of liquor, and that the liquor commission purchased all the liquor it had money to buy and allocated it among various companies as demand for said products warranted."[157]

Swiveling the chair slightly to the right, the jurist peered intently at Sigler and his assistants. "The People have not established the claim as set out in their information," Simpson explained to the gloomy prosecutors. "McKay and any of these defendants had nothing to do in appointing Ehrmann to his job. The only man, from the evidence in this case, that asked Mr. McKay for his O.K. was Mr. Webber. But even if he did so, that certainly is not criminal. The prosecution makes claims for inferences

177

and the like, but from the evidence here, there is nothing for the jury to draw inferences from. In this case, there are no criminal facts, and there are no inferences of guilt for the jury to infer. In my opinion, no case should be submitted to a jury where the verdict or charge must be based on conjecture or guess."[158]

"All of the facts here show no criminal offense committed," Simpson declared, still staring at the prosecution table. "Therefore, under the law and my burden of duty, I must grant the motion for a directed verdict of not guilty as to all of these defendants. The information, as now constituted, does not show that the defendants committed any criminal or wrongful acts. As heretofore stated, all of the testimony is devoid of any criminality, and, therefore, there is no proof to substantiate the same. Therefore, I will dismiss jurors number thirteen and fourteen and require the jury to stand and unto the direction of the Court issue a verdict of not guilty as charged in the People's information."[159]

Floyd J. Poole, Jackson County Clerk, instructed the jury to rise. As he asked each individually if they agreed to the verdict, all responded in the affirmative.[160]

VI Immediately after court was dismissed the half-filled auditorium erupted into pandemonium as spectators and reporters mobbed both the defense and prosecution tables. Flashbulbs exploded in the smiling faces of the defendants as they accepted congratulations from well-wishers. Frank McKay was embraced and kissed by his wife, who had been present throughout the trial.[161]

Sigler, who had sat slumped in his chair, his face expressionless, throughout Simpson's reading of the thirty-two page decision, accepted his initial grand jury defeat with outward calm. "Oh, well," he said, belying his true feelings, "it was just another law suit. We will hit the next one."[162] He then bustled off to meet with the jurors to discuss the case. This session, which had been ordered by Simpson, consisted primarily of the Special Prosecutor telling the veniremen how much he had enjoyed working with them and expressing his belief that they "would have had quite an argument" if the case had not been taken out of their hands.[163] Most jurors did not share that belief, however, as they told reporters that they considered the State's case very weak, and they agreed with the directed verdict.[164]

"You might not believe this," Simpson, relaxing in his chambers, told newsmen, "but I don't know of any case I've enjoyed more. I informed Sigler and Garey that their arguments were helpful and enlightening, and that even though I had to keep them at arm's length, there was no harm in that."[165] With a slight smile, he added: "I think I've done my share for the state now. The Ingham Court should be able, with its new additional circuit judge, to handle future trials by itself."[166]

The only note of discord present was a prepared statement, issued by McKay within minutes of the verdict, in which the Republican boss viciously assailed Judge Carr and the grand jury. "The charges of bribery against me, after I had already been acquitted by a jury, illustrate the dangers inherent in the so-called one man grand jury." McKay asserted. "It followed more than one year of investigation in which no evidence of bribery was, or could be, found. The examination produces no such evidence. Yet, Judge Carr, without a particle of evidence to support him, held me up for trial on that charge. It is unthinkable that a regular grand jury would ever tolerate the making of such a false charge against a citizen, for such a grand jury votes an indictment only after at least some evidence is offered to support the charge. I regard my acquittal more than a vindication for myself. It is a reflection on the judicial integrity and courage of Judge Simpson. It should be reassuring to all people to know that our courts can still dispense justice unhampered by the subtle influences which were aligned against me. This is, I hope, the end of my political persecution."[167]

In private correspondence to supporters, McKay repeated his animosity toward Carr. "At no time did I worry about what would happen," McKay wrote to an acquaintance, "because I knew I had done no wrong. But the thing that bothered me most is that Judge Carr, acting as a one man grand jury, could willfully and knowingly indict me on a bribery charge when he knew that not a single witness had appeared before him to testify that I had offered a bribe. They now admit it after they have given me all the publicity in the newspapers on a charge of bribery."[168] To others, McKay bitterly attacked Carr's motives and hinted at vengeance against his tormentor. "It is my opinion," McKay wrote Judge William B. Brown of Grand Rapids, "that Carr did not care how many dead bodies he stepped over as long as he could obtain a seat up there in the Capitol at Lansing."[169] McKay wrote to a Detroit friend in more threatening terms: "I was smeared in the newspapers throughout the state and considerable prejudice was built up against me. They then decide to withdraw the charge of bribery. This, in my opinion, was very unfair on the part of Judge Carr, and it's my opinion that he walked over my dead body in order to get a seat in the Capitol Building in Lansing. He will never enjoy it."[170] On a more practical note, the multimillionaire complained to a confidante that "Sigler is alleged to have said that if he didn't convict me he was at least going to make me spend a lot of money. Well, he did this, and I don't thank him for it."[171]

V II In an effort to maintain Sigler's image as the defender of justice and crusader against evil, several of his "pet" newspapers raised issues regarding the verdict. The Special Prosecutor's hometown press, *The Hastings Banner*, editorialized: "Under Judge Simpson's interpretation of the law, individuals, politicians, pressure groups, etc. have the right to use any influence short of direct bribery and intimidation to secure advantageous purchasing or sales relationships for themselves or their clients with state bureaus or departments entrusted with purchasing functions. . . . The weaknesses in the state law, as brought out in the McKay trial, are not peculiar to Michigan; it is probably common to most states, and is certainly a special problem to those under the domination of boss rule. Judge Simpson's verdict makes it clear that existing laws are not sufficient to do the job. But one can't help but wonder whether the jurist held himself to such a narrow interpretation of the evidence that he failed to see the forest for the trees, figuratively speaking. . . . The grand jury Special Prosecutor, even though he lost in this important case, has performed a valuable service in bringing to public attention a fundamental weakness in our state law."[172]

The *Cheboygan Observer* echoed the *Banner*'s sentiment: "Judge Simpson's decision that Prosecutor Sigler failed to produce evidence sufficient to hold the defendants may have been justified under the law, but it is not approved by the public, at least that public that cannot reconcile itself to the idea that extracting thousands of dollars out of a state business under fictitious names is honest and honorable conduct and is not worthy of court notice."[173]

The *Ingham County News* ran an editorial entitled "There May Have Been No Crime, But . . . " which concluded: "The people will not quarrel with the directed verdict. Salesmanship is not criminal or illegal, nor is friendship. The Judge is right. But the brand of friendship which juggles around hundreds of thousands of dollars a year in liquor sales commissions has no place in government, and there would be no place for it if the state were not in the liquor business. . . . No, there may not have been any crime proved against McKay and his co-defendants, but most people can draw their own conclusions when they find a trout in the milk."[174]

Lloyd Buhl, editor of the *Deckerville Recorder*, discussed the moral side of the verdict: "Judge John Simpson may be within his rights as a circuit judge to free McKay and four other defendants in the infamous liquor conspiracy trial . . . but it would seem to us, as a common ordinary layman, that the case should have at least gone to the jury and let them decide whether or not those men were guilty. To me, it does not represent democracy when one man can, by spending a sum of money, elect a Governor of the state, and then, because of this, draw commissions from liquor distillers on the liquor they sell to the State of Michigan. This is politics at its lowest, and while the courts in the country may rule it legal, it isn't morally right by a long shot."[175]

Sigler's honor was not the only thing now at risk, however, as shortly after the verdict, supporters of McKay in the State Senate passed a resolution to investigate the Special Prosecutor and his use of more than $400,000 in state appropriations to the grand jury. Having won his battle with Sigler, "Boss" McKay was intent on winning his war as well.

CHAPTER NINE

. . . BUT SIGLER IS

Upon learning of the resolution to create a three-man subcommittee, vested with subpoena power and composed of Republican Senators Ivan A. Johnston of Mt. Clemens and Harold D. Tripp of Allegan and Democrat Robert J. McDonald of Flint, for the purpose of looking into "the manner, method, and object" of expenditures made from the $442,000 grant for the grand jury, Sigler outwardly was nonplussed.[1] "The one man grand jury investigating bribery and other illegal acts in recent state administrations is not through by any means. I will keep driving away until I complete the job. It is natural at this time to expect some new opposition," the Special Prosecutor said in an ominous tone to a horde of reporters gathered at the grand jury headquarters in Lansing. "We've had that sort of thing since the beginning of the grand jury. There are certain people right now who would like to know what we are doing and going to do—to find out what we're working on. Some of the gentlemen mixed up in the bank and gambling matters would like very much to hamstring our efforts. If they had an accounting at this time, they could find out. When we are through, there will be an accounting for every dime."[2]

As the newsmen began filing out of the room, Sigler called them back for a parting remark. "Remember, boys," he said with a smile of assurance, "I don't care how far the Senate committee investigates just as long as they do not interfere with cases in progress, in particular cases investigating certain members of the House and Senate."[3] Having planted the seed that a cover-up was the motivating factor behind the new probe, Sigler confidently awaited the next day's press accounts to reap his harvest.

To the Special Prosecutor's astonishment, his innuendo elicited no railing against Senator Johnston's probe. Therefore, Sigler, undaunted, tried another approach, and successfully urged his long-time friend Senator Murl DeFoe to speak out on the Senate floor against the investigation as a ploy by the friends of McKay to exact revenge.

The aging lawmaker, still smarting from his humiliation at the liquor conspiracy trial, eagerly rose to the occasion. "The action of this Senate in attempting to glorify Frank D. McKay and, at the same time, insult Justice Leland W. Carr, should not be allowed to pass by without more notice," DeFoe said in a soft, but firm, voice. "I have come to feel that the action was beneath the dignity of this Senate, but it did serve, at least for the nonce, to acquaint the people as to precisely how some of the Senate feels toward the grand jury and its operatives. The real purpose of the resolution," DeFoe asserted, leaning on his cane for support, "is to weaken the grand jury and its work in the minds of the people by majoring on the costs rather than the jury's record."[4]

Suddenly becoming viciously personal, the Charlotte Republican aimed a broadside at his fellow party member, who sat stunned by the unexpected attack. "The integrity of Judge Carr and Sigler has never been under question. On the other hand, Senator Johnston has a good deal to explain," DeFoe said, his voice reaching a high pitch. "Before his election to the legislature, he served two terms as prosecuting attorney of Macomb County. During his regime it was open knowledge that gambling and vice flourished in and near Mt. Clemens. Handbooks and disorderly houses operated with impunity within sight of Johnston's office window. Yet, Johnston never took any decisive action, either against the vice operators themselves or against the law enforcement officials who permitted the rotten conditions to go unchecked. Johnston, at various times, served as legal representative for underworld characters in Macomb. He knew who they were, he knew where they operated, yet he never ordered the long due cleanup."[5]

Pointing his finger at the red-faced committee chair, DeFoe continued. "When the members of the Senate committee sought to impede the work of the Carr-Sigler investigation, they opened the door wide to a full probe of Johnston's own bailiwick and his personal administration, as well as of the other Sigler charges." he said menacingly. "The iron curtain, before which charges and countercharges have been hurled, should be raised to permit the people of Michigan to see what is actually going on behind it. It should be done so that the voters can apply their own remedy before the primary election."[6]

If war had been declared by Johnston, then Sigler, through DeFoe, had the honor of firing the initial salvo. However, Johnston quickly recaptured the offensive.

The depth of the Macomb Republican's hostility was apparent when he denied a request by Judge Coash that Ingham County Prosecutor Victor C. Anderson be permitted to attend the closed committee sessions, on behalf of Sigler, in order to prevent leaks of information which might have an impact on pending cases. Anderson protested this, arguing that the only way "to protect the confidential information now under investigation is to have someone present who knows what's going on in the grand jury."[7] Sigler, in the midst of a Florida vacation, was notified immediately by his legal confidante of what was taking place, and he wired back: "I'll be there quickly. I'm starting now."[8] He then prepared a press release in which he asserted that the Senate probe was "a deliberate attempt to sabotage the future value of the grand jury."[9]

Sigler had no more than packed his automobile and headed northward when Johnston exploded another bomb under the grand jury by proclaiming that the committee work would be done in open hearings. "Strong indications of irregular expenditures by the grand jury have been found," he piously explained. "We considered it our duty to let the public know."[10]

On Wednesday, February 27, the cramped hearing room was filled beyond comfortable capacity by pushy reporters, flashbulb-popping photographers, and curious spectators when Johnston rapped his gavel to have the proceedings commence. The Senator began with a statement cautioning witnesses not to reveal anything they might know regarding current or future cases under investigation by the grand jury. "We must emphasize again," he added, with apparent sincerity, "that we are not interested in grand jury secrets but are only concerned with the expenditures of money and how they were made by the grand jury."[11]

The first witness, George MaDan, special auditor and grand jury accountant, stated that the grand jury had spent approximately $325,000 of the legislative appropriation of $448,000. When asked to cite specific examples of large expenditures, MaDan revealed that Sigler had garnered $62,150 in salary plus $7,415 in expenses, while his two chief assistants, H. H. Warner and Thomas J. Bailey, had received $37,978.42 and $3,724.36 respectively. The Olds Hotel had been paid $25,361.89 for rooms and services, and hotel bills for grand jury travel amounted to $3,500.[12]

The most sensational disclosures, however, came from Detective Sergeant Leo VanConant, who had headed the grand jury State Police detail until October, 1945. Under questioning by Lansing attorney Roy T. Conley, who had offered his services to the Senate committee without pay, VanConant disclosed that he alone had paid grand jury money totalling $6,450 to Charles F. Hemans for "special services."[13]

"Did that include hotel rooms, transportation, and meals?" inquired Conley.

"No, sir," the State Trooper replied. "Those items were paid under the heading of expenses."

"Well, Sergeant," the attorney asked, "what were these payoffs for, and how were they made?"

"I paid Hemans an average of $150 monthly from May 2, 1944 to January 29, 1945. This was in addition to paying for his entertainment and drinks. In addition, on March 2, 1945 I was given a check for $450 which I cashed and paid him in cash. Major Hemans was to 'go to work' for the grand jury, assigned as an attorney to check into a bill they were working on at the time."[14]

"How exactly were these payments made?" Conley inquired, turning to look at the press eagerly taking notes.

"I would be given a check, made out to me, by the grand jury. I would then cash the check and turn the money over to Hemans. The money was charged officially to expenses for special services and informant fees. In April, 1945 Heman's pay was increased to $600 a month. Sometimes I would deposit the money in the Michigan National Bank and give Hemans a receipt."[15]

"Did you make any other unusual payments?" continued counsel.

"Yes, I paid for entertainment and liquor for Hemans while acting as his bodyguard," VanConant related in a firm voice. "Hemans was also given a room at the Olds Hotel, which he still occupies, where he was afforded room service for meals, telephone service, and prostitutes. Hemans' long distance telephone bills averaged $50 to $60 a month. They seemed so high that I brought them to the attention of Judge Carr, but they continued to be approved and paid for out of grand jury funds."[16]

"Payments to Hemans were not in line with the usual witness fees paid by the court, were they?" interrupted Johnston.

"No, sir," the State Trooper smiled. "The usual witness fee was $3.00 per day, plus mileage."

"Now let me understand you clearly," the Senator went on. "Except for the month Hemans served as a grand jury attorney, he was being paid simply to divulge information which he himself already had?"

"That's about right."

"Did you ever accompany Hemans on trips?"

"Yes, Senator. I once drove Hemans to Washington, D.C. in a State Police car. While there I paid three or four checks for entertainment, drinks, and meals for him. I purchased $18 worth of liquor for Hemans, but he repaid me and said he would charge it to his grand jury account."

"Did you go there on grand jury business?" asked Johnston, his expression assuming a look of an animal about to pounce on its prey.

"No," VanConant responded coldly. "Hemans had some personal business in Washington. I was sent as his bodyguard. He later went to Texas alone, but was given police protection while there. When he came back I told him he would no longer have a bodyguard or any special privileges, but after Senator Warren G. Hooper was killed, a bodyguard was again assigned to Hemans."[17]

"And these expenses were all approved by someone, were they not?" Johnston questioned, leaning back in his chair, knowing what the response would be.

"Yes, sir. Judge Carr authorized all of them right up to the time he took over his Supreme Court duties."

VanConant was excused and his successor as grand jury investigator, Fred C. Kelly, was sworn in. He testified that since he replaced VanConant, he had paid Hemans $2,400, at the rate of $600 monthly. Like his predecessor, he received checks made out in his name, cashed them, and gave the money to Hemans. He added that, to the best of his knowledge, Hemans was still accorded a free room and privileges at the Olds Hotel.[18]

Johnston barely had ordered the committee recessed for "several days" when comments were sought by reporters from the two grand jurors. Carr issued only the terse statement: "The investigation of the Senate is still in progress. Any items it questions will be explained at the proper time."[19] Coash, however, distributed a carefully crafted release proclaiming his innocence in any wrong-doing. "I had the assurance of both Judge Carr and Special Prosecutor Sigler that all expenditures were properly within the scope of the grand jury and necessary to its investigation," Coash wrote. "Naturally I cannot at this time divulge the nature of the investigations which are still before me as the grand juror. But when I questioned some expenditures, I was assured they were proper. Any explanation of the use of funds before I became grand juror will have to come from Carr and Sigler. Since I have become the grand juror I have received only $43.22, for expenses on trips I took in behalf of the grand jury. Prosecutor Anderson has received only $87.11 throughout his entire service to the grand jury."[20]

When approached for his views, Anderson clearly remained furious over Johnston's headline-grabbing tactics. "It is significant," the prosecutor snarled, his eyes reflecting the depth of his anger, "that the Senate committee's findings were made partially public when Sigler was on the way back to Michigan and had no opportunity to be present." The implication was obvious: when the grand jury maestro arrived, a different tune would be played.

IIISigler arrived in Lansing late Friday night, March 1, and immediately closeted himself with his grand jury aides. In reply to dogged appeals by newsmen, the Special Prosecutor was uncommonly short. "When I left, after almost five months of straight court work in two trials, I was given to understand that the Senate committee was not going to touch matters bearing on future work of the grand jury," he snapped. "I must find out whether this has been done, and, if so, how extensive the damage has been. Then I will be ready to say things."[21]

The following morning, a press conference was called, in which Sigler spewed forth a stream of vituperation against the committee members. "These men have broken faith with the grand jury, and their action clearly discloses they have but four purposes in mind. They are seeking to bar further investigation of the legislature by the grand jury," Sigler raged, reading from a prepared statement which would later be distributed to newsmen. "They are seeking to squelch and destroy the forthcoming bank indictment and gambling indictment, to discredit the accomplishments of the grand jury thus far, and to shake the confidence of the people in the one-man jury system and thus prevent any further disclosure by this or any other grand jury."[22]

Singling out individual committee members, Sigler enumerated how each was motivated by vested self-interest. "Senator Johnston is very much personally interested in the indictment involving anti-branch bank bills and gambling," Sigler stated, his tanned features frozen in hatred. "He was a former prosecuting attorney in Macomb County. For some time past we have been investigating gambling in Macomb County during the time he was prosecutor. It was my intention and plan to call Senator Johnston before the grand jury as soon as I returned from my rest and ask him to explain a number of things. Why was he named chairman? The reason is obvious: we expect to have a bank indictment out shortly and an indictment on gambling. Senator Tripp was my opponent for the state senate in 1942 and ran a bitter campaign. The grand jury enemies are most usually the ones who are most active in a smear campaign against us. Senator McDonald is part of this conspiracy because we expect to indict a couple of legislators who come from his hometown of Flint. Even the committee counsel, Mr. Conley, is generally recognized for his hostility toward the grand jury."[23]

Having assailed his foes with a broadside of innuendo, Sigler vigorously defended the treatment he had afforded Hemans. "Charlie Hemans has given us more help than a dozen other investigators could possibly give. He has saved to the people of this state many times what we paid him," the Special Prosecutor, his voice rising steadily, contended. It is generally understood by the enemies of the grand jury that Major Hemans is a key witness in the future bank indictment. The committee has attempted to obtain information which would discredit Mr. Hemans in the eyes of the public and interfere with his usefulness as a witness for the people in the bank indictment. They have not waited until the investigation was completed, but have given to the public such information as they believed would harm the grand jury, discredit Hemans, and shake public confidence in the work we are doing. The truth is that Charlie Hemans testified before the grand jury before he received a dime, except for a few incidental expenses. With his knowledge of persons and graft, and with his legal ability and experience, he was able to render vital assistance. He has done so. Few men know more about graft and corruption in the legislature than he."[24]

Concluding his tirade, Sigler stormed from the room, refusing to answer shouted queries from reporters. Frustrated by this reception from the normally loquacious Special Prosecutor, the newsmen hurried to locate the victims of Sigler's verbal barrage. Tripp initially declined to comment when told what Sigler had attributed to him, but then smiled and replied: "I hold no grudge against Mr. Sigler. I defeated him. Maybe he has a grudge against me."[25] Johnston, reached by telephone at his home in Mt. Clemens, said derisively: "Our answer may be by way of further exposure of irregularities."[26] Conley piously stated that his "services were offered solely in the interests of good government."[27]

When tracked down at his Flint residence, McDonald, obviously forewarned to expect a telephone call from Lansing scribes, offered a surprisingly lengthy discourse on his role on the committee. "I have no axe to grind with anyone concerning the grand jury," he explained somberly. "I was given the distasteful duty to perform, requiring some personal sacrifice, and I have endeavored to follow the dictates of my conscience as to its performance. Any facts disclosed by our committee to date were not meant to hamper the work of the grand jury, but to give the people of Michigan facts which we, in our best judgment, felt they were entitled to know. I certainly have no desire to protect anyone, and any attempts to ascribe such motives to me are ridiculous."[28]

IV On March 5, the committee lashed back at Sigler by way of a public statement rebutting the Special Prosecutor's allegations that it had broken faith with the grand jury by revealing that Hemans was an important witness in the long-awaited anti-branch banking case. In a scathing attack, Johnston and his cohorts strongly contended that if any one had committed a breach of faith it had been Sigler with the citizens of Michigan by utilizing hired testimony, a practice which the committee said "was un-American and smacked of Fascism."[29]

"Mr. Sigler fails to deny that Charles Hemans, a state witness and admitted briber, has received more than $8,850 from the grand jury funds in addition to being provided with luxurious living in a hotel" the report began. "Mr. Sigler has failed to deny that Hemans was sent to Washington on private business in a State Police car at grand jury expenses and that the grand jury replaced a mattress ruined by Hemans during one of his periods of indiscretion. He has failed to deny that Hemans was paid through an intermediary so that the books of the grand jury would not disclose he was on the payroll. He has failed to deny that the grand jury has incurred a bill exceeding $25,000 at only one of the several hotels of which he has made use. He has failed to deny that State Police officers were permitted to spend taxpayers' money to purchase liquor for the entertainment of private investigators employed by the grand jury. Since Mr. Sigler fails to deny these charges, it may be taken that he admits them."[30]

"The committee hopes that Mr. Sigler may admit with greater frankness and less subterfuge that Charles Spare, commonly known as 'Nightshirt Charlie' and alleged to have been a former president of the Detroit chapter of the Ku Klux Klan and accused by some of having been a murderer and instigator of race riots, was reinstated on the grand jury payroll last August at a salary of $400 per month and expenses which have averaged over $300 per month, and that he has been paid under the name 'Mary Duke' so that the records do not disclose that persons of ill-repute were again in the employ of the grand jury," the statement continued. "We hope that he will admit that he placed the late Senator Miles Callaghan on the grand jury payroll and paid him a salary, in addition to his hotel bills and car storage bills, while he was a witness for the grand jury."[31]

"We hope that he will admit that former Senator Joseph Roosevelt, admittedly a conspirator, was placed on the grand jury payroll," the litany went on, "and that Mr. Roosevelt was paid a salary and provided with hospital, clinical, and ambulance service, together with other expenses, while he, too, was a witness for the grand jury. We hope that he will reveal the names of other witnesses who similarly drew salaries from the grand jury."[32]

"We further hope," the statement set forth, "he would admit that within the last six months he has taken three vacation trips to Colorado, Nebraska, and Florida, with a State Policeman as a driver, and that on the trips to Florida and Nebraska he drew $4 a day from grand jury funds for living expenses. We hope he will tell us why grand jury funds were used to purchase four or more scrapbooks and fifty newspaper cuts of his own photograph."[33]

In conclusion, the report requested the public to remember a critical fact. "It has been said that the committee has broken faith with the grand jury. Yet we ask Mr. Sigler who it was that revealed Hemans was to be a witness in the anti-branch bank case. We did not know that fact until we learned it from Sigler's statement attacking the committee. If anyone has broken faith with Judge Coash, it is the Special Prosecutor himself."[34]

Coash, who had temporarily suspended all grand jury activity the previous day and had not only evicted all State Police detectives assigned to the grand jury, but also had returned eight of the twelve rooms occupied by the grand jury to the Olds Hotel, held a press conference after receiving a copy of the Senate's statement. "The grand jury will continue," he assured newsmen. "I do not claim at this time that any expenditures were improper or that anyone got a dime illegally, but I want to make certain to my own satisfaction that all expenditures are proper and that the state is getting its money's worth for funds expended."[35] When informed of numerous rumors circulating in the Capitol that Sigler had been removed, Coash replied angrily that "no one has been fired, but that is not to say that changes in personnel might not occur."[36]

Teetering on the brink of losing every political goal he had so painstakingly calculated for himself, Sigler played a desperate gambit. He would attempt to link Coash to the grand jury opponents in an effort to force the jurist to oust him as prosecutor. In turn, this might shift public sentiment back in his favor. The risk was substantial, but oblivion was the alternative.

The following morning Sigler played his trump card by making public the contents of a letter he had delivered to the grand juror. "Soon after the development of facts relating to the gambling conspiracy," Sigler wrote in his calculated correspondence to Coash, "you began to lose interest in the grand jury and talked continuously about winding it up. Your suspension of the grand jury, for all practical purposes, means an end of the investigation. I am sure your action is a result of poor advice or counsel from some quarter. Valuable time is being lost and incalculable harm results while you have looked over expense accounts which you have known about and approved. As a judge, you would not have

191

approved these matters without knowing what you were paying. Your attitude has encouraged the making of baseless and slanderous statements concerning myself."[37]

Belying his contention that "this matter is beyond personalities," the Special Prosecutor then launched into a self-serving diatribe against his employer. "Your public utterances have created and encouraged distrust in me to the enemies of the grand jury. I have repeatedly told you to call upon the members of my staff or myself to explain any of the items you wished to know about," Sigler asserted. "The members of the staff and myself have worked long hours diligently over two years and more to expose graft and to bring about a clean and honest government in Michigan. It has been a thankless and difficult task. I have sacrificed my law practice and been away from my home and family for over two years. Uncovering graft is of far more importance than you, the Senate committee, or myself, and of more importance to the people of the State of Michigan. The citizens of this state have the right to expect that graft will not be tolerated. It has been our duty to uncover it and bring the offenders to the bar of justice. You know how difficult that is. I humbly believe that I owe to the people of this state the duty of continuing the fight. From its inception, the progress of the investigation has been met with every obstacle."[38]

Throwing down the gauntlet, after having slapped the jurist with it, Sigler issued his ultimate challenge to Coash's authority. "I believe it to be my duty to take such action as will salvage the grand jury. I am working upon a petition to submit to the Supreme Court of this state asking it under Section 4 of Article VII, of the Constitution of the State of Michigan, to take general superintending control over this proceeding. I will become personally responsible for any grand jury exhibits now in my possession until this matter is disposed of."[39] The only question now remaining was how much longer the tail would be permitted to wag the grand jury dog.

For forty-eight hours, much to Sigler's discomfort, the grand juror maintained a stony silence. When finally pressured into a comment, he would merely say that he was too busy with his regular court work to reply to the charges and that he could not yet say whether Sigler would continue in his present capacity.[40] In private, however, Coash was feverishly working to oust his disloyal aide.

Saturday night, March 9, Coash drove to a Lansing dinner party at which former Ingham County prosecutor Richard B. Foster was a guest. The judge summoned Foster to his car, where they conferred for nearly three hours in frigid temperatures, regarding the grand jury. Coash expressed a desire to throw Hemans in jail as a way to force him to testify, and asked Foster's opinion as to that course of action. Foster concurred, but warned that he doubted it would obtain the desired results. With the assurance that Foster would do his bidding regarding the state's so-called star witness, Coash informed the attorney that he would be named Sigler's successor as Special Prosecutor, at the identical $100 per day salary, within a matter of days.[41]

Meanwhile, Johnston continued to boil the oil with which to roast Sigler. On March 9, the committee disclosed that the actual amount of grand jury money given Hemans was nearly $16,000, or almost double what had been previously thought. Hemans, the committee said, had not only taken trips to Texas and Washington D.C. on grand jury money, but also had received funds under the alias of R. Millard and F. Benson, and the possibility remained that other payments had been received under additional assumed names.[42] "The record clearly shows," Johnston stated, "that Hemans was wined and dined in regal fashion since he was first returned to Michigan as a witness. Moreover, the committee has uncovered other startling evidence of irregularities in the grand jury expenditures which will be developed and disclosed as the investigation progresses. The committee also wishes to make it clear that it subscribes fully with the past and future objectives of the grand jury, but that even the best results should not conceal from the people the fact that there has been waste and extravagance in the expenditure of taxpayers' money."[43]

Hearing from eager reporters of the committee's latest revelations, Sigler dramatically slammed his fist on his desk. "The great statesmen of the Senate committee have been unable to find anything on me so they're raising the ante on Hemans," he said sarcastically. "If they were accurate they would have stated that Hemans went to Texas to testify before a federal grand jury investigating small loans, and we almost lost him as a witness entirely on that occasion. He went to Washington on his Army status. The actions of the Senate committee have now become tantamount to obstructing justice."[44] All protestations of innocence aside, it was now obvious that Sigler's tenure was all but over.

On Tuesday morning, Sigler received his hoped for pink-slip from the grand juror. "After very deliberate consideration I have deemed it advisable to reorganize the staff of the Ingham County grand jury," Coash coldly informed his insufferable legal assistant. "This is to inform you that your services as special prosecutor of the Ingham County grand jury are no longer required and your appointment as such has been terminated. I am requesting, and an order has been so entered, requiring that you surrender to me forthwith all books, documents, keys, and any and all other property of the Ingham County grand jury that you may have in your possession or which may be under control of the Ingham County grand jury."[45]

As the ever-present cadre of reporters flocked around the dapper ex-Special Prosecutor for what many surmised might be the last time, Sigler was remarkably cheerful. The more insightful scribes noted that Sigler appeared almost relieved by his dismissal and quickly realized the naive Coash had been maneuvered skillfully into turning Sigler into a martyr in the eyes of his tens of thousands of faithful admirers. "I am not surprised by anything Judge Coash would do," he said with feigned fury. "If he believes he can do better without me, that's all right, so long as grafters do not get off the hook. I will, of course, abide by Judge Coash's wishes. I will, however, proceed with my petition, and I will present it merely from Mr. Sigler, private citizen, since I have no further connection with the grand jury. I am not interested in holding public office, although there is a tremendous amount of pressure trying to make me run for Governor on both tickets. I am just going to go back to Florida to get a good rest and then return to my law practice in Battle Creek."[46]

V The immediate response to the removal was gratifying, yet unsettling, for Sigler and his political aspirations. On the positive side, fifteen editors and publishers of small, rural weekly newspapers signed a resolution condemning the Senate for creating the investigating subcommittee, damning Coash as being "weak and vacillating," and urging the reinstatement of Sigler so that he be permitted "to finish the task he has started."[47] The *Battle Creek Enquirer* praised Sigler as a man "who tackled the problem so that it knew it had been tackled."[48] The *Hastings Banner* chided the committee for attacking Sigler's salary, noting that "maybe the size of the fee wasn't quite as much out of line as you tried to imply," since Foster was given the same stipend.[49] The *Lapeer County Press* lamented the firing, adding: "If the new staff of the grand jury lets this crusade peter out, we venture this prediction: Kim Sigler will be the next Governor of Michigan."[50]

Most supportive was the *Detroit Free Press*, long a staunch ally of the former Special Prosecutor. "The discharge of Kim Sigler can only be interpreted as a victory for those who have something to fear from the continuation of the investigation. It has been no mystery that certain elements in the state have had the axe out for Sigler for some time. The splendid record which he made by securing 41 convictions of criminals who, had it not been for him, would have escaped unscathed, made a campaign to get him inevitable. During the time that Sigler headed the grand jury investigation, he served this state well. The people will not forget that."[51]

Conversely, the *Grand Rapids Press*, while congratulating Sigler for his "commendable record of convictions and confessions obtained," chastised him for recent overt contempt of the grand juror which "doubtless left Judge Coash with no alternative but to remove him"[52] The *Ingham County News* warned the ex-Special Prosecutor to be a "good sportsman" and support his "relief pitcher." Reminding Sigler of his own words to Judge Coash, the editorial concluded: "Feuds and personal animosities have no place in the investigation of state graft. Every man who has entered into a conspiracy to gain some unfair advantage out of corrupting the legislature or any state agency should be brought to justice, and most of us are not particularly interested as to what men serve as the instruments of justice."[53] Of course, it was left to the acerbic Edwin Goodwin of the *Michigan State Digest* to pen the most biting obituary for the Sigler grand jury era. "The ambitious little man who had stultified the grand jury operation for the sake of personal gain and political advancement is gone. Gone are the theatricals. Gone the courtroom ensembles. Gone the police squads. Gone the showmanship."[54] Yet both friends and foes knew that this apparent setback marked only the conclusion of another act in Sigler's well-orchestrated scenario to achieve personal glory.

VI

On March 21, Sigler, looking statesmanlike in a charcoal gray pinstripe suit with a bright paisley cravat, announced his candidacy for the Republican nomination for Governor.[55] "The campaign this year will be a people's fight—not mine, nor that of any individual or group of individuals," Sigler promised, reading from a prepared script. "Foes of the grand jury, whether men or newspapers, will fight me in this campaign as bitterly as they have opposed my efforts to bring criminals to justice. Now, as in the past, my friends are the ones who want to strike out graft and corruption in our great state. Those who now stand ready to smear me and flood the state with money to defeat me have reason to be both bitter and fearful. When you encounter these smears and jibes, remember they are inspired by those who want to protect graft, or worse yet, by those who have been made their messenger boys. More particularly, they want to block an indictment concerning a payoff on the anti-branch banking bill of 1941 or seek to block exposure of a gambling conspiracy. These men can be dangerous only if the people permit them to remain in power."[56]

Having labelled all who might oppose him as allies of corruption, Sigler forged ahead with unabashed self-praise. "In my two years of hard work as prosecutor, I have learned what the obstacles are. I know who creates the obstacles—and why! During this campaign I shall explain to the people how these enemies hope to throttle the present grand jury and whitewash malfeasance in public office. How they had hoped to use me as their scapegoat, and how, finally, they planned to kill the grand jury law. Some people do not like grand juries because they never know how far they will go. Guilty conscience promotes fear. I want to make it perfectly clear, however, that my interest is not who brings the guilty to justice, but that it is made sure that they are brought to justice. I am responsible only to my own conscience and the people, not to any organization or political machine."[57]

The initial potshot at candidate Sigler came from a former ally, Nelson Brown, publisher of the *Ingham County News* and son of Lieutenant Governor Vernon J. Brown, who was a rival for the G.O.P. gubernatorial nomination. On March 27, the younger Brown distributed a letter to editors of every newspaper in the state, in which he laid out for public scrutiny the issue of Sigler's ethical behavior by dragging a skeleton from the ex-prosecutor's closet. "All during the trials," Brown recalled, "the four or five that I sat in on, Sigler intimated that even the defense lawyers were almost conspiring against the people by daring to cross-examine state witnesses. It was a holy crusade in which he was engaged, Sigler insisted, and no-one had or has the right to question his motives or his handling of the $400,000 put up for finding out about the 'barrel of money.' In the back of my mind, as I watched Sigler perform in court, lurked the thought that after the Special Prosecutor was hired at $100 per day he had to withdraw from the defense of former Representative William Green. Had any other man than Sigler been hired as Special Prosecutor, Sigler most likely would have been among the defense attorneys at the trial."[58]

In keeping with his newly created populism, Sigler sought to dispel his image of lofty superiority. "People have noticed," he informed his pal Al Nieber of the *Detroit News* in an exclusive interview, "that my fabled wardrobe is dated. Well, let me tell you something about that. Back in 1942 I successfully defended a man who, because of his poverty, asked if a relative of his who was a tailor could pay my fee in clothing. I got twenty-one suits out of it, and I haven't bought a suit since, and I won't for some time, regardless of changing styles. Mr favorite, by the way, is the gray pinstripe I wore when I announced for Governor." Twitting his good friend, he added with a smile: "Your story, Al, about forty-seven suits in my closet was a pretty wild guess and must have included pajama suits and union suits."[59] Candidate Sigler—hard on criminals, but otherwise just a "regular guy"—was being packaged for the electorate.

The campaign was spirited with not only Brown, but also Detroit Mayor Edward Jeffries and Raymond J. Kelly contesting for their party's prize. In virtually every speech, Sigler played upon his sacrifices and service as grand jury prosecutor. At one stop he philosophized to his audience: "None of you realize the terrific pressure that can be brought to bear to prevent the uncovering of graft in government. Perhaps I should be glad that I'm out of a job where someone calls you on the phone in the night and says, 'Listen cowboy, a sideswipe from a truck some dark night can take care of you.'" At another rally, he intimated that Coash was aligned with the forces of evil, saying: "I was discharged because I was naming names." At yet another gathering, he invoked the spectre of his favorite nemesis, recalling with a folksy flair: "You know, Frank McKay hired a detective to get some dirt on Judge Leland W. Carr and myself. We couldn't take a walk without being followed. We grabbed the fellow, and he was so dumb that he carried his instructions from his clients with him. McKay and his friends were moving heaven and earth to smear us."[60]

As the primary neared, Sigler's adversaries used the Senate committee report in a vain attempt to stem the maverick's tide, but the front-runner had a biting retort for each allegation. Yes, he had taken State Trooper Kenneth Templin with him on his trips, but it was because numerous threats had been made on his life. However, no tax dollars had been spent for Templin's expenses. Yes, he had hired a clipping service to preserve newspaper articles in leather scrapbooks, but it was so the grand jury staff could have ready access to what local press throughout the state was writing about their work and what prospective jurors were reading. Yes, witnesses had been paid, but that was common practice in grand juries because criminals needed incentives to squeal on their pals.[61]

As to the charge that he had spent $95.00 one evening at a dinner party, Sigler scoffed derisively: "I don't need to tell you folks that I spent the entire month of October, 1945, in fact six weeks, right in Oakland County preparing for, and trying, the case which sent five hoodlums to prison. McKay's friends in the Senate want you to think I spent the state's money buying whiskey and having a good time. If any one of them had been through that ordeal, working day and night to be prepared, he would know that I didn't have any time for partying, even if I had been in the mood. You know, McKay doesn't care who is governor, so long as it isn't Sigler. He's got his stooges all over the state working because he knows there won't be room in Lansing for his methods, or for anyone to cash in on influence, if I am elected."[62] It was vintage Sigler, and it fired fervor in the faithful.

Any lingering doubt as to who would oppose the Democratic nominee, former Governor Murray D. VanWagoner, was blasted away one week before the primary when Macomb County grand juror Herman Dehnke, a political ally of Sigler, issued a warrant charging Ivan Johnston with accepting bribes while serving as county prosecutor from 1939 to 1943. Ensuing stories afforded Sigler not only further credence as a prophet scorned, but also thousands of dollars of free publicity. The primary election of June 17 was now anti-climatic, and on election day Sigler swept past his nearest challenger, Lieutenant Governor Brown, by 50,000 votes.

The Republican nominee would not have a unified party, however, as Brown, through his son's newspaper, tried to undermine Sigler's hold on the party regulars. In a circular letter to editors across the state, the younger Brown asserted that his father lost because he was a gentleman and did not enumerate several significant aspects of Sigler's character and past: (1) for nearly all his life Sigler had been a Democrat; (2) he paid vacation expenses and bar bills for, and leaked secret grand jury information to, *Detroit Free Press* reporter Ken McCormick to assure the support of that influential newspaper; (3) Sigler used "four-flushing, double-crossing, brow-beating, and bludgeoning tactics to convict the small fry caught up in the grand jury mesh"; (4) at age twenty-two, Sigler chose to remain at the University of Michigan rather than enlist in the armed forces in 1917; (5) Sigler was the tool of former reform Governor Alex Groesbeck, an avowed enemy of G.O.P. conservatives; and (6) Sigler's chief ally in the Senate was Murl DeFoe, a mediocrity "who can smell a political job from farther off than any other man in Michigan." Had his father shown the voters the real Kim Sigler, Brown claimed with certainty, the results would have been reversed.[64]

The whining of the defeated candidates notwithstanding, Sigler's triumph over the G.O.P. machine was impressive, and since three times as many Republicans cast a ballot in the primary as did Democrats, a victory in November over his Democratic rival seemed assured. The only question remaining was whether the gubernatorial campaign would eclipse the grand jury probe in the public mind, but that became moot in mid-July with the startling news that indictments were to be issued in the oft-postponed branch banking bill conspiracy case.

CHAPTER TEN

CHARLIE TAKES THE FIFTH

On July 21, 1946 the *Detroit Times* reported that the Joint Congressional Pearl Harbor Investigating Committee had concluded that the blame for the lack of preparedness of that naval base on December 7, 1941 rested with Admiral Husband E. Kimmel and General Walter C. Short, and that committee member Senator Homer Ferguson of Michigan placed the burden of guilt squarely on the shoulders of President Franklin D. Roosevelt. Although shocking to the nation as a whole, this revelation was relegated to a secondary position on the front page of the *Times*, as its banner headlines blared the news Michiganians had waited nearly three years to hear: "Bohn, 23 Others Indicted in $50,000 Bank Bill Bribe."

Named in the warrant, signed by Judge Coash at 3:00 p.m. Saturday, July 20, were five well-known figures in the state's financial community and seventeen current or former members of the state legislature. The non-legislative defendants cited were: Charles B. Bohn, sixty-six year old Detroit multimillionaire industrialist and Chairman of the Board of Michigan National Bank; Howard J. Stoddard, Bohn's son-in-law and President of Michigan National Bank; Simon D. DenUyl, a socially prominent Grosse Pointe resident and secretary/treasurer of Bohn Aluminum & Brass Corporation; Byron L. Ballard, legal advisor to both Michigan National Bank and Governor Murray D. VanWagoner; and Francis P. Slattery, assistant vice president of the Grand Rapids branch of Michigan National Bank. The contingent of lawmakers included the familiar names of James A. Burns, Charles C. Diggs, Leo J. Wilkowski, William G. Buckley, Edward Walsh, Ernest G. Nagel, Francis J. Nowak, Walter N. Stockfish, Adam W. Sumeracki, Earl C. Gallagher, Joseph J. Kowalski, and Carl F. DeLano, all of whom had been indicted at least once before by the grand jury. New faces to the list of graft suspects who had operated under the Capitol dome were Charles F. Blondy, Gilbert H. Isbister, Robert B. McLaughlin, William C. Stenson, James B. Stanley, Earl McEwen Sr., and Raymond J. Snow. Listed as co-conspirators, but not charged in the indictment, were Harold Vandenberg, George O. Harma, William C. Green, and the prosecution's star witness, Charles F. Hemans.

Few of the defendants had anything to say immediately after being served with the warrant, but those who did volunteer a statement predictably proclaimed their innocence. Ballard, reached at his Lansing home, seemed stunned. "This comes as a complete surprise to me," the bespectacled, wavy-haired attorney and former treasurer of the Michigan Democratic party said softly. "I don't know anything about the nature of the complaint. I haven't seen the charge and I have no knowledge of the charge and cannot comment further. I'm innocent of any wrongdoing. The matter of corrupting the legislature was never even thought of, nor has anyone suggested paying or giving anything whatever for the purpose of influencing the bank bill or any other legislation."[1] Stoddard defiantly averred: "I have been president of the bank since it was organized, and I don't know of a single improper thing that was ever done. I did no such thing. I emphatically deny the whole thing. I am in a position to know that not one dollar of either the bank's, or my own, funds have been used for any improper legislative or political activity. Mr. Ballard has been the general counsel of this bank before he was requested by Governor VanWagoner to serve as his legal advisor, and he fully advised the Governor and the Attorney General, Mr. Herbert Rushton, of his relation with the bank. As soon as I study the charge and know what it is all about, I will prepare a statement."[2] Bohn, presented with his summons upon returning from a business trip to South America, smiled and told newsmen: "I knew the grand jury had been investigating during the past three years, but I hadn't paid much attention to it. It is all Greek to me."[3] Democratic Representative Stanley of Kalamazoo was almost in tears as he stammered: "I am innocent. I don't understand this. If they say I am guilty of bribery, that is not true. I am an innocent man."[4] Ex-representative McEwen, a Flint Democrat, seemed bewildered by his alleged involvement. "I want to talk to my attorney before deciding what to do," he muttered. "All of this is new to me. I never got into one of these holes before. I don't know anything about the banking bill. I have always voted according to my own conscience. Gallagher and Snow sat right around me during the 1941-1942 legislative session, and they never mentioned the bank bill to me. I'm just trying to find out what all this is about."[5] Another

200

indicted Flint Democrat, former State Senator McLaughlin, snarled to reporters: "Of course I'm not guilty. I don't know what this is all about. I voted yes on the bank bill."[6]

Not surprisingly, both gubernatorial candidates readily responded to the grand jury indictments. Sigler, campaigning in the upper peninsula, gloated that he was "extremely gratified that warrants have resulted from matters on which Judge Leland W. Carr and I spent so much time."[7] Former Governor VanWagoner, realizing the need for instantaneous damage control, released a formal statement. "Of the five major bank indictments, I only know one of the men intimately. I have known Byron Ballard for the last thirteen years and know him as a man of the highest integrity. When he says he is innocent, I am one citizen of Michigan who believes him. When he has his trial before a jury of twelve honest American citizens, I venture to predict he is one man who will be found innocent," VanWagoner asserted in defense of his friend. Then, discussing his own role in any purported conspiracy, VanWagoner claimed he stood on the side of the angels and urged that this matter should not become a campaign issue. "If there was skullduggery going on behind the scenes in connection with the anti-branch banking bill or any other measures passed by the legislature during my administration as Governor, I certainly shall do everything in my power to help bring any guilty individuals to justice," he promised. "I firmly believe in the justice of our courts. There should be fair trials for all. This investigation and subsequent indictments are not a matter for politics."[8]

On Monday, July 22, during the initial arraignments, the phalanx of denial was broken dramatically when Representative Snow, a three-term Flint Democrat, appeared before Coash and pleaded guilty to accepting money to vote against the bank bill. The grand juror quickly postponed the proceedings and took the former beer distributor, potato chip manufacturer, dishwasher, and Coast Guardsman into his chambers to explain the consequences of his decision.[9]

In an exclusive interview later that afternoon with Don Gardner of the *Detroit Times*, Snow related a sordid tale of innocence lost. "I was only twenty-six years old when I came to Lansing in 1941. I left behind many months of hard work on an assembly line at Buick, and I was anxious to do what I could to make the lot of the working man a little easier, if I could. My only previous experience was an appointment to the Genesee County Board of Supervisors, and I was ignorant of the way they did things at the Capitol. But it didn't take me long to get initiated."

"The very first thing I found out," he continued, with noticeable bitterness, "was that every hotel room not occupied by a legislator contained a lobbyist. There was always plenty of whiskey and beer around and always something to do. I spent a lot of time in those rooms drinking and playing cards and even shooting craps. I often wondered where the legislators were who sat down with each other and talked over the laws they were going to pass. No one I saw seemed much interested."

"I was approached by lobbyists with bribe money, but I turned them down. I still had ideals. But then one night in a room at the hotel I had been playing cards and drinking, when I suddenly found myself in the room alone with a lobbyist. He offered me money to vote against the anti-chain bank bill, and I was dumb enough to take it," Snow confessed. "I don't know why I did it, because I've been sick about it ever since. I'm not going to say how much it was, but believe me it was a darned small part of the $50,000 that was supposed to have been spent by the banks. Now the quicker I can get this thing over with and start fresh, the happier I will be. It's good-bye to Lansing for this guy."

Becoming pensive for a moment, Snow offered an explanation why lawmakers succumbed to temptation. "The pressure a legislator encounters in Lansing is terrific, and it takes a strong man to stand up against it—particularly when the legislator is trying to live on the $3 a day he gets," Snow admitted. "The people have either got to give their representatives more money or be content to elect farmers and retired businessmen to the legislature. They are the only ones who can afford it."[10]

To his hometown journal, Snow elaborated on his past and future actions. "I took their money, but I didn't vote on the bill. I'm not guilty of bribery, because I didn't carry through. However, the grand jury officials advise me that I'm guilty of conspiring to defeat the bill despite that fact," he said ruefully. "If the legislation had included drug stores and grocery stores as well as banks I might have been for it, but before I was approached by the individual who gave me money I made clear my position of opposition. Whatever the consequences to me in this matter, I sincerely hope the disclosures of the grand jury will cause the public to become aware of the defects in our present legislative system and to take adequate steps to prevent a reoccurrence. I hope the public will consider my complete record when passing judgment on me. I feel I gave representation to the best of my ability. I particularly would like them to consider my record on social legislation and such things as school aid. I just want to get it all over with as soon as possible."[11]

III For the next six weeks nothing was heard from the grand jury. Then, on September 3, Special Prosecutor Foster publicly admitted what had been rumored for several weeks: Charlie Hemans was refusing to testify in the bank case. Foster told Judge Coash that he and his chief aide, Charles F. Cummins, had been unable to induce the state's star witness, who had resigned from the Michigan Bar Association to avoid disbarment proceedings, to appear, and that Hemans had told him that he would return to Michigan from his newly adopted home of Washington, D.C. only if the United States Supreme Court ordered him to do so under a new federal statue which made it a felony for a person to flee a state because he did not wish to testify in a criminal suit. However, Foster related, Hemans threatened to "fight extradition in every state if necessary."[12]

Questioned in his hotel room by Sigler confidante Al Nieber of the *Detroit News*, Hemans explained his motives for refusing to return to the witness stand for the state. "I'm not running away from the grand jury," Hemans declared, adding that his decision had been reached months earlier. "I warned them time after time I would not testify. I did not want a grant of immunity, but they gave it to me anyhow. The day before the indictment was signed by Judge Coash, I said to him: 'I hope you fellows know what you're doing, because I'm telling you I won't testify in this case. I'm through! I'll let my lawyers and the grand jury lawyers worry about things from now on.'"[13]

Asked if his position was in any way a means to achieve retribution against Coash and Foster for the way they had treated him, Hemans was pleasant but evasive. "Oh, if Judge Carr and Sigler had continued to hold those roles things might have been different," he replied, sipping on a glass of scotch. "I had faith in them, but I am not going to say any more about that." Suddenly becoming sullen, the lobbyist anticipated Nieber's next query and precluded any possibility of being used by the gubernatorial candidate as a political pawn. "However, not even personal appeals from Judge Carr and Sigler could alter my decision not to testify. My old pal Kim has made me angry by citing 'men of the type like Hemans' in his campaign speeches."[14]

In response to the query as to why he was so adamant, Hemans assumed his familiar posture of prophet scorned. "After all I've done to help clean up this state and correct a sorry state of affairs at Lansing, where tribute had to be paid to obtain enactment of meritorious legislation, I found myself referred to in newspapers and editorials as a stool pigeon and a rat," he said indignantly. "I made up my mind then and there that I'd taken the wrong course. Ever since, I've been made the whipping boy. You know, Dick Foster called Monday night [September 9] to see if I'd changed my mind. I told him again that I would return only if the United States Supreme Court tells me I have to. But I also told him that even if I was forced to return, I would still refuse to testify under my Fifth Amendment rights against self-incrimination."[15] Quickly breaking into his famous grin, Hemans boasted to Nieber: "After I hung up, I told friends in the room that I would rather rot in jail than testify after all I've taken."[16]

Hemans grew defensive once more when asked to comment on published reports that he had been paid to leave Michigan. "No one paid me a dime to leave, and no one will pay me," he shouted. "I came here because I made a lot of friends while I was in the Army. However, I will have to move out of this hotel suite and get a job. No money has been coming in since February 4 when Judge Coash cut me off the grand jury payroll, and I can't stand the financial strain."[17]

IV On Tuesday, September 10, the examination began in the Lansing courtroom of Circuit Judge Chester P. O'Hara, who had been assigned as presiding magistrate. Fifteen defense counsel were seated across the room, with Eugene L. Garey and William Henry Gallagher, who had achieved notoriety as McKay's barristers and now were representing the Grand Rapids politico's close friend Charles Bohn and the other non-legislative defendants, located directly in front of the jurist.

As soon as court was gaveled into session, Foster moved for dismissal of all charges against Wilkowski, Nowak, and Buckley, all of whom were serving sentences in Southern Michigan Prison following their conviction in two other conspiracy cases. The Prosecutor then read into the record that all these men had been granted immunity in return for turning state's evidence.

Foster's first of thirty-five scheduled witnesses was the secretary of the State Senate, Fred I. Chase, who, despite repeated objections by defense counsel Gallagher and Garey, traced the course of the 1941 anti-branch bank bill through the Senate. The significance of the fact that Bohn had retained McKay's attorneys to represent all the non-legislative defendants was not lost on anyone, especially candidate Sigler, who bled the "McKay angle" for all it was worth in his tirades as he stumped against corruption in state government.

Following Chase to the stand were Frederick R. Elliot, State Banking Commissioner from 1939 to May 1941, and former clerk of the State

House of Representatives Myles F. Grey, who traced the history of the bank bill and its course through the House respectively. Apparently bored by the recitation, Bohn, who was growing deaf, turned off his hearing aid and read a detective magazine. After court was adjourned, Foster bravely declared that even though Hemans was an important witness, the prosecution's case was not "shot" without him.[18]

Once the groundwork painstakingly had been laid for two days, Foster brought forth his first big gun, former Senator Leo J. Wilkowski. The heavy-set, beady-eyed Detroit Democrat lumbered to the stand and sat with a snarl on his thin lips as Foster moved toward him.

"When did you first meet with Charlie Hemans regarding this bank bill, Senator?" Foster, looking most un-Sigleresque in a rumpled brown suit, asked softly.

"Oh, early sometime in the 1941 session," the convict replied gruffly. "He seemed depressed because he had no money to finance his campaign for re-election as University of Michigan regent. I told him if he got off his ass he could get some accounts, and I told him I had been asked to contact DenUyl over the phone, and that I had contacted him. A week or so later, Hemans told me he had been retained by DenUyl to stop the passage of Senate Bill No. 1, the bank bill. He then promised to pay me $200 to keep the bill in committee. He paid me two more $200 payments for my no votes and refusal to vote to override VanWagoner's veto. He also promised me campaign contributions in my next election. So, in the summer of 1942 I spoke with Francis Slattery in Grand Rapids and I told him Hemans had said I could expect campaign contributions, and Slattery told me he would be glad to help me out and would see what he could do. Later, in Detroit, Slattery gave me $250."

"Did you ever speak with the defendant Byron Ballard, the former legal advisor to Governor VanWagoner?" Foster continued.

"I had several conversations with him," Wilkowski said, his lips curling into a barely visible sneer. "I saw him on more than one occasion at committee hearings where he made some not very lengthy remarks. They were more confirmations of what Mr. Stoddard had testified to. I talked with him several times also in the Senate chambers about the possibility of keeping the bill in committee, defeating it on the Senate floor, or sustaining the Governor's vetoes—not just in the bank case, but all of them."[19]

Before Foster completed his examination of the witness, Judge O'Hara recessed court for the weekend so that he and any interested counsel could attend the Michigan Bar Association annual conference which was being held in Lansing. As he left the courtroom, Foster told reporters that he was disappointed that the judge had refused to admit as evidence more than $40,000 in Michigan National Bank checks, several of which had been made out to Ballard. "Despite the court's contention that the state has not yet shown that Ballard has committed a crime," Foster said, his darkly handsome features brightening, "we will prove these charges made to the bank were for Ballard's legal services, and we will present evidence to show a crime."[20]

While court was adjourned in Lansing, events were happening rapidly in Washington, D.C. On Friday afternoon, September 13, F.B.I. agents seized Hemans at his hotel, the arrest warrant charging that the lobbyist had violated the Federal Fugitive Felons Act by "taking flight to avoid giving testimony in a criminal proceeding now pending in Michigan."[21] After posting $5,000 bond, Hemans reiterated his earlier statements to fight extradition and added quietly: "You know, I've taken more than I can stand."[22]

When court reconvened, Garey moved to limit the time covered in the charge from three years to eight months, the length of the legislative session in 1941, arguing that after the legislature adjourned any conspiracy would have ceased. Foster objected, stating that the actual attempt to defeat Senate Bill 1 was only a part of the charge and that "as long as the agreement existed, it does not matter when the payments were made." O'Hara pondered for a moment and said that he would reserve his ruling on the motion until all testimony had been presented.[23]

Wilkowski then resumed the stand and completed his testimony. The ex-Senator, in response to Foster's queries, hammered on the role of Ballard, stating that the Lansing lawyer "urged the defeat of the bank bill."[24] The witness said that "Ballard told us the bank bill was practically unnecessary and that the chain bank he was connected with was in a position to make certain loans which other banks in the state could not make."[25] He also swore that he received $55 in an envelope handed him by a female employee of Bohn Aluminum and Brass after he had telephoned DenUyl "requesting money for my vote."[26]

During the next two days, three of the non-indicted co-conspirators, all of whom had been granted immunity in return for their testimony, were called as witnesses. First to take the stand was Harold Vandenberg, an executive of the Kalamazoo Paper Company, who, in 1941, had been the roommate of Kalamazoo Republican Carl F. DeLano, one of the defendants.

"Sometime in April, 1941," Vandenberg began, speaking hesitantly, his voice low, "Carl, who had been ill much of the session, asked me to call Charlie Hemans to our room. Carl said, 'I want you to know that

Hemans owes me an undetermined amount of money, and if anything happens to me I want you to let Mrs. DeLano know about it."[27]

"Was that the end of it?" Foster pressed the reluctant witness.

"No," Vandenberg admitted, again engaging in a lengthy pause before elaborating. "I told DeLano that he should work for the bill for the future of his political career, but he said he didn't think so because Dunlap Clark, president of the American National Bank of Kalamazoo, was against it. After the session ended, DeLano told me he and Hemans had gone to Detroit and met with some bankers, where they agreed on the determination of some money. To the best of my recollection he used the figure $3,500. The only thing I can add is that Carl said it was certainly too cheap, or words to that effect."[28]

Following Vandenberg was Ferndale Republican Senator George N. Higgins, who in 1941 was a member of the Michigan House of Representatives. "The day before the bill was to come up for a vote, I was getting my shoes shined in the cloakroom when Francis Slattery came up and asked me how I was going to vote on the bank bill," the dour Senator recalled vividly. "I told him I would vote for it, although I had no personal interest in it, and I told him why. A few minutes later Slattery was standing next to the cloakroom door as I headed for the assembly room, and he said he would make it interesting for me to vote against the bill. He was thumbing a roll of $50 bills. I told him I was not interested."

"Had you known Slattery prior to this time?" asked Foster.

"I had seen him around and knew him as a well-dressed man," Higgins said, sitting ramrod straight in his chair, "But I didn't know his name until he approached me."[29]

"Was that the end of this matter for you, Senator?" Foster inquired expectantly.

"No," Higgins stated, his face becoming florid. "Bill Stenson, one of my three roommates in 1941, came back to the hotel room waving a $50 bill. I at once accused him of getting money from Slattery on the anti-branch banking bill, and he kind of smiled. So I said: 'Listen, Stenson, if you go in there tomorrow and vote against the bill, I'll expose you on the floor of the House.' Stenson voted for the bill."[30]

Bespectacled sixty-six year old William Green, his mouth set in its familiar crooked smile, walked slowly to the stand to replace his former colleague. "I was just the go-between for Hemans and some legislators," the former Republican lawmaker and crony of Frank McKay claimed, giving the judge his now familiar grand jury look of a man scorned. "Sure Hemans promised me $500 to vote against the bank bill, and he asked me if I knew any other fellows who would go along."

"So, what did you do?" snapped the Special Prosecutor.

"Well, I went to Bill Stenson. He first asked $1,000 for his vote, but he later lowered his demand to $400, which Hemans agreed to pay."

"What happened after that?"

"Well, I paid him the $400, but he voted yes on the bill," Green continued, his lips still curled in the smile-sneer. "Later, Hemans told me Stenson better return the money or he would do for a one-way ride. So I made him give it back."

"Did you give anyone else any bribe money, Mr. Green?" Foster growled, exhibiting an obvious displeasure with his witness' smugness.

"Oh, yes," Green said matter-of-factly, "I gave George Harma $100 too."[31]

Harma, a look-alike for Hollywood leading man George Brent, with his slicked black hair and pencil-thin moustache, was the next to testify. "I voted for the bill the first time it came up," the forty-one year old ex-Democratic lawmaker from Houghton stated. "After the vote, I went to the Olds Hotel and saw Francis Slattery in the lobby. I told him I was ready to change my mind on the bank bill for $100, but I got the cold shoulder. He told me that he had heard from Representative James Stanley of Kalamazoo that Hemans was handling the money for the Democrats."

"Go on, if you please, Mr. Harma," Foster said politely, pleased with this witness far more than his predecessor on the stand.

"Well, five days later I talked with Bill Green, and Bill said to me: 'So you want to change your vote on the bank bill?' I said maybe, and he said there would be $100 for me."

"Did you earn your money?"

"I voted against the bill, if that's what you mean," Harma said, his voice suddenly lowering. "I got the payment the last day of the session. Bill Green pulled five crumpled $20 bills from different pockets and handed them to me."

"Did you ever talk directly with Hemans about this bill?" Foster inquired.

"No, sir," was the ready reply. "Not about the bank bill. I had made a deal with him on another matter though."[32]

Tuesday's list of prosecution witnesses concluded with Raymond Snow, who had previously pleaded guilty, relating how Hemans had given him $100 in the lobbyist's now-famous bathroom, and William G. Buckley, who had been granted immunity, telling how Hemans had paid him $200 in two equal installments to vote against the bank bill.[33]

On Wednesday, Foster suffered a setback when Judge O'Hara refused to admit records of the law firm of Shields, Ballard, Jennings, and Taber.

"I can see where Mr. Ballard can very easily be connected with the events," the jurist ruled, "but there is nothing in the items which the prosecution wishes to introduce—charges of conferences with senators and other officials concerning the bank bill—at this time to show any unlawful act. The offer is premature under these circumstances."[34] O'Hara also explained that he was "letting in much testimony out of order because the connecting link between the legislators and the bankers—if there is such a link—is now in Washington in the person of Charles F. Hemans. However, we have got to cut this out soon before I get in a daze myself."[35]

Hounded by reporters after court recessed, Foster displayed public exasperation for the first time. "I don't know why we should refuse to admit what is a fact," he replied when asked if the absence of his star witness was interfering with the presentation of his case. "I intend to continue the examination for the time being, although I may have to seek a continuance if Hemans' appearance is long delayed."[36]

Foster's misfortunes continued the following day when O'Hara ordered the prosecution to call former Attorney General Rushton and possibly former Governor VanWagoner to testify as to the terms of Byron Ballard's employment. The judge did so in response to a request by defense counsel William Henry Gallagher, who averred that his client "took the employment as legal advisor with the express understanding with Rushton that the duties would not interfere with his employment as attorney for the Michigan National Bank."[37] O'Hara silenced Foster's objection by asserting: "I believe it is absolutely necessary for me to know the facts. The examination really has developed into a trial because we have questions here which ordinarily would be presented to the trial court, and I am entitled to know if there was any such agreement."[38] Soon afterward the judge declared court in recess for the weekend.

When the examination resumed on Monday morning, a haggard Rushton, who had been ill for several weeks, stepped uncertainly to the witness stand. "I gave Ballard permission to retain his clients, including Michigan National Bank," Rushton admitted, his once gruff voice now barely a whisper. "Ballard told me he didn't want the job because some proceedings might come along and he'd have to appear for one of his clients and that might embarrass me. I told him it wouldn't embarrass me any. So I appointed him at the request of VanWagoner, but it is significant to remember that Ballard was reluctant to accept until he had spoken to me."[39]

Another prosecution witness who was too sick to appear in person, Carl DeLano, submitted a statement, which Foster read into the record over the strenuous objection of Garey and Gallagher. "Charlie Hemans picked me up in an automobile and drove me and Simon DenUyl to west Lansing." DeLano wrote. "We parked the car, and we discussed my price for voting against the bill. I wanted $10,000, but we settled on $7,500. I made no effort to collect the money until after the session, in the autumn of 1941, when I drove to Detroit and met with Hemans in a room at the Statler Hotel. Hemans pulled out his billfold and handed me $3,500. I told him the price was $7,500. Hemans and I haggled over the sum. We agreed to call DenUyl to settle the matter. DenUyl came up to the room and said I had to take Hemans' figures. Hemans thereupon agreed that I had done a good job and should be given an additional $2,000. But I received only $300 more."[40]

On Wednesday, September 25, the inevitable occurred when Foster moved for a delay until October 9. Gallagher rose to speak against the motion. Turning abruptly to confront Foster, defense counsel thrust out an index finger and yelled: "You knew that Hemans wasn't going to be here, yet you went ahead with the examination. We are entitled to speedy action." The Special Prosecutor fired back insinuatingly that the State "believes that other forces are responsible for Hemans' failure to appear."[41]

Gavelling for order, Judge O'Hara consented to the recess. "The case against many of these defendants cannot be established without Mr. Hemans," the magistrate stated. "Mr. Hemans seems to have the peculiar idea that he is a hero. He must have a funny quirk to believe that." He added caustically, "I do not propose to let Charles Hemans, who at least was once an attorney, to obstruct the court and the prosecution. Therefore the court is going about meeting a situation brought about by an individual who thinks he is bigger than the law. We've heard a lot of rumors about what Hemans is or is not going to do when he gets here. I'll take care of that. He is not going to make the law a laughing stock. I'm going to do everything possible to get him here."[42]

VDuring the recess, the saga of Hemans was forced to share headlines with stories relating to two other figures well-known to Michiganians. Kim Sigler kept up his campaign ranting, in which he relegated all his critics to abettors of crime. "You know," he shouted to a rally at Albion, the home of the martyred Warren Hooper, "the racketeers do not want me to become Governor of Michigan. Shysters, gangsters, and crooked politicians are at work to prevent me from becoming Governor. I'm not concerned with closing bingo in churches as my enemies claim, but I am concerned with things which make grafters out of honest men."[43] In Jackson he appealed to the female voters, pointing out that "not one woman has been indicted, and mighty few have been questioned, in the six grand juries in Ingham, Wayne, Oakland, Macomb, Washtenaw, and Bay Counties."[44] Of course, he failed to mention that these inquiries were into the actions of elected officials, and virtually no women fell into that category. In Bay City, the Republican nominee vehemently asserted that the State Police were part of the criminal conspiracy. "I promised in the primary campaign to clean up the State Police," he reminded his audience. "This is a great organization of fine young men—90 percent of whom are clean, honest, and fine. Yet the Superintendent of that police was sitting in the Capitol taking bribes."[45] To those in the know, this allegation against the highly respected Oscar Olander was baseless, but because the "White Knight" said it, many automatically accepted it as fact.

At a Democratic party gathering in Battle Creek Sigler's pristine purity came under attack as Thurmond B. Doyle, his party's candidate for Attorney General, posed a question for the electorate to ask the crusading Republican: "Did you, Kim Sigler, or did you not, as an attorney, receive $500 as a retainer fee from the Michigan National Bank prior to the grand jury investigation of the anti-chain bank bill?"[46] Calhoun County Circuit Judge Frank Kulp took Sigler to task over the Hooper murder probe. "Who killed Senator Hooper?" he bellowed to the cheering assembly. "If the State Police know and Kim Sigler knows, as he says he does, why isn't that person arrested?"[47] Former Jackson County Prosecutor Harold Steinbacher incited the partisans by inquiring: "What has Sigler done that he needs a State Police bodyguard every time he goes for a walk?"[48]

Not content with leaving Sigler to the tender mercies of surrogates, VanWagoner savagely lit into his opponent in a speech at Muskegon. "The Democratic party is placed in the difficult position of removing the self-imposed halo from the curls of the former Democratic Kim," stated the man who wished to regain his seat in the Executive Office. "He may have sprung from the common people, but once started on grand jury money he managed to spring a good long way from them. Instead of being caught with his hand in the grand jury cookie jar, Kim will tie himself to a stake and pretend that the lions are being loosed on him."[49]

Startled by this assault on his integrity, Sigler chose to avoid the first two queries, but was willing to respond to the third at a speech in Detroit. "The only reason I am a candidate," he stated hotly, trying to reclaim he initiative by diverting attention back to his only real issue, "is that I was stopped in the middle of my work exposing graft in the Michigan government. The job of getting evidence is tough and keeping it ready is a bigger job. My chances wouldn't be worth a nickel in certain spots if the right opportunities presented themselves. I've told certain yahoos that they aren't going to get away with things they have been doing any more. They don't need to worry about that bodyguard."[50]

Amidst this firestorm of political oratory came news from Florida that McKay henchman William McKeighan was facing extradition to Michigan to face charges of conspiring to violate state gaming laws by bribery and corruption of public officials. McKeighan's attorney, William Pruit of Miami Beach, where his client owned 350 feet of oceanfront property valued at more than $400,000, told reporters that he believed the charges were a frame-up by Sigler for political purposes. "If he knew he was going to face trial right away and get it all over, he would fly back to Michigan," the lawyer claimed. "But he feels that he might serve a year in sixty day stretches, without ever having had a trial, because Herman Dehnke, the Macomb County grand juror who issued the order, would hold him in contempt." McKeighan went so far as to feign a heart attack to prevent proceedings from moving forward, but he made a remarkable recovery upon learning that Florida authorities would not support extradition.[51] It seemed that no-one previously associated with the Ingham County grand jury ever wanted to "come home again."

VI The prosecution's fortunes apparently took an upward turn when federal marshals returned Hemans to Detroit on October 1 to be arraigned before Federal Judge Frank A. Pickard on a federal fugitive witness charge.[52] Unable to post a $7,500 bond, the once-prosperous reluctant witness was remanded to the Wayne County Jail, where he spent his first day playing poker with fellow inmates and visiting with both his wife Ruth and his attorney Seymour Person. "Ruth told me she had a chance to sell part of the farm for $6,000," he instructed his counsel to tell reporters. "I told her to get rid of it. I'm fast running out of money. You can't pay bonds and high attorney fees forever with no income. I'm going to liquidate completely."[53]

Upon learning of Hemans' arrival in Michigan, Gallagher requested, and received, from Judge O'Hara a one week delay in reopening the hearing. Foster readily consented, remarking that the continuance would benefit the prosecution as well. "We plan to have Hemans up here [in Lansing] before the examination starts again to visit with him, since we haven't talked with Hemans since we saw him in Washington before the examination first began," Foster commented. When asked if he was made more hopeful by Hemans' presence, the prosecutor shook his head. "Well, the delay means Hemans will have sat in jail a week longer—if he doesn't make bond—and whether that will make any difference in his decision to talk, I don't know," was the candid reply. Somewhat wistfully, Foster added: "You know, from now on, Hemans makes the decisions on what happens, not me. If he doesn't talk, it's one thing. If he does, it's another."[54]

Exactly one week after his arraignment, Hemans was escorted from his cell by United States Deputy Marshal John D. Page for a trip to Lansing to answer a writ of habeas corpus issued by Coash. Beset by hollering newsmen, the former man-about-town flashed a toothy grin and waved. "I am unaccustomed to talking these days," he said cheerfully. "I will say, however, that I have no statement to make before I see the grand juror and prosecutor."

"Will you be doing much talking today?" screamed someone from the crowd.[55]

"Oh, you won't get me into that one," shot back the jovial lobbyist.

After a grueling two hour interrogation, Hemans emerged from the grand jury room, having abandoned his good-humored bravado. "I told you when I went in I'd have nothing to say, and now that I've been in there, I have even less," he growled, sliding into the rear seat of the automobile which would take him back to his Detroit jail cell. "I'm still in federal custody. I will make no statement, as it might tend to incriminate me in view of the federal charge."[56]

VII The next day, Coash, frustrated by his inability to coerce Hemans into testifying, penned a letter to Governor Kelly urging the "Little Legislature" to grant an additional $50,000 so that the grand jury could complete its labors. "Only $8,000 remains from the $444,000 original appropriation made in 1943," Coash explained to Kelly. "This sum is insufficient to carry to completion the work undertaken by the grand jury, and there are several very important matters which must be carried to a conclusion."[57]

When the "Little Legislature" convened on Friday, October 11, Governor Kelly distributed another message from the grand juror, this time addressed to the assembled lawmakers. "On or about October 5, the grand jury obtained and received information relative to matters highly important to the people of Michigan," read the tantalizingly mysterious missive, "the nature of which requires action by the grand jury and an extensive and thorough examination. The information was not known to the grand jury before the above date, but it is of such importance, I believe a judicial investigation should commence."[58]

Because the grand juror's request had been submitted after the mandatory ten day legal notice to members prior to the beginning of the session, unanimous consent was required before discussion could ensue. Senator Charles F. Blondy, who had been indicted by the grand jury in the anti-chain bank case, objected. "The grand jury has spent a large amount of money and hasn't accomplished much," the Detroit Democrat sneered, much to the consternation of his colleagues who sat dumbfounded at the gall he exhibited by trying so overtly to undermine the body investigating his behavior. "It has had $450,000, and that's a lot of money. The schools need it, and lot of others do, too."[59]

Republican Senator Otto Bishop personally appealed to Blondy to cease his obstructionism, but Blondy remained obdurate. Only after Bishop pointed out that if Blondy persisted, the Governor would merely call the "Little Legislature" back for a second session in ten days, did the former Wayne County constable relent. After a brief debate, the motion for the latest appropriation carried.[60]

VIII

On Wednesday, October 16, the hearing resumed, and Hemans was called as a witness for the State. He responded to interrogation concerning his background and law practice, but balked as soon as the Special Prosecutor quizzed him about his work as a lobbyist.

"Did you have an argument with Simon DenUyl, treasurer of the Bohn Aluminum and Brass Corporation, and receive money from him to pay legislators?" Foster inquired sharply.

I refuse to answer that question," Hemans replied with a slight smile.

"Did you pay legislators in accordance with an agreement with DenUyl?"

"I refuse to answer that question."

"Do you recall talking with DenUyl and Charles Bohn in Bohn's office to explain how you spent DenUyl's money to do his work?"

"I don't remember."

"Did you speak with Byron Ballard regarding the anti-chain bank bill?" continued Foster in frustration.

"Mr. Foster," came the calm response, "I have under the constitution certain rights, and I am informed by my counsel I must avail myself of them and refuse to answer any questions which might tend to incriminate me."[61]

Foster urged the presiding magistrate to compel the witness to answer, but, to Foster's dismay, O'Hara sided with Hemans. "If I permitted him to answer questions at this time," the judge ruled, after citing several federal and Michigan cases as precedent, "when prosecution in federal court is not only imminent, but actual, I would be remiss in my duty. He cannot be compelled to answer any questions tending to show that he could give testimony in this case. Moreover, as long as that prosecution is pending, he is entitled to the privilege of refusing to testify."[62]

Casting a disapproving glare at Hemans, who sat back in his chair with a broad grin, O'Hara sought to make his decision perfectly clear. "I am making this ruling regardless of the personal thoughts of this court of what might or ought to happen to Mr. Hemans," the judge said, his eyes squinted in scorn. "I hold no brief for the position of Mr. Hemans, and I do not approve of his conduct in leaving the jurisdiction of the state after his immunity was granted and the warrant issued in this case. But the law dictates my ruling."[63]

"The People cannot successfully proceed without the testimony of Hemans, who is a vital, key witness, Your Honor," Foster pleaded, "and we believe if his testimony is available it would justify the court to find probable cause against all the defendants named. Therefore, I will begin immediately the appeal process to the Michigan Supreme Court against your ruling, and I request a delay in these proceedings until such time as the higher court may rule."[64] O'Hara, exhibiting no offense at the remarks, recessed the hearing until Monday, January 6, 1947.[65]

Crushed by reporters following the session, Hemans was subdued. "I can only say that I'm deeply gratified by Judge O'Hara's action," Hemans stated. "Six hundred acres of my farm near Aurelius is being sold, so I expect to be able to post my $7,500 bond within a few days. Then I'm going on a rest before my federal court trial in Detroit on October 31. I'll see you boys then."[66]

IX Early November brought no surprises to observers of Michigan's political and legal scenes. On the fifth of the month, Kim Sigler steamrolled VanWagoner by nearly 400,000 votes to become Governor-elect. Three days later, the former Special Prosecutor's "golden boy," Charlie Hemans, was found guilty by a jury of ten women and two men, after only twenty-six minutes of deliberation, of violating the Federal Fugitive Law.[67]

Four weeks later, before sentencing was imposed by Federal Judge Theodore Levin, Hemans' attorney, O. R. McGuire, made an impassioned plea for leniency. "I seek mercy for my client, Your Honor," the lawyer began. "He has passed the fifty year mark. He has never been found guilty before of any crime, and he was for many years an honored member of the bar. I ask the Court to be as compassionate as possible."[68]

Levin, however, was unmoved. "This defendant, Hemans, just flouted the law. He did obstruct justice. I can't imagine a situation where a man could have less regard for a statute than Mr. Hemans has shown," the judge stated, his animus evident in every word he spoke. "I don't feel that my duty would be recognized if I did act leniently in this case. Therefore, I sentence the defendant, Charles Fitch Hemans, to serve four years at Lewisburg Federal Penitentiary and to pay a $1,000 fine. Bail will not be set because I am sympathetic to the fears expressed by the prosecution that Mr. Hemans might flee again, this time to Canada, if given his freedom while the appeal is pending."[69]

On December 11, the day after Hemans' sentencing, Foster went before Judge O'Hara and argued that because Hemans had been convicted "anything he might say here in Lansing would no longer tend to incriminate him and his privilege under the Fifth Amendment ceases."[70] In the midst of expounding his rationale in detail, the former Ingham County Prosecutor was summarily halted. "Don't waste any time on that," burst in the jurist, evincing scorn at having to listen to such an ill-advised motion. "There is always the danger of self-incrimination until the time for filing an appeal for a conviction expires. A verdict is considered vacated until such time as the appeal is decided."[71]

Following this rebuff, Foster drove to Detroit to visit Hemans again. Hemans, looking tired and paler than normal, did his best to maintain his facade of devil-may-care jauntiness. "Charlie," Foster implored, "why won't you testify against those $50,000,000 friends of yours? They couldn't pay you enough, Charlie, to take the fall for them—and I know you got paid to keep quiet. Why go to jail to keep your rich pals free?"

"Four years," Hemans replied with a wave of his hand. "Hell, Dick, I can do that standing on one hand."[72]

With Hemans staying mum, on January 6 Foster requested yet another stay, this time until April 28, to permit completion of appeals involving his reluctant witness. Ignoring the protestations of Gallagher that his clients were entitled by law to a "speedy trial," O'Hara granted the motion and the waiting game moved into its next phase.[73]

X An earlier aspect of the grand jury had resurfaced on January 2, 1946 when Sigler, as his first act as Governor, made public a letter he had sent to State Police Commissioner Oscar G. Olander demanding his resignation. "I do not understand how you could be at the head of the chief law enforcing agency of the state and not realize fully what was going on around you," Sigler wrote. "For some time prior to his indictment on gambling charges, Captain [Laurence] Lyon, the first officer under you [head of the Uniform Division], had been accepting bribes. It was so generally known that it became a matter of common gossip. Other officers in the department were involved and some have been indicted. Such conduct on the part of these officers is a disgrace to the State of Michigan and you, as head of the department, should have been the first to exterminate this condition. This, frankly, you failed to do. I appreciate all that you have done for the department in the past, but I cannot tolerate graft and corruption in any department of Michigan's government."[74]

Kenneth McCormick, Pulitzer Prize winning reporter for the *Detroit Free Press*, who had won the award for his coverage of the grand jury by penning stories filled with secrets leaked to him by his friend Sigler, published an article January 4 tracing the Sigler-Olander feud to the McKay liquor conspiracy trial. "On the eve of the trial of Frank D. McKay, Olander cancelled the State Police detail assigned to the grand jury. These investigators were the backbone of the jury. They ran down clues, checked records, questioned witnesses, and worked day and night under the direction of Sigler," McCormick stated, clearly implying that the Commissioner was abetting McKay. "Olander's decision was hushed at the time. Sigler was on his way home to Battle Creek from Lansing in a State Police car when he heard a broadcast over the police radio: 'To all commanders: Honor no more requests by Kim Sigler. Orders from Commissioner Olander.'"

"Sigler called Olander from his home, and Olander asserted that his move was prompted by a manpower shortage," the exposé continued. "Sigler promptly subpoenaed Olander before the grand jury. When he arrived at grand jury headquarters, Olander asked to speak with Sigler in chambers. After letting Olander cool his heels for some time, Sigler came in punching with both hands. 'You pull that detail away from me now,' he said, 'and I'll blast you right out of this state.' Olander then agreed to drop the matter for the good of the grand jury. The Commissioner then told his men he was sorry, and he promised Sigler more men if necessary."[75]

Two days after McCormick's sensational revelation Olander resigned and Captain Donald S. Leonard, in whom Sigler placed implicit trust, was named to head the State Police. Ironically, unbeknownst to Sigler, his pent-up fury had caused him to commit a monumental blunder. Olander was not then, nor never had been, a tool of McKay, but his successor probably was.[76] The prima donna Governor was proving quickly that he had abandoned neither his prosecutorial vindictiveness nor his shoot-from-the-hip tactics when he ascended to his new position.

XI On February 1, 1947, the *Detroit Times* ran a brief item stating what most Michigan residents already suspected: that the grand jury was all but completely dissolved. "I have begun the job of being a plain circuit judge," Coash said with evident relief. "The Ingham County grand jury is now interested in cleaning up the unfinished cases as quickly as possible. All of the cases are in some court or other, and from now on it is a matter of legal procedure and waiting."[77] The grand juror added that his staff consisted only of Foster and State Trooper Fred C. Kelly, both of whom were on a part-time basis, and that he had expended less than $5,000 of the $50,000 voted to the probe the previous October by the "Little Legislature."[78]

In keeping his pledge to make the slate clean, on March 19, 1947 Coash quashed charges against Frank D. McKay, Floyd Fitzsimmons, and William Green, indicted on conspiracy charges regarding a horse racing bill, and William Burns, who had been indicted for purportedly bribing State Representative Warren Hooper for his vote on health insurance legislation. Also relieved of possible legal action were Emmanuel N. Rosenthal, Charles Layton, and Samuel Schreier, of the Mohawk and Arrow Liquor Corporations, who had been indicted on charges of conspiring to corrupt the legislature on a bill to reduce distillery license fees.[79]

As to the ever-present spectre of Charlie Hemans, the scheduled resumption of his hearing had been postponed from April to June and then to November 13, all on the perpetual promise of Foster that the witness would finally agree to squeal on his friends.[80] When Hemans took the stand on the appointed day in the autumn and sullenly parroted his earlier refrain of silence, Judge O'Hara exploded with a fury rarely seen on the bench.

"You haven't been fair with the state or the defendants or this court," O'Hara snapped, furiously brandishing his index finger at the prison-pale ex-lobbyist. "You have a duty to this state and especially to the defendants, who could be freed at once if your testimony did not implicate them. But you have been trying in every way that you know how to thwart the law of this state in this lawsuit. I intend to see that you, nor any other individual, cannot do that."

Seeing a nervous grin forming on Hemans' face, the judge grew more incensed. "I don't think you ever believed you had a constitutional basis for refusing to testify. I think it was a ploy," O'Hara fairly bellowed. "But because of circumstances—the prison sentence you are now serving—I am unable to send you to jail today. But when the day comes and you will be free on parole or at the end of your sentence, a warrant for contempt of this court will be waiting for you as you step out of the prison. I believe I have the power under the law, as I interpret the statutes, to send you to the county jail until you testify or until you die. Think about that and appear here again this Friday."[81]

After pondering his fate, Hemans remained unchastened. O'Hara, having stood as much as he could, quietly informed the prisoner that he alone could determine how long he would remain behind bars. "If you change your mind tomorrow or in two weeks or two years," the judge pledged, "you can purge yourself of this contempt by answering the questions which were asked of you in this case. I assure you that you will be kept in jail until you talk or die." Disgusted, the judge, after observing that this case could not go on forever, decreed it would hang on at least until March 24, 1948, when Hemans would be paraded forth once more.[82]

In the meantime, Foster, on October 9, filed an affidavit with the Ingham County Circuit Court in which he set forth what Hemans had told him he would say in court about the bank case. This document, which was published in full by the *Michigan Tradesman*, demonstrates why the State was willing to attempt to outlast Hemans' silence. Foster's sworn statement contained political dynamite, as it not only reaffirmed in detail the testimony given by legislative recipients of graft, but also portrayed the non-legislative defendants, especially DenUyl, in a most damning light.

"Mr Hemans made such arrangements and payments to Senators Leo Wilkowski, Charles Diggs, Gilbert Isbister, Charles Blondy, Ernest Nagel, and James Burns. Most of the payments were made in the bathroom of his, Mr. Hemans', hotel room, and the price agreed upon with each was from $600 to $800, excepting for Senator Nagel which was $200," Foster related being told by the lobbyist. "Mr. Hemans also made arrangements with a few members of the House of Representatives, although he at this time told Mr. DenUyl that he expected that the principle action upon the bank bill would occur in the Senate. He made arrangements with Representatives Edward Walsh, Francis Nowak, William Buckley, Earl C. Gallagher, Joseph Kowalski, Walter Stockfish, Adam Sumeracki, Raymond Snow, William Green, and Earl McEwen for about $500 each in consideration of their opposition to the bank legislation, and about $800 or $1,000 with Representative James Stanley. Representative Stanley told him he was not keeping any of the money but that he would pass it on to members of the Committee on State Affairs."[83]

"Sometime prior to April 10, 1941, Mr. Hemans saw Senator Carl DeLano in his, Senator DeLano's, room at the Hotel Olds, who told him that he understood Mr. Hemans was representing the interests opposed to the bank bill and that he would vote against the bill and secure two or three other votes against the bill for the sum of $50,000," the affidavit stated. "Mr. Hemans told him that such a figure was out of the question, that he had no authority to make any such commitments, but that he would report it to his principle, Mr. DenUyl. Either that night or the next night, Mr. DenUyl came to Lansing, and the three, Mr. DenUyl, Senator DeLano, and Mr. Hemans, drove in Mr. Hemans' car to a point west of the city of Lansing near the Air Port Road, where the car was parked and discussion occurred between Mr. DenUyl and Senator DeLano upon the price to be paid to Senator DeLano. The discussion lasted some time, Senator DeLano demanding first $50,000, then $30,000, and finally $25,000, but no agreement was reached, and Mr. DenUyl told Senator DeLano that he and Mr. Hemans would discuss the matter and that Mr. Hemans would notify him. After leaving Senator DeLano, Mr. DenUyl told Mr. Hemans to make the best deal he could. Mr. Hemans met with Senator DeLano several times during the next few days, and Senator DeLano finally stated that he would agree to $7,500. Mr. Hemans telephoned Dr. DenUyl, and Mr. DenUyl told him that was satisfactory."[84]

"During the course of the legislative session Mr. Hemans received the monies that he used to pay the legislators upon the bank bill from Mr. DenUyl at his office in the Lafayette Building. He made numerous trips to Mr. DenUyl's office, sometimes going into Detroit on the afternoon train and coming back to Lansing the same night, and on other occasions driving into Detroit and remaining over the weekend. The money was always given to him in cash, usually in twenty dollar bills, and was given to him in white envelopes," Foster testified Hemans had said.[85]

"During the legislative session, Mr. Hemans talked with Mr. Howard Stoddard at his office in the bank six or eight times about the bank bill," the document set forth. "Mr. DenUyl had told Mr. Hemans to see Mr. Stoddard and to keep him advised of his progress in his efforts to defeat the legislation. On some occasions thereafter when he was in the bank Mr. Stoddard would send for him and the two discussed the legislative maneuvers relating to the bill and the names of the legislators who would vote for the bill and who had promised to vote against the bill."[86]

220

"In his conversations with Mr. DenUyl during the session, Mr. DenUyl repeatedly told him that he, Mr. DenUyl, was representing Mr. Bohn's interests and others connected with the bank, and that Mr. Byron Ballard was handling all legal matters for them in connection with the legislation," Foster recounted Hemans as saying. "On several occasions Mr. Hemans met with Mr. Ballard, and Mr. Ballard told him on one occasion that he knew Mr. Hemans was working on the banking legislation."[87]

"Mr. Hemans said he met Mr. DenUyl in his office in Detroit, and Mr. DenUyl asked him how much it would cost to secure enough votes to be certain that the veto would not be overridden when the legislature convened. Computations were made by Mr. DenUyl and Mr. Hemans as to what sums had been spent and what he, Mr. Hemans, believed would be necessary yet to spend and it totaled about $30,000. He told Mr. DenUyl that he believed it would be necessary only to spend money in the Senate," the affidavit read, "but Mr. DenUyl stated that so they should be sure to also cover the key members in the House of Representatives, and that if it could be done with a total expenditure of about $30,000 to go ahead and do it."[88]

"After the grand jury proceedings had commenced," the statement declared, "Mr. DenUyl visited Mr. Hemans in Washington about three times. Mr. Hemans generally met him in the Mayflower Hotel. Mr. DenUyl told him that everything would be taken care of because they were going to get the investigation stopped and for Mr. Hemans to make no statement of any kind. On one occasion he told him that they had decided that if he, Mr. Hemans, was ever questioned by anyone concerning the banking legislation, he was to state that he had been employed by Mr. Joseph Brewer of Grand Rapids, and that Mr. Brewer was the only person that Mr. Hemans dealt with on behalf of the bank or those interested in defeating the bank legislation. Mr. Hemans told him he would be unable to do this because he had never met Mr. Brewer or seen him, and if they flashed a picture on him he would be helpless."[89]

"DenUyl also told him," Foster averred, "that his associates had spent a lot more money in connection with the bill than they had originally intended or that Mr. Hemans knew about, but that if Mr. Hemans kept quiet everything would be all right. Mr. Hemans asked him who had spent the money, and Mr. DenUyl stated that he didn't know but presumed it was an individual he named. Mr. Hemans also called Mr. DenUyl on the telephone from Washington several times, and at one time reached him at the Ambassador Hotel in Los Angeles. He told him that things were getting too hot, but Mr. DenUyl told him everything would be taken care of; that perhaps the investigation still could be stopped, and for Mr. Hemans not to say anything."[90]

With Hemans telling this story from the stand, the guilt of each defendant was assured. It is little wonder that Foster was convinced that Hemans had received for his refusal to testify a payoff so large that it could not be made even in Hemans' fabled bathroom.

XII Foster's hand was forced, however, when on April 5, 1948 the Michigan Supreme Court ordered that trials for the defendants in the bank case had to be held within sixty days.[91] Immediately upon hearing of the high court ruling, Judge O'Hara instructed the prosecution that unless it completed its testimony by April 19 he would dismiss all warrants issued against the indictees.[92]

On the day of the court appointed deadline, Foster rose and informed the jurist that it would be impossible to continue the case without the testimony of Hemans, and therefore he was requesting the court to quash all indictments against those accused. O'Hara granted the motion, and the twenty-one month legal ordeal was over.[93]

XIII All that was left now for Coash was to tie up the remaining loose ends of the grand jury. Some of the "ragged edges," as Foster referred to the unfinished work, were amusing, such as Raymond Snow requesting $489 in back salary on the grounds that he had never resigned his seat and that his guilty plea became invalid when the bank case was dismissed,[94] but others represented a vivid reminder of the vindictiveness engendered by the probe. An example of this occurred on May 28, 1948 when Governor Sigler refused to commute the sentences of Dr. Mihkel Sherman and Floyd Fitzsimmons, both of whom had undergone nervous and physical breakdowns, and Carl DeLano, who had suffered a paralytic stroke which rendered his right arm and leg useless and deprived him of the ability to speak. The Governor admitted that appeals had been made on behalf of these men, but it was his position that he "could not establish a precedent." Sigler did promise, however, that he would personally see that each of the aged men received proper medical care in prison.[95]

On November 30, 1948 Chester M. Howell was placed on probation and ordered to pay $1,500 in court costs. Appearing before the grand juror, the former lawmaker looked every day of his sixty-six years. "I never considered the money I received as graft," he said, his head almost resting on his chest. "It had long been the custom in the legislature to accept gifts and gratuities. I realize that in the eyes of the grand jury there is no difference between gratuities and bribes. But I want to say that I made no effort to get any money."[96]

Ten days later, Sigler, who had suffered a stunning upset in his bid for re-election by Democrat G. Mennen Williams, refused to pardon thirteen individuals, including Fitzsimmons, DeLano, Jerry Logie, and Charles Diggs, who had been convicted on graft grand jury charges. "Justice must be served without favoritism or preference," the repudiated Chief Executive stated harshly in his best prosecutor's tone. "The law must apply equally to all persons, regardless of who they are or their station in life. Those sentences came after jury trials in which these men were found guilty beyond a reasonable doubt. Executive clemency cannot be founded on sympathy, but I realize that it is almost impossible to explain to friends of these men the facts so that they will fully understand the position I am compelled to take."[97]

The new year brought forth both a Democratic administration in Lansing and a period of more compassion toward the victims of the grand jury. On January 6, 1949 Coash threw in the towel and dismissed charges against the remaining fifteen defendants awaiting trial for conspiracy in cases involving intangible taxes, dental advertising, and liquor distribution. Freed were Julian H. Thompson, Armand Robichaud, Abraham Cooper, John E. Hancock, George Omacht, Charles C. Diggs, Leo J. Wilkowski, Ernest G. Nagel, William G. Buckley, Earl C. Gallagher, Francis J. Nowak, Edward J. Walsh, Walter N. Stockfish, Dr. Edwin J. Chamberlain, and Charles Leiter.[98] One week later, the State Supreme Court erased O'Hara's "testify or stay in jail until you die" sentence against Hemans on the grounds that the case in which the lobbyist refused to speak was dismissed.[99]

On Valentine's Day, 1949, the State Parole Board, upon recommendation from the sentencing judge, John Simpson, freed DeLano, Logie, and Fitzsimmons. Regarding the disabled DeLano, Simpson wrote: "Apparently here is a case which has been punished as much as humanly possible. Because of the nature of the case and the report of the doctor, I do not see where the state will gain anything by keeping him in prison if his family is willing to assume the burden and care for him."[100] Of Logie, the jurist said: "He has undoubtedly been punished as much as though he were to remain in prison for the rest of his life. He was unfortunate in getting mixed up with men such as Hemans and Howell. I understand his family will care for him, as medical records show he is suffering from nervous instability, low pulse rate, and hyperthyroidism, and thus relieve the state of providing facilities in the hospital for him."[101] As to the pathetic, bedridden Fitzsimmons, Simpson stated: "This man has been punished as much as he can ever be punished. The fact that he has been in prison will show to the public that when a man has committed a crime, he will be punished. That is the significant fact. With his physical condition what it is [hypertension, peptic ulcer, myocarditis, coronary sclerosis, arteriosclerosis, chronic arthritis, and anemia], he has been punished sufficiently for the nature of the crime. Of course, we could keep him and let him die in prison, but that would not do society any good."[102]

In early November, yet another aging convict was permitted to die as a free man. William Green, sixty-eight years old and in rapidly failing health, received a parole after serving only ten months of his three to five year sentence on the grounds that the Parole Board had "no desire to see him die in prison."[103]

XIV

The name of Charles Hemans rose Phoenix-like again in September 1950 when Circuit Judge John Simpson granted new trials to John E. Hancock and George Omacht, both of whom had been convicted in the finance conspiracy case in 1944. His decision, the judge stated, was based on his belief that the convictions were a result of "purchased testimony."[104]

"I gave serious consideration to the new testimony of Monroe [Monty] Wendell, who, with his father Leo, had been discharged as grand jury investigators 'for betraying grand jury secrets' by then Special Prosecutor Sigler. Mr. Wendell said there had been an agreement between Hemans and Prosecutor Sigler," Simpson explained to Ingham County Prosecutor Charles R. McLean at the retrial hearing. "Wendell claimed that Hemans promised to give favorable testimony in return for a promise that Sigler would use his influence to keep Hemans from being disbarred as an attorney; that Sigler agreed to get Hemans a job for life with a good Michigan company; that Hemans was granted immunity from prosecution; that he was paid $600 monthly while he was a grand jury witness; and that Sigler would try to get the Army to transfer Hemans, then a major, to Michigan. Wendell stated that Hemans told him he was supplied with liquor and women, and that the State Police had orders to take him any place he wanted to go. Hemans also told Mr. Wendell that he had not informed the finance company officers that he was bribing legislators. Monty Wendell's testimony, if given to a jury, might have given a different aspect to the trial."[105]

Reached at his law office in Lansing, Sigler shook his head in disbelief upon being told of the reversal. "Well, I'm surprised, to say the least," he said. "In point of fact, there is absolutely not a word of truth in any of

Monty Wendell's charges, except that Hemans was promised immunity. However, that immunity extended only to the cases in which Hemans cooperated fully."[106]

McLean filed an appeal with the State Supreme Court contending that Simpson "abused his discretion" in granting new trials. The high court sustained Simpson's ruling, but the prosecution opted to drop all charges, saying that a retrial would be "not worth the expense."[107]

Heman's legal wars finally ended on April 10, 1951 when Circuit Judge Herman Dehnke put the ex-lobbyist on five years' probation and fined him $1,000 in court costs as a consequence of pleading guilty in May 1950 to offering a $200 bribe to Representative George O. Harma in 1941 to influence his vote on the intangibles tax bill. "I have delayed sentencing for nearly a year to see how you would comport yourself," Dehnke stated sternly. "From what I see, your actions have been acceptable, but not completely satisfactory."

"You made partial atonement by giving important aid—up to a point— to the cause of honesty and integrity in government," the jurist continued. "Yet, I cannot forget that your bribery record undermined the integrity of good government. And I cannot forget that your stubborn refusal to testify in one case led to the dismissal of the defendants. What is the personal cost of your actions? You have to live with the knowledge of having disgraced yourself, your family, and the memory of an honorable, respected father. You have been disbarred from the practice of law with no prospect of reinstatement, thereby having lost your means of livelihood in that profession."

Peering down on the defendant, who stood impassively listening to the recitation, Dehnke concluded by telling Hemans the true tragedy of his life. "The trouble," the judge said, "is that you are still trying to convince yourself that the offenses you committed were, after all, not very serious."[108]

After receiving his sentence, Hemans asked permission to address the court. "Your honor," he said to the astonishment of the jurist, "I wish you to know that if needed again, I will be available to testify against grafting former state legislators."[109] Charlie Hemans was truly one of a kind.

XV The Ingham County grand jury passed into history. It issued 127 warrants. Of those arrested, fifteen pleaded guilty, thirty-four were indicted, sixty-six had their cases dismissed or never were brought to trial, and twelve were acquitted. One witness was murdered, and several others died under mysterious circumstances. One grand juror was elevated to the Michigan Supreme Court and a Special Prosecutor used the grand jury to catapult him to the governorship.

Over eight years, the monetary cost to the taxpayers was a staggering $495,189. Attorney fees totalled $228,418, of which Sigler received $71,276 and Foster $55,242, while attorney expenses added up to $15,524. Other expenditures included $18,992 for auditing, $37,822 in hotel fees, $36,925 for State Police expenses, $48,894 for court stenographers, $14,825 in trial expenses, $10,616 for witness fees, and $47,057 in investigator salaries and expenses.[110] Moreover, approximately 5,800 man days were put in by State Police troopers, or nearly sixteen years if it had been done by a lone officer. Nearly 500,000 miles were put on state owned vehicles and 1,300 subpoenas were served by the State Police for the grand jury.[111]

Yet, even after its passing, intrigue hovered over the grand jury. In 1957 Circuit Judge Coash, allegedly on orders from the State Supreme Court, went to a storage vault in downtown Lansing late at night, loaded what he believed were all copies of the grand jury records into a truck, and supervised their destruction in the Oldsmobile incinerator.[112] When former prosecutor Foster, who was out of town, learned of the judge's deed, he was troubled, because he was convinced that there was a statute that instructed such records to be filed with the county clerk.[113] The grand jury corpse, having been exhumed and then cremated, at long last reached its official final rest, fittingly as the result of a questionable legal action on the part of an elected official.

EPILOGUE

VICTOR C. ANDERSON, a graduate of Michigan State University and the University of Michigan Law School, served as Ingham County Prosecutor from 1942 to 1947, at which time he became Governor Kim Sigler's chief legal advisor. Following Sigler's defeat in 1948, Anderson joined with the former Governor and Leland Carr Jr. to form the Lansing law firm of Sigler, Anderson, and Carr. Three months before his death on September 27, 1981 at the age of seventy-seven, Anderson granted an interview to the authors. In his conversation, he asserted that, despite being part of the grand jury staff, he had not been aware that grand jury funds had been used to support Charlie Hemans. Furthermore, he claimed that he and Sigler were convinced that Frank McKay put up the money to have Hooper murdered, but while they believed there was enough evidence to cause the arrest of the Grand Rapids politician, there was not enough to assure his conviction.

LELAND W. CARR, a graduate of Eastern Michigan University and the University of Michigan Law School, served as Ingham County Circuit Judge from 1921 until joining the State Supreme Court in 1945. After serving two years as Chief Justice, he retired from the state's highest court in December 1963, disappointed that President Dwight D. Eisenhower had overlooked him for a seat on the nation's highest tribunal. He continued to practice law in Lansing until his death, at the age of eighty-five, on Memorial Day, 1969.

LOUIS COASH, of Saginaw, graduated from Alma College and the University of Detroit Law School. Moving to Lansing in 1938, he practiced law with the firm of Haight and Coash until ascending to the Municipal Court in April 1941 at the age of thirty-seven. Known more for his calm demeanor and mastery of judging human nature than for exper-tise in the technicalities of law, Coash had been on the Ingham County Circuit Court for less than a year when he was named Carr's successor as grand juror. He remained on the Circuit Court bench until suffering a fatal heart attack on March 28, 1968.

RICHARD B. FOSTER, a graduate of the University of Michigan Law School, served as Ingham County Prosecutor from 1939 until his resigna-tion on July 1, 1942 when he enlisted in the United States Army Air Corps. He served in the judge advocate general's department and was released from active duty, at the rank of major, in October 1945. He resumed practicing law in his hometown of Lansing and held the position of grand jury prosecutor from March 12, 1946 until the dissolution of that body in 1953. As of this writing, he is senior partner in the Lansing law firm of Foster, Swift, Collins, and Smith. He had known Charles Hemans for years as a lawyer and had high regard for his legal skills and honesty; based on this, Foster remained convinced that Hemans was telling the truth regarding his lobbying activities. Foster further stated to the authors in an interview that he knew Sigler had rewarded all state witnesses not necessarily with monetary payments, but with positions at companies such as Ford and General Motors.

CHARLES FITCH HEMANS was working for the Butzel law firm in Detroit when one of the firm's client's became interested in a bill pending before the state legislature. Hemans was sent to Lansing to influence the measure's defeat, and while there, in the words of Kenneth McCormick, "came to love the gay life of entertaining prominent state office holders" and decided to become a full-time lobbyist. After serving his sentence at Lewisburg Federal Penitentiary, he married for the third time and spent the remainder of his life as an antique dealer, expert glassblower, and contractor, building homes on a portion of his Aurelius farm which he turned into a residential subdivision. At the time of his fatal heart attack on January 29, 1971, the seventy-four year old Hemans resided in Eaton Rapids, where he was regarded as a model citizen and neighbor.

HARRY F. KELLY, a graduate of the University of Notre Dame Law School, enlisted in the army the day after the United States declared war on Germany in 1917. He earned the Croix de Guerre, the Purple Heart, and the Distinguished Service Cross for his valor, but he also lost his left leg as a result of wounds incurred on the battlefield at Chateau-Thierry. After serving four years as assistant Wayne County Prosecutor, during which time he was named special prosecutor for the twenty-three man grand jury investigating the gangland slaying of Detroit radio commentator Jerry Buckley, in 1935 he was appointed by Governor Frank Fitzgerald as manager of the Detroit office of the State Liquor Control Commission. In 1938 and 1940 he was elected Michigan's Secretary of State, and in 1942 defeated Democratic incumbent Murray D. VanWagoner to begin the first of two terms as Michigan's chief executive. After stepping down in 1946, he returned to private practice, but took an active role in the 1948 intraparty revolt to help Democrat G. Mennen Williams oust Kim Sigler, whom he and other conservatives deemed too liberal. In 1950 Kelly sought to regain the governorship, but was narrowly defeated. Two years later he was elected to the Michigan Supreme Court, where he served until his retirement in January, 1971. On February 8, 1971 he suffered a massive stroke and died at the age of seventy-five.

FRANK D. MCKAY continued to exert covert influence on the state Republican scene until the mid-1950s. He masterminded the defeat of Sigler in 1948 by urging conservative Republicans to stay away from the polls. His plans to recapture the governorship for the G.O.P. failed, however, when his conservative candidates, including Harry Kelly, with whom he had mended his political fences, Fred Alger Jr., and Donald S. Leonard, could not unseat the popular liberal G. Mennen Williams. McKay died January 12, 1965, at the age of eighty-one, at his Miami Beach residence. In his will he established an annuity trust to The University of Michigan for the creation of the Frank D. and Agnes C. McKay Medical Research Foundation. In an obituary, Kenneth McCormick of the *Detroit Free Press* wrote: "McKay always went out of his way to tell you the good things he had done for the underprivileged and to insist on his straight-laced conduct." His papers, housed at The University of Michigan, attest to this, as they contain virtually nothing but congratulatory messages on his legal triumphs, plus letters and newspaper accounts of his philanthropic activities.

WILLIAM H. MCKEIGHAN, elected mayor of Flint for the first of five non-consecutive terms in 1915 at the age of twenty-nine, was one of the most colorful, and most often indicted, politicians in Michigan's history. Between 1915 and 1920 he was charged with violating the local option law, vote fraud, and conspiring to violate prohibition statutes, but was acquitted in each instance. In 1918 he was convicted of assault and robbery and sentenced by Circuit Judge Edward Black to two to fourteen years at the Ionia Reformatory. After one week behind bars he was released when the state supreme court permitted him to post bond pending an appeal. Two years later his conviction was overturned when the supreme court ruled that Judge Black had improperly charged the jury. McKeighan later boasted that during his brief prison stint he had dined daily in the warden's house and slept in his guest room. Despite his questionable record, he was re-elected mayor of Flint in 1922, 1927, 1931, and 1932, but failed in two tries to be elected Genesee County sheriff. A maverick with a silver tongue, he chose to enter the 1932 G.O.P. primary against incumbent Governor Wilber M. Brucker, running on a platform of abolishing prohibition, the state property tax, the State Police, and the Public Utilities Commission, while establishing a state sales tax and a system of old age pensions, but was soundly trounced. Along with Frank D. McKay and Detroit attorney Edward Barnard, McKeighan controlled Republican politics in Michigan for nearly two decades. Along with McKay he was indicted by both the federal government and the Ingham County grand jury for conspiracy to violate state liquor laws, but was acquitted. In 1946 after being indicted by a Macomb County grand jury on gambling conspiracy charges, McKeighan took up residence in Miami and fought extradition for eight years. Finally, in 1954 "to get things over with" he returned to stand trial before Circuit Judge Edward T. Kane. After a stormy trial, the charges were dropped for lack of evidence, but not before Kane told the smirking defendant: "The Divine Power will give you your just desserts. In society you cannot hold your head up any more than a worm that crawls out from under a log." On September 15, 1971, at the age of seventy-one McKeighan succumbed to the effects of a third stroke, dying before he could complete his dream of constructing a $7,000,000 hotel in Miami Beach.

HERBERT C. RUSHTON attended the University of Michigan and received his law degree in 1907 in the state of Washington. In 1908 he returned to Michigan and set up practice in Menominee County, specializing in corporate law. Moving to Escanaba a few years later, he served twenty-one years as city attorney as well as being elected Delta County Prosecutor. A vice president of the Escanaba National Bank, Rushton was sent to the state senate for three terms (1927-1933) and then voluntarily retired to private life. An avid lover of horse racing, Rushton was a familiar figure at tracks throughout the state and became acquainted with major promoters of the "Sport of Kings," including Floyd Fitzsimmons. In May 1940 Governor Dickinson appointed him Director of the State board of Tax Administration, which position he held until being elected in November of that year as attorney general. Choosing not to seek re-election for a third term in 1946, he again returned to private practice in Escanaba, where he died on December 11, 1947 at the age of seventy.

KIM SIGLER served two turbulent years as governor, expending most of his energy ferreting out criminals and suspected communists in the state. Known to his legal adversaries as a master psychologist who deftly could play on the weakness of witnesses, once in politics all of Sigler's flaws were put to public scrutiny. His flashiness, egotism, short temper, and apparent disdain for the average citizen combined to wear thin on voters, as did his constant complaint that being Michigan's chief executive was a "crummy job" because there were too many legal restrictions on his ability to act on issues. As his frustration mounted, he spent more time flying his airplane and less in Lansing, which made him increasingly susceptible to criticism from both his own party and the opposition. After his crushing 160,000 vote defeat in 1948, Sigler entered private law practice, and while he never ran again for office he maintained that he intended to solve the Hooper murder case, which would instantly catapult him back into the limelight. A daring pilot who had flown as far as the southern tip of Chile and past the rim of the Arctic Circle, the fifty-nine year old former state idol was returning to Lansing on November 30, 1953 from a business trip to Louisiana when he crashed his plane into a recently erected, fog-shrouded television transmitter tower northwest of Battle Creek. Sigler, his longtime personal secretary and reputed mistress Ruth Prentice, and two other passengers perished instantly in the ensuing inferno. Guy H. Jenkins, Capitol correspondent for the Booth newspapers and a critic of Sigler, came forth with the most accurate description of the late governor: "Kim Sigler was one of a kind. He will always be remembered as the political skyrocket of Michigan. He went sky high, spewing brilliantly colored sparks all the way, and then quickly faded out."

JOHN SIMPSON, born in 1891, worked his way through high school, Albion College, and the University of Michigan Law School, receiving his degree from the latter in 1919. In 1920 he acted as a Police Judge and the following year was elected Jackson County Prosecutor, a post he relinquished after his election to the state legislature in 1926. After serving one term in Lansing, he returned to private practice, but Governor Fred W. Green shortly thereafter appointed the thirty-eight year old Simpson to the Jackson County Circuit Court, making him the youngest man in Michigan's history, to that date, ever to serve in that capacity. Known as a stern, no-nonsense jurist who believed in a strict adherence

231

to the letter of the law, Simpson's refusal to permit his courtroom to become "a three-ring circus" greatly inhibited the flamboyant Sigler's theatrical endeavors to convict McKay and McKeighan on liquor conspiracy charges. After stepping down from the bench, Simpson resided in Jackson until his death, caused by a cerebral hemorrhage, on April 3, 1975.

MURRAY D. VANWAGONER, regarded at the time as a conservative Democrat, was elected State Highway Commissioner in 1933, and during his seven-year tenure became known for establishing the first roadside park in the nation. In 1940 he defeated aged incumbent Republican Governor Luren Dickinson in a most unusual race which saw the G.O.P. candidate not only refuse to campaign, but actually urge the electorate not to vote for him. Two years later, VanWagoner lost the governorship to Harry F. Kelly, and then in 1946 he was again defeated in a gubernatorial race, this time by Kim Sigler. In 1950 VanWagoner, affectionately known to his friends as "Pat," was appointed to fill a one-year vacancy on the University of Michigan Board of Regents and also to be a member of the Mackinac Bridge Authority, serving on the latter until his death on June 12, 1986 at the age of eighty-eight.

Chapter 1 - Notes

1. *Flint Journal*, 24 August 1943.
2. *Detroit Free Press*, 7 August 1939; *Detroit Free Press*, 29 April 1941.
3. *Detroit Free Press*, 13 August 1939; *Detroit Free Press*, 15 August 1939; *Detroit Free Press*, 18 August 1939; *Detroit Free Press*, 20 August 1939. Ferguson immediately sought guidance from New York Governor Thomas E. Dewey, himself a former crime-busting prosecutor, but all Dewey could impart was his preference for the twenty-three man grand jury system used in New York, saying: "It's mighty hard to deceive twenty-three men sitting around a table" (*Detroit Free Press*, 22 August 1939).
4. *Detroit Free Press*, 22 February 1940.
5. *Detroit Free Press*, 29 April 1941.
6. Ibid.
7. *Detroit Free Press*, 29 April 1941.
8. *Detroit Free Press*, 15 April 1941.
9. *Detroit Free Press*, 3 April 1941.
10. Ibid.
11. Ibid.
12. *Detroit Free Press*, 22 April 1941.
13. Ibid.
14. "Removal Proceedings of Duncan McCrea, Wayne County Prosecutor," Records of the Attorney General Office, Criminal Law, Accession No. 59-16, Box 8, Book XXVI, pp. 4144, 4146, State Archives of Michigan, Bureau of History, Department of State.
15. *Detroit Free Press*, 25 April 1941.
16. *Detroit Free Press*, 16 April 1941.
17. Ibid.
18. *Detroit Free Press*, 27 April 1941.
19. *Detroit Free Press*, 29 April 1941. Only Charles Moceri was acquitted. Following the trial one of the female jurors, Mrs. Alma Mulligan, was outspoken regarding the role of women in the legal system. "Women are too emotional and sentimental to act as agents of justice," she contended. "Men are much better able to determine facts and weigh them in evidence" (*Detroit Free Press*, 29 April 1941). Interestingly, later in the trials involving graft, Kim Sigler, conscious of his suave manner and

handsome features, purposely sought to have as many women as possible as jurors in hopes that they might succumb to his arguments more readily than men.

20. *Detroit Free Press*, 26 April 1941.
21. Ibid.
22. *Detroit Free Press*, 29 April 1941.
23. *Flint Journal*, 14 August 1943.
24. *Flint Journal*, 17 August 1943.
25. Ibid.
26. *Michigan State Digest*, 19 August 1943.
27. Ibid.
28. *Flint Journal*, 19 August 1943.
29. *Detroit Free Press*, 14 September 1943.
30. *Battle Creek Enquirer*, 21 July 1946.
31. *Michigan State Digest*, 14 May 1942.
32. *Flint Journal*, 23 August 1943.
33. Ibid. Rushton's first two appointees as special prosecutors were Democrats John D. Voelker, who later served on the Michigan Supreme Court and achieved fame under the pen-name Robert Traver for writing *Anatomy of a Murder*, and Dean W. Kelly, president of the State Bar Association of Michigan.
34. Interview with Al Kaufman, 24 February 1984.
35. Interview with Don Gardner, 19 November 1982.
36. *Flint Journal*, 30 August 1943.
37. Ibid.
38. *Michigan State Digest*, 2 September 1943.
39. Ibid. Former *Detroit Times* reporter Don Gardner concurred with Goodwin, and stated that Stenson's story "had to be a lie because his vote wasn't worth $500. He didn't serve on any committees that would have anything to do with reporting out a banking bill. Why he concocted this story, I don't know. Maybe somebody put the money in the wrong coat pocket" (Gardner interview, 19 November 1982). Both Gardner and Goodwin proved to have the proper assessment of Stenson's character, as on May 13, 1944 Stenson was named by Judge Carr in a perjury warrant for recanting his story of receiving money to influence his vote on the anti-chain bank bill. When asked by reporters about his earlier testimony about "a man in a gray coat" stuffing money in his overcoat pocket, Stenson angrily denied ever saying such a thing happened. "I don't know anything about this," he sputtered. "It's a frame-up. That's all I can think of. My conscience is clear" (*Detroit Free Press*, 14 May 1944; *Flint Journal*, 14 May 1944).
40. *Flint Journal*, 13 September 1943; *Detroit Free Press*, 14 September 1943.
41. *Flint Journal*, 14 September 1943.

42. *Flint Journal*, 13 September 1943; *Detroit Free Press*, 14 September 1943.
43. *Detroit Free Press*, 14 September 1943.
44. *Flint Journal*, 23 September 1943.
45. Ibid.
46. *Flint Journal*, 27 September 1943.
47. *The People of the State of Michigan vs. William J. Burns*, Ingham County Circuit Court, Docket Number 4423, 6 (hereafter referred to as *Burns*).
48. Ibid., 8.
49. Ibid., 9.
50. Ibid., 64-67.
51. *Detroit Free Press*, 1 December 1943.
52. Ibid.; *Detroit News*, 1 December 1943.
53. *Detroit Free Press*, 1 December 1943; *Detroit News*, 1 December 1943; *Ingham County News*, 2 December 1943.
54. *Ingham County News*, 2 December 1943.
55. Ibid.; *Flint Journal*, 2 December 1943. Although serving in the legislature was considered a full-time position, it was not uncommon for members to hold part-time jobs, especially during periods of adjournment, to supplement their meager state salaries.
56. *Ingham County News*, 2 December 1943; *Flint Journal*, 4 December 1943; *Detroit Free Press*, 4 December 1943.
57. *Detroit News*, 4 December 1943.
58. Ibid.
59. *Flint Journal*, 10 December 1943; *Detroit News*, 10 December 1943.
60. *Detroit News*, 10 December 1943.
61. Ibid.
62. *Ingham County News*, 2 December 1943.
63. Ibid.
64. *Detroit News*, 10 December 1943.
65. *Ingham County News*, 23 December 1943.
66. *Flint Journal*, 26 November 1943.
67. Ibid.
68. *Detroit Free Press*, 8 December 1943; *Flint Journal*, 9 December 1943.
69. *Flint Journal*, 8 December 1943; *Ingham County News*, 9 December 1943. The *Free Press* assertion was not without basis, as on September 28 the attorney general had proclaimed "virtual completion" of the grand jury's work.
70. *Detroit Free Press*, 11 September 1943.
71. *Flint Journal*, 8 December 1943; *Flint Journal*, 9 December 1943. Linsey admitted handling "two small matters for McKay" and added that he was "glad to work for him because he always paid a good fee on time" (*Flint Journal*, 9 December 1943).

72. *Flint Journal*, 8 December 1943.
73. Ibid.
74. *Detroit Free Press*, 17 November 1963.
75. *Detroit Free Press*, 13 January 1965; Frank B. Woodford, *Alex J. Groesbeck* (Detroit: Wayne State University Press, 1962), 245-51. Ironically, the *Detroit Free Press*, which would be McKay's most bitter enemy, supported him in his anti-Groesbeck campaign because it believed the Governor's road building program would benefit outstate residents more than those in Detroit.
76. *Detroit Free Press*, 17 November 1963.
77. *Detroit Free Press*, 18 January 1965.
78. Ibid.; Dr. Willard B. VerMeulen interview taken by Dr. Thomas F. Soapes, 26 January 1980, Gerald R. Ford Presidential Library, Ann Arbor, Michigan. Dr. VerMeulen was a leader in the Grand Rapids "Home Front" movement, which opposed McKay.
79. *Detroit Free Press*, 13 January 1965; *New York Times*, 13 November 1940; *New York Times*, 28 November 1940; *Newsweek*, 9 December 1940; *New York Times*, 13 July 1941; *Michigan State Digest*, 28 May 1942. On May 29, 1942, McKay wrote H. S. Babcock, editor of the Alma, Michigan *Recorder*, "I am advised they spent between 1.5 and 2 million dollars in attempting to satisfy the whims of a certain gentleman in Washington who was disappointed in a Michigan election." Four days later, he penned a note to a Grand Rapids friend, Burt Decker, in which he described his trial as a "federal farce" (Frank D. McKay Papers, Michigan Historical Collections, Bentley Historical Library, The University of Michigan, Ann Arbor, Michigan).
80. *Detroit Free Press*, 17 November 1963.
81. *Flint Journal*, 11 December 1943; *Flint Journal*, 12 December 1943.
82. *Flint Journal*, 17 December 1943; *Ingham County News*, 23 December 1943.
83. *Flint Journal*, 13 December 1943.
84. *Flint Journal*, 14 December 1943.
85. Ibid.
86. Ibid.; "Biographical Sketch of Kim Sigler," 1946, Biography File, Library of Michigan, Lansing, Michigan; Interview with Richard B. Foster, 30 September 1982.
87. *Flint Journal*, 14 December 1943; *Detroit News*, 15 December 1943. Sigler told Ken McCormick of the *Free Press* that he was taking the job "because it sounds like too much fun to turn down" (Frank Angelo, *On Guard: A History of the Detroit Free Press* [Detroit: Detroit Free Press, 1981], 191).
88. *Flint Journal*, 14 December 1943.
89. *Detroit News*, 15 December 1943.

90. *Newsweek*, 24 February 1947; *Lansing State Journal*, 2 December 1953; *Grand Rapids Press*, 3 July 1954; *Detroit Free Press*, 15 February 1959; *Lansing State Journal*, 29 November 1963; Interview with Victor C. Anderson, 4 June 1981.

91. Kim Sigler to William R. Cook, 2 May 1944, Cook Papers, Michigan Historical Collections, Bentley Historical Library, University of Michigan, Ann Arbor.

92. Kim Sigler to William R. Cook, 25 December 1943, Cook Papers, Michigan Historical Collections, Bentley Historical Library, University of Michigan, Ann Arbor. Sigler's altruism was short-lived as in his 2 May 1944 letter to Cook he referred to his press conferences and completion of a series of photographic sessions with Carr.

93. Kim Sigler to William R. Cook, Cook Papers, Michigan Historical Collections, Bentley Historical Library, University of Michigan, Ann Arbor.

94. Kim Sigler to William R. Cook, Cook Papers, Michigan Historical Collections, Bentley Historical Library, University of Michigan, Ann Arbor; Angelo, *On Guard*, 191.

95. *Detroit Times*, 21 December 1943.

96. Ibid.

97. Ibid.; *Ingham County News*, 23 December 1943.

98. *Detroit News*, 21 December 1943. Despite a reputation for honesty, Rushton committed some questionable acts. For example, before hiring Dalton as a $400 per month grand jury investigator, in mid-June 1943 at an angry press conference he fired Dalton from serving as his chief clerk, at a $3,800 annual salary, after discovering he had been serving as a go-between for distilling company agents seeking to sell $2,500,000 of whiskey to the state (*Michigan State Digest*, 17 June 1943; *Detroit News*, 21 December 1943).

99. *Flint Journal*, 22 December 1943; *Detroit Times*, 22 December 1943; *Detroit Times*, 23 December 1943; *Detroit News*, 27 December 1943; Gardner interview, 19 November 1982. Following Dalton's dismissal, the Office of Price Administration announced it was considering a probe to determine if the McKay trip was a violation of gas rationing laws. Also, William P. Lovett, whose complaints had launched the grand jury probe, began a series of public statements charging Rushton with trying to sabotage the grand jury to protect his friends.

100. *Detroit Times*, 21 December 1943; *Detroit Times*, 22 December 1943.

101. *Ingham County News*, 23 December 1943.

102. *Ingham County News*, 30 December 1943; *Detroit News*, 31 January 1944.

103. *Detroit Times*, 26 December 1943.

104. Ibid.

105. *Detroit Times*, 2 January 1944.

106. *Detroit News*, 4 January 1944.
107. Ibid.
108. *Detroit Times*, 2 January 1944.
109. Ibid.
110. Ibid.
111. *Detroit Times*, 9 January 1944.

Chapter 2 - Notes

1. Ingham County Circuit Court Warrant, 22 January 1944; *Detroit Times*, 23 January 1944; *New York Times*, 23 January 1944; *Ingham County News*, 27 January 1944.
2. *Detroit Times*, 23 January 1944.
3. Ibid.
4. *Detroit Times*, 24 January 1944; *Detroit Times*, 25 January 1944.
5. *Detroit Times*, 24 January 1944.
6. *Ingham County News*, 27 January 1944.
7. *Detroit Times*, 25 January 1944.
8. *Flint Journal*, 25 January 1944.
9. Ibid.
10. Ibid.; *Detroit Times*, 24 January 1944; *New York Times*, 25 January 1944.
11. *Detroit Times*, 28 January 1944; *New York Times*, 25 January 1944.
12. *New York Times*, 25 January 1944.
13. Ibid.
14. Ibid.
15. Ibid.
16. Ibid.
17. Ibid.
18. Ibid.
19. *Kalamazoo Gazette*, 30 January 1944; *Detroit Times*, 30 January 1944; *Flint Journal*, 30 January 1944.
20. *Flint Journal*, 30 January 1944; *Report of the Michigan State Senate Investigating Sub-Committee*, 5 March 1946, Guy H. Jenkins Papers, Michigan Historical Collections, Bentley Historical Library, The University of Michigan., Ann Arbor, Michigan.
21. *Detroit Times*, 2 February 1944; *Ingham County News*, 3 February 1944.
22. *Detroit Times*, 2 February 1944.
23. Ibid.
24. *Report of the Michigan State Senate Investigating Sub-Committee*, 5 March 1946.
25. *Lansing State Journal*, 28 February 1944.
26. *Detroit Times*, 27 January 1944.

27. *Flint Journal*, 25 January 1944; *Lansing State Journal*, 28 January 1944.
28. *Lansing State Journal*, 28 January 1944.
29. Ibid.
30. Ibid.
31. Ibid. Companies cited as making deposits into Hancock's account included: Citizens Loan and Investment Company of Lansing, Citizens Investment Company of Flint, Citizens Budget Company of Monroe, Saginaw Financing Corporation, Citizens Loan and Investment Corporation of Saginaw, Grand Rapids Investment Company, T.H. Bird and Company of Ypsilanti, Fidelity Corporation of Grand Rapids, Liberty Loan Association of Chicago, National Discount Corporation of South Bend, and Union Investment Corporation, General Finance Corporation, Lloyd Fast Company, McDonald-Robbins Company, and the Contract Purchase Corporation, all of Detroit.
32. Ibid.; *Detroit Times*, 29 January 1944.
33. *Detroit Times*, 28 January 1944; *Detroit Times*, 29 January 1944.
34. *Detroit Free Press*, 1 March 1944.
35. *Flint Journal*, 1 March 1944; *Detroit Times*, 1 March 1944; *Detroit Free Press*, 1 March 1944.
36. *Detroit Free Press*, 1 March 1944; *Detroit Times*, 1 March 1944.
37. *Detroit Times*, 1 March 1944.
38. Ibid.; *Detroit Free Press*, 1 March 1944.
39. *Detroit Times*, 2 March 1944.
40. *Detroit Free Press*, 2 March 1944.
41. *Detroit Free Press*, 3 March 1944.
42. *Detroit Times*, 3 March 1944.
43. Ibid.; *Detroit Free Press*, 3 March 3 1944.
44. *Flint Journal*, 3 March 1944; *Detroit Times*, 4 March 1944; *Detroit Free Press*, 4 March 1944.
45. *Detroit Times*, 2 March 1944.
46. Gardner interview, 19 November 1982. Gardner recalled asking Hemans what it took to become a successful lobbyist, and got the following reply: "It takes a sense of humor, a cast iron stomach, and an understanding wife.
47. Gardner interview, 19 November 1982
48. *Detroit Free Press*, 16 March 1958.
49. *The People of the State of Michigan Versus John Hancock, et al.*, Ingham County Circuit Court, Docket 7813.
50. *Report of the Michigan State Senate Investigating Sub-Committee*, 5 March 1946.
51. Ibid.
52. Ibid.
53. *Michigan State Digest*, 13 March 1946.

54. *Detroit Times*, 2 March 1944; *Detroit Times*, 5 March 1944.
55. *Flint Journal*, 3 March 1944.
56. *Flint Journal*, 5 March 1944; *Detroit Times*, 5 March 1944.
57. *Detroit Free Press*, 5 March 1944; *Detroit Times*, 5 March 1944; *Flint Journal*, 5 March 1944; *Newsweek*, 20 March 1944.
58. *Detroit Times*, 5 March 1944; *Detroit Free Press*, 5 March 1944.
59. Ibid.
60. *Flint Journal*, 5 March 1944; *Detroit Free Press*, 5 March 1944; *Detroit Times*, 5 March 1944; *Lansing State Journal*, 5 March 1944.
61. *Lansing State Journal*, 5 March 1944; *Detroit Times*, 5 March 1944.
62. *Detroit Times*, 5 March 1944.
63. Ibid.; *Detroit Free Press*, 7 March 1944.
64. *Detroit Free Press*, 7 March 1944.
65. Ibid.; *Flint Journal*, 6 March 1944.
66. *Detroit Free Press*, 6 March 1944.
67. *Detroit Free Press*, 7 March 1944; *Detroit Times*, 7 March 1944.
68. *Ingham County News*, 9 March 1944.
69. *Detroit Times*, 5 March 1944; *Detroit Times*, 7 March 1944.
70. *Detroit Times*, 7 March 1944.
71. Ibid. This view was shared by Carl M. Saunder, editor of the *Jackson Citizen-Patriot*, who, on 8 March 1944, wrote Booth Newspaper Capitol correspondent Guy H. Jenkins: "You kept telling me how rotten everything was in the legislature, but I never suspected that the market had gone down to the point where votes could be bought for fifty dollars" (Guy H. Jenkins Papers, Michigan Historical Collections, Bentley Historical Library, The University of Michigan, Ann Arbor, Michigan).
72. *Detroit Free Press*, 6 March 1944.
73. *Detroit Times*, 8 March 1944; *Detroit Free Press*, 8 March 1944; *Flint Journal*, 8 March 1944.
74. *Detroit Times*, 8 March 1944.
75. Ibid.; *Flint Journal*, 8 March 1944.
76. *Detroit Free Press*, 12 March 1944.
77. *Detroit Free Press*, 8 March 1944; Gardner interview, 19 November 1982.
78. *Detroit Times*, 9 March 1944.
79. *Michigan State Digest*, 9 March 1944.
80. *Ingham County Circuit Court Warrant*, 2 May 1944; *Detroit Times*, 2 May 1944; *New York Times*, 2 May 1944.
81. *Detroit Times*, 2 May 1944.
82. *Detroit Free Press*, 16 May 1944; *Detroit Times*, 16 May 1944; *Flint Journal*, 19 May 1944. The hearing on the second finance case was held in late-May and early-June 1944. Although Judge Carr bound the defendants over for trial, he set no court date and no trial was held.
83. *Detroit Times*, 17 May 1944; *Flint Journal*, 17 May 1944; *Ingham County News*, 18 May 1944. It is not coincidental that the announcement

of the liquor probe marked the first of many calls for the dissolution of the grand jury by the *Michigan State Digest*, whose editor, Edwin Goodwin, was a staunch ally of Frank McKay (*Michigan State Digest*, 18 May 1944).

84. *Ingham County Circuit Court Warrant*, 3 June 1944; *Detroit Times*, 3 June 1944.
85. *Detroit Times*, 4 June 1944.
86. *Detroit Times*, 6 June 1944; *Michigan State Digest*, 8 June 1944.
87. *Detroit Times*, 7 June 1944; *New York Times*, 8 June 1944.
88. *Detroit Times*, 5 June 1944.
89. Ibid.
90. *Michigan State Digest*, 8 June 1944.
91. *Detroit Times*, 11 June 1944.
92. Ibid.
93. *Detroit Times*, 18 June 1944. The jurors were: Mrs. Esther Jones, Aurelius Township; Mrs. Mattie LeMunion, Leslie Township; Mrs. Mabel V. Graham, Lansing; Mrs. Florence E. Hughes, Mason; Mrs. Florence Wilcox, White Oak Township; Cleyo Sanders, Aurelius Township; Mrs. Viva Lantis, Lansing; Nathan E. Allen, Lansing; Mrs. Grace Beduhn, LeRoy Township; Mrs. Ethel Haynes, Ingham Township; and Mrs. Pearl Smith, Lansing.
94. *Ingham County News*, 22 June 1944.
95. *Detroit Times*, 20 June 1944; *Detroit Times*, 22 June 1944.
96. *Ingham County News*, 22 June 1944.
97. *Ingham County News*, 6 July 1944.
98. *Detroit Times*, 8 July 1944.
99. *Ingham County News*, 13 July 1944.
100. *Detroit Times*, 12 July 1944; *Ingham County News*, 13 July 1944.
101. *Lansing State Journal*, 11 July 1944.
102. Ibid.
103. Ibid; *Detroit Times*, 14 July 1944.
104. *Lansing State Journal*, 11 July 1944.
105. *Detroit Times*, 12 July 1944.
106. *Detroit Times*, 14 July 1944.
107. *Detroit Times*, 12 July 1944.
108. *Detroit Times*, 16 July 1944; Al Kaufman Interview, 24 February 1984.
109. *Detroit Times*, 16 July 1944.
110. *Detroit Times*, 21 July 1944.
111. *Detroit News*, 21 July 1944.
112. Ibid.; *Detroit Times*, 21 July 1944.
113. *Detroit Times*, 21 July 1944.
114. Ibid.
115. Ibid.; *Ingham County News*, 27 July 1944.
116. *Ingham County News*, 27 July 1944.

117. Ibid.
118. Ibid.
119. *Detroit Times*, 28 July 1944.
120. *Detroit Times*, 27 July 1944.
121. Ibid.
122. *Detroit News*, 8 August 1944.
123. *Ingham County News*, 10 August 1944.
124. Ibid.
125. Ibid.
126. *Detroit News*, 9 August 1944.
127. Ibid.
128. Ibid.
129. Ibid.; *Ingham County News*, 10 August 1944.
130. *Detroit News*, 9 August 1944.
131. Ibid.
132. *Ingham County News*, 10 August 1944. Al Kaufman disagreed with this characterization of Cooper, saying that the financier was "a nice guy, but dumb" (Kaufman interview, 24 February 1984).
133. Ibid; *Detroit News*, 9 August 1944.
134. *Ingham County News*, 10 August 1944.
135. *Detroit News*, 11 August 1944.
136. *Ingham County News*, 17 August 1944.
137. *Detroit News*, 11 August 1944; *Ingham County News*, 17 August 1944.
138. *Ingham County News*, 17 August 1944.
139. Ibid.
140. Ibid.
141. Ibid.
142. *Detroit News*, 11 August 1944.
143. *Ingham County News*, 17 August 1944.
144. Ibid.; *Detroit News*, 11 August 1944.
145. *Ingham County News*, 17 August 1944.
146. Ibid.
147. Ibid.
148. Ibid.
149. *Detroit News*, 14 August 1944.
150. Ibid.
151. Ibid.
152. Ibid.
153. Ibid.
154. *Ingham County News*, 17 August 1944.
155. *Hastings Banner*, 17 August 1944.
156. *Ingham County News*, 17 August 1944.
157. Kaufman Interview, 24 February 1984.

Chapter 3 - Notes

1. *Ingham County News*, 16 November 1944.
2. *Ingham County News*, 30 November 1944.
3. *Battle Creek Enquirer*, 11 January 1959; Statement of Callienetta Hooper to Kim Sigler, Oscar G. Olander, and Harold Mulbar, 26 January 1945, Attorney General Records, Criminal Division, 105-07, pp. 13-15.
4. Statement of Callienetta Hooper to Kim Sigler, Oscar G. Olander, and Harold Mulbar, 26 January 1945, Attorney General Records, Criminal Division, 105-07, pp. 16-18.
5. Ibid., p. 20; Interview with Betty Keys (the Hooper's regular babysitter), 26 August 1984; Interview with George V. Mather (editor of the *Albion Evening Recorder* during Hooper's years in that city), 21 August 1984; Statement of Callienetta Hooper, 26 January 1945.
6. *Burns*, 20.
7. Mather interview, 21 August 1984. Mather noted that he "didn't imagine Warren did much to dissociate himself with those stories."
8. Will Muller-Al Nieber Confidential Memo to Fred Gaertner, Michigan State Police Records, 22 January 1945.
9. *Detroit News*, 16 March 1946.
10. Muller-Neiber Memo, 22 January 1945.
11. Ibid.
12. Transcript of Testimony of Warren G. Hooper, 14 November 1944. Michigan State Police Records.
13. Ibid., 5-8.
14. Ibid., 8-9.
15. Ibid., 10.
16. Ibid., 11.
17. Ibid.; Mrs. Wickens later testified that she did not hear any of the conversation between Hooper and Fitzsimmons (Statement of Agnes Wickens to Kim Sigler, Oscar G. Olander, William Hansen, and Lyle Morse, 13 January 1945, Attorney General Records, Criminal Division, 17).
18. Transcript of Testimony of Warren G. Hooper, 14 November 1944, p. 12.
19. Ibid., pp. 13-16.
20. Transcript of Testimony of Warren G. Hooper Before Kim Sigler and Victor C. Anderson, 15 November 1944, Michigan State Police Records.
21. Transcript of Testimony of Warren G. Hooper Before Kim Sigler, 15 November 1944, Michigan State Police Records.
22. Ibid.
23. Transcript of the Examination of Harry Fleisher, et al., May 15, 1945 conducted before the Honorable William H. Bibbings, Justice of the

Peace in and for the County of Calhoun, State of Michigan, at the Circuit Court Room, City Hall, Battle Creek, Michigan, pp. 15-16, 21 (hereafter referred to as Examination Transcript).

24. Muller-Nieber Memo, 22 January 1945.

25. Statement of Callienetta Hooper to Kim Sigler, et al., 26 January 1945, Attorney General Records, Criminal Division, pp. 46-54.

26. Statement of Callienetta Hooper to Kim Sigler, et al., 16 January 1945, Attorney General Records, Criminal Division, pp. 33-36; Statement of Callienetta Hooper, 26 January 1945, pp. 50-54.

27. *Ingham County Circuit Court Warrant*, 2 December 1944; *Detroit Free Press*, 4 December 1944.

28. *Detroit Free Press*, 3 December 1944; *Detroit News*, 3 December 1944.

29. *Detroit News*, 3 December 1944.

30. *Detroit Free Press*, 3 December 1944.

31. Ibid.; *Detroit News*, 3 December 1944.

32. *Ingham County Circuit Court Warrant*, 8 December 1944.

33. *Michigan State Digest*, 13 December 1944; *Detroit Free Press*, 15 December 1944.

34. *Michigan State Digest*, 13 December 1944.

35. *Michigan State Digest*, 25 April 1945.

36. Ibid.

37. Statement of Louis Brown, Inmate #48529-J, to Kim Sigler, et al., with handwritten notes by State Police Commissioner Donald S. Leonard, Donald S. Leonard Papers, Box 19, Bently Historical Library, University of Michigan, Ann Arbor, Michigan. A detailed analysis of the conspiracy, the actual murder, and the court trials which followed may be found in Bruce A. Rubenstein and Lawrence E. Ziewacz, *Three Bullets Sealed His Lips* (East Lansing: Michigan State University Press, 1987).

38. Rubenstein and Ziewacz, *Three Bullets Sealed His Lips*.

39. Ibid.

40. Ibid.

41. Examination Transcript, 148-52.

42. Ibid., 152-53.

43. Ibid., 154-55.

44. Ibid., 244-50.

45. Ibid., 251.

46. Ibid., 254-56.

47. Rubenstein and Ziewacz, *Three Bullets Sealed His Lips*, 195-99. Of the two bullets recovered, the coroner located one in Hooper's neck and the other in his shoulder.

48. *Detroit Times*, 13 January 1945.

49. Ibid.; *Detroit News*, 12 January 1945.

50. Muller-Nieber Memo, 22 January 1945.

51. Ibid.
52. Ibid.
53. *Detroit Times*, 13 January 1945.
54. Ibid.
55. McKay hired many Purple Gang members as bodyguards, most notably Charles Leiter and Isador Schwartz.
56. *Detroit News*, 13 January 1945; *Albion Evening Recorder*, 13 January 1945.

Chapter 4 - Notes

1. *Detroit Free Press*, 18 December 1944; *Detroit Times*, 18 December 1944.
2. *Detroit Times*, 18 December 1944; *Detroit Free Press*, 29 December 1944.
3. *Detroit Times*, 18 December 1944; *Detroit Free Press*, 19 December 1944.
4. *Detroit Free Press*, 19 December 1944.
5. Ibid.
6. *Albion Evening Recorder*, 29 January 1945.
7. Ibid.
8. Ibid.; *Detroit Times*, 30 January 1945.
9. *Flint Journal*, 30 January 1945; *Detroit Free Press*, 30 January 1945.
10. *Detroit Free Press*, 30 January 1945.
11. Ibid.
12. *The People of the State of Michigan versus Floyd Fitzsimmons*, Docket 9019, Ingham County Circuit Court (hereafter referred to as *Fitzsimmons*); *Ingham County News*, 1 February 1945.
13. *Fitzsimmons*.
14. Ibid.; *Detroit News*, 1 February 1945.
15. *Detroit News*, 1 February 1945.
16. Ibid.; *Fitzsimmons*.
17. *Battle Creek Enquirer*, 2 February 1945.
18. *Fitzsimmons*; *Detroit Times*, 1 February 1945; *Detroit News*, 1 February 1945.
19. *Detroit Times*, 1 February 1945; *Detroit News*, 1 February 1945.
20. *Fitzsimmons*; *Detroit News*, 1 February 1945; *Detroit Times*, 1 February 1945.
21. *Fitzsimmons*; *Detroit Times*, 1 February 1945; *Detroit Times*, 1 February 1945; *Albion Evening Recorder*, 1 February 1945; *Battle Creek Enquirer*, 1 February 1945.
22. *Battle Creek Enquirer*, 1 February 1945; *Detroit News*, 1 February 1945; *Fitzsimmons*.
23. *Fitzsimmons*; *Battle Creek Enquirer*, 1 February 1945; *Detroit News*, 1 February 1945.

24. *Albion Evening Recorder*, 1 February 1945; *Battle Creek Enquirer*, 1 February 1945; *Detroit Times*, 2 February 1945. Handy claimed that he "had never seen DeRosa" but did not deny making the threat (*Flint Journal*, 31 January 1945).

25. *Detroit Free Press*, 2 February 1945.

26. *Albion Evening Recorder*, 1 February 1945; *Detroit Free Press*, 2 February 1945; *Flint Journal*, 2 February 1945; *Detroit Times*, 2 February 1945.

27. *Detroit News*, 1 February 1945; *Albion Evening Recorder*, 1 February 1945; *Albion Evening Recorder*, 2 February 1945; *Detroit Times*, 2 February 1945; *Flint Journal*, 2 February 1945.

28. *Flint Journal*, 2 February 1945.

29. Ibid.; *Detroit Free Press*, 2 February 1945.

30. *Detroit Free Press*, 2 February 1945.

31. *Albion Evening Recorder*, 2 February 1945.

32. *New York Times*, 2 February 1945; *Flint Journal*, 2 February 1945; *Detroit Times*, 3 February 1945.

33. *New York Times*, 2 February 1945.

Chapter 5 - Notes

1. *Ingham County Circuit Court Warrant*, 10 February 1945.

2. *Flint Journal*, 11 February 1945.

3. Ibid.

4. Ibid.

5. *Michigan State Digest*, 14 February 1945.

6. *Flint Journal*, 16 February 1945.

7. Ibid.; *Albion Evening Recorder*, 16 February 1945; *Detroit Times*, 17 February 1945.

8. *Detroit Times*, 17 February 1945.

9. *Albion Evening Recorder*, 16 February 1945.

10. Ibid.; *Albion Evening Recorder*, 22 February 1945.

11. *People of the State of Michigan versus E. J. Chamberlain, et al.*, Docket 8066, Ingham County Circuit Court, 127-28 (hereafter referred to as *Chamberlain*).

12. *Chamberlain*, 129-32.

13. *Detroit Times*, 17 February 1945.

14. Ibid.

15. *Chamberlain*, 134.

16. *Detroit Times*, 18 February 1945; *Chamberlain*, 229.

17. *Albion Evening Recorder*, 17 February 1945; *Detroit Times*, 18 February 1945; *Chamberlain*, 229.

18. *Chamberlain*, 223. Of course, since Barnard was a powerful political figure, and because the Olds Hotel was a gathering site for many legislators, there is nothing sinister about his presence at the hotel.

19. *Chamberlain*, 228-32; *Albion Evening Recorder*, 17 February 1945; *Detroit Times*, 18 February 1945.

20. *Detroit Times*, 18 February 1945; *Chamberlain*, 234-38.

21. *Chamberlain*, 240-41; *Detroit Times*, 18 February 1945.

22. *Detroit Times*, 18 February 1945.

23. Ibid.

24. *Albion Evening Recorder*, 17 February 1945; *Detroit Times*, 18 February 1945.

25. *Detroit Times*, 18 February 1945.

26. *Chamberlain*, 258-71.

27. *Chamberlain*, 274; *Detroit Times*, 18 February 1945.

28. *Detroit Times*, 18 February 1945.

29. *Michigan State Digest*, 21 February 1945.

30. *Detroit Times*, 22 February 1945.

31. Ibid.

32. *Chamberlain*, 299-300.

33. Ibid., 300-3.

34. Ibid., 304-5.

35. *Chamberlain*, 330-32.

36. Ibid., 332.

37. Ibid., 333-37; *Detroit Times*, 22 February 1945.

38. *Chamberlain*, 374.

39. Ibid., 400-1.

40. Ibid., 405-9.

41. Ibid., 409-11.

42. Ibid., 411-12.

43. Ibid., 472-75.

44. *Albion Evening Recorder*, 23 February 1945.

45. *Flint Journal*, 23 February 1945.

46. *Chamberlain*, Sentence of Clarence J. Wright and M. S. DeViliers by Circuit Judge Louis E. Coash, 8 December 1948.

47. Walter H. Taylor to Henry W. Jackson, November 1, 1951, Attorney General Records, 68-28-11-7. Another of the defendants, Senator Stephen Benzie died of a heart attack on 19 April 1945.

Chapter 6 - Notes

1. *Ingham County Circuit Court Warrant*, 6 December 1944. Naturopathy is a form of treatment utilizing herbs, vitamins, salts, and manipulation. In 1939 and 1941, when regulatory legislation was intro-

duced to legalize the practice, approximately 95 percent of Michigan's naturopaths were chiropractors.

2. *Detroit Free Press*, 7 December 1944.
3. Gardner interview, 19 November 1982.
4. *Detroit Free Press*, 7 December 1944; *Detroit Free Press*, 9 December 1944.
5. *Detroit Free Press*, 9 December 1944.
6. Ibid. Sigler stated that he became suspicious of Howell because the Senator had been protesting his innocence too strongly (*Detroit News*, 16 March 1946).
7. *Michigan State Digest*, 20 December 1944.
8. *Detroit Free Press*, 9 December 1944.
9. *Michigan State Digest*, 7 February 1945.
10. *Ingham County News*, 7 December 1944.
11. *Detroit Free Press*, 13 January 1945.
12. *Detroit Times*, 12 December 1944.
13. Ibid.; *Detroit Free Press*, 14 January 1945; *Albion Evening Recorder*, 14 January 1945; *Detroit Times*, 16 January 1945; *Hastings Banner*, 18 January 1945.
14. *Detroit Free Press*, 26 December 1944.
15. *Detroit Times*, 13 January 1945.
16. *Flint Journal*, 12 January 1945.
17. *Detroit Times*, 22 December 1944; *Detroit Free Press*, 22 December 1944.
18. *New York Times*, 28 January 1945; *Detroit Free Press*, 30 January 1945.
19. *Detroit Free Press*, 23 December 1944.
20. *Albion Evening Recorder*, 15 February 1945; *Albion Evening Recorder*, 20 February 1945.
21. *Flint Journal*, 26 February 1945; *Detroit Times*, 27 February 1945; *Albion Evening Recorder*, 27 February 1945; *Ingham County News*, 1 March 1945.
22. *Flint Journal*, 26 February 1945; *Albion Evening Recorder*, 27 February 1945.
23. *Albion Evening Recorder*, 27 February 1945.
24. *Detroit News*, 2 March 1945; *Albion Evening Recorder*, 2 March 1945.
25. *Detroit News*, 2 March 1945.
26. *Albion Evening Recorder*, 6 March 1945; *Detroit News*, 6 March 1945.
27. Ibid.
28. *Detroit News*, 6 March 1945.
29. Ibid.; *Albion Evening Recorder*, 7 March 1945 .
30. *The People of the State of Michigan versus Mikhel Sherman, et al.*, Docket 8043, Ingham County Circuit Court, 20-30, 40 (hereafter referred to as *Sherman*).

31. Ibid., 53-55.
32. Ibid., 60.
33. Ibid., 62.
34. Ibid., 67-69.
35. Ibid., 70.
36. Ibid., 70-71.
37. Ibid., 101-4; *Albion Evening Recorder*, 7 March 1945.
38. Gladys B. Pike to Governor Harry F. Kelly, 1 December 1943, Harry F. Kelly Papers, File 42, State of Michigan Archives.
39. *Sherman*, 106-7.
40. *Albion Evening Recorder*, 8 March 1945.
41. Ibid.; *Sherman*, 119, 175.
42. *Sherman*, 579-80.
43. Ibid., 633-34.
44. *Detroit News*, 11 March 1945.
45. Ibid.
46. Ibid.; *Sherman*, 673-74.
47. *Albion Evening Recorder*, 13 March 1945.
48. *Albion Evening Recorder*, 12 March 1945; *Detroit Free Press*, 14 March 1945.
49. *Detroit Free Press*, 15 March 1945; *Detroit Free Press*, 16 March 1945. The jurors were: Mrs. Juanita Stone, Mrs. Fern Wellington, Mrs. Imogene Barr, John Warner, Mrs. Lucille Avery, Roy Rusch, Mrs. Nora DeLashmut, Roy Wilson, Mrs. Kathryn Richner, Kenneth Squires, O. E. Ames, and Mrs. Genevieve Hefty.
50. *Detroit Free Press*, 16 March 1945.
51. *Albion Evening Recorder*, 15 March 1945.
52. Ibid.
53. Ibid.
54. *Grand Rapids Press*, 20-22 March 1945; *Detroit Free Press*, 25 March 1945.
55. *Michigan State Digest*, 11 April 1945.
56. *Flint Journal*, 19 April 1945.
57. Ibid.
58. *Flint Journal*, 20 April 1945.
59. Ibid.
60. Ibid.
61. Ibid.
62. *Detroit Times*, 20 April 1945.
63. *Battle Creek Enquirer*, 21 April 1945. Sigler mistakenly listed Schenley as a "Democrat." He meant to say Seagram's.
64. Ibid.
65. Ibid.
66. *Detroit News*, 23 April 1945.

67. *Detroit News*, 24 April 1945.
68. Ibid.
69. *Detroit News*, 25 April 1945.
70. Ibid.
71. Ibid.; *Flint Journal*, 26 April 1945.
72. *Detroit News*, 25 April 1945.
73. Ibid.

Chapter 7 - Notes

1. *Ingham County News*, 7 June 1945.
2. Ibid.; *Detroit Free Press*, 5 June 1945.
3. *Ingham County News*, 7 June 1945.
4. *Michigan State Digest*, 6 June 1945.
5. *Ingham County News*, 7 June 1945; *Detroit Free Press*, 5 June 1945.
6. *Detroit Free Press*, 5 June 1945.
7. *Ingham County News*, 7 June 1945.
8. *Detroit Times*, 6 June 1945; *Ingham County News*, 7 June 1945.
9. *Ingham County News*, 7 June 1945.
10. Ibid.; *Detroit Times*, 6 June 1945; *People of the State of Michigan vs. Jerry T. Logie and Charles C. Diggs*, Ingham County Circuit Court, Docket 8105 (hereafter referred to as *Logie*).
11. *Ingham County News*, 7 June 1945.
12. *Detroit Times*, 6 June 1945.
13. Ibid.; *Ingham County News*, 7 June 1945; *Logie*.
14. *Detroit Times*, 6 June 1945; *Detroit Times*, 7 June 1945.
15. *Detroit Times*, 7 June 1945.
16. *Ingham County News*, 7 June 1945.
17. *Detroit Times*, 7 June 1945. Don Gardner, who after leaving the newspaper scene worked as lobbyist for the Detroit Race Course, recalled that Sigler's assertion was correct. "The wires from the betting booths to tally the take went into the ground, period. The Detroit Racing Association was booking the bets themselves. The state never got a dime out of it" (Gardner interview, 19 November 1982).
18. *Detroit Times*, 7 June 1945.
19. *Ingham County News*, 7 June 1945.
20. Ibid.; *Detroit Times*, 7 June 1945.
21. *Detroit Free Press*, 7 June 1945.
22. *Logie*.
23. Ibid.
24. Ibid.
25. *Detroit Times*, 8 June 1945; *Detroit Free Press*, 8 June 1945.

Chapter 8 - Notes

1. *Battle Creek Enquirer*, 27 June 1945.
2. Ibid.
3. *Grand Rapids Press*, 27 August 1945.
4. *Grand Rapids Press*, 28 August 1945.
5. *Detroit Free Press*, 28 August 1945; *Detroit Free Press*, 1 September 1945.
6. *Grand Rapids Press*, 27 August 1945; *Grand Rapids Press*, 28 August 1945.
7. *Grand Rapids Press*, 27 August 1945.
8. Ibid.
9. Ibid; *Detroit Free Press*, 28 August 1945.
10. *Detroit Free Press*, 28 August 1945.
11. Ibid; *Grand Rapids Press*, 28 August 1945.
12. *Grand Rapids Press*, 28 August 1945; *Detroit Free Press*, August 29, 1945; *Detroit Times*, 1 September 1945.
13. *Detroit Free Press*, 23 August 1945; *Hastings Banner*, 30 August 1945.
14. *Hastings Banner*, 30 August 1945.
15. Ibid.
16. Ibid.
17. *Grand Rapids Press*, 28 August 1945.
18. *Grand Rapids Press*, 1 September 1945.
19. *Detroit Free Press*, August 29, 1945.
20. *Albion Evening Recorder*, 32 August 1945; *Grand Rapids Press*, 4 September 1945.
21. *Grand Rapids Press*, 31 August 1945; *Detroit Free Press*, 1 September 1945.
22. *Grand Rapids Press*, 31 August 1945.
23. *Detroit Free Press*, 2 September 1945; *Detroit Times*, 3 September 1945.
24. Don Gardner interview, 19 November 1982.
25. *Detroit Times*, 7 September 1945.
26. *Michigan State Digest*, 5 September 1945.
27. *Grand Rapids Press*, 6 September 1945.
28. Ibid; *Albion Evening Recorder*, 6 September 1945.
29. *Grand Rapids Press*, 6 September 1945.
30. Ibid.
31. Ibid.
32. Ibid.
33. Ibid.
34. Ibid; *Detroit Free Press*, 6 September 1945; *Albion Evening Recorder*, 6 September 1945.
35. *Grand Rapids Press*, 6 September 1945; *Detroit Free Press*, 6

September 1945; *Albion Evening Recorder*, 6 September 1945; *Detroit Times*, 7 September 1945.

36. *Grand Rapids Press*, 6 September 1945.

37. *Detroit Free Press*, 8 September 1945; *Detroit Times*, 8 September 1945; *Michigan State Digest*, 12 September 1945.

38. *Albion Evening Recorder*, 20 September 1945.

39. *Detroit Times*, 26 September 1945; *Michigan State Digest*, 26 September 1945; Richard B. Foster interview, 30 September 1982; Marvin J. Salmon interview, 14 October 1982.

40. Richard B. Foster interview, 30 September 1982; Marvin J. Salmon interview, 14 October 1982; Al Kaufman interview, 24 February 1984.

41. *Michigan State Digest*, 2 January 1946.

42. Ibid.

43. *Grand Rapids Press*, 10 January 1946; *Detroit Free Press*, 11 January 1946.

44. Ibid.

45. *Detroit Free Press*, 11 January 1946.

46. *Detroit Free Press*, 12 January 1946.

47. *Detroit Free Press*, 11 January 1946.

48. *Grand Rapids Press*, 10 January 1946; *Detroit Free Press*, 11 January 1946.

49. *Battle Creek Enquirer*, 14 January 1946.

50. Ibid; *Detroit Free Press*, 15 January 1946.

51. *Battle Creek Enquirer*, 14 January 1946; *Detroit Free Press*, 15 January 1946.

52. *Detroit Times*, 16 January 1946; *Detroit Times*, 20 January 1946; *Detroit News*, 17 January 1946; *Battle Creek Enquirer*, 20 January 1946.

53. *Detroit News*, 17 January 1946; *Battle Creek Enquirer*, 17 January 1946.

54. *Detroit News*, 17 January 1946.

55. Ibid.

56. *Detroit Times*, 18 January 1946. The jurors were: Archibald C. Martin, retired railroad conductor; Dwight Harr, farmer; Forest Miller, farmer; Clarence Pulver, farmer; Leland Clark, farmer; Fred A. Fletcher, meat market owner; Mrs. Elizabeth S. Burnett; Mrs. Margaret A. Southard; Mrs. Marguerite Probert; Mrs. Mabel Hagadon; Mrs. Kathleen McCurdy; Mrs. J. M. Haag; Mrs. Louise L. Williams; and Mrs. Alice Musolf.

57. Ibid.

58. *Battle Creek Enquirer*, 16-17 January 1946; *Detroit Free Press*, 17 January 1946.

59. Ibid.

60. *Battle Creek Enquirer*, 16 January 1946.

61. Ibid.; *Detroit Free Press*, 17 January 1946.
62. *Battle Creek Enquirer*, 20 January 1946.
63. *Battle Creek Enquirer*, January 19, 1946.
64. *Detroit Times*, 21 January 1946; *Detroit Times*, 22 January 1946.
65. *Detroit Times*, 22 January 1946.
66. Ibid.
67. *Detroit Times*, 22 January 1946.
68. Ibid.
69. Ibid.
70. Ibid.
71. Ibid.
72. Ibid.
73. Ibid.
74. Ibid.
75. *Detroit Times*, 24 January 1946.
76. Ibid.
77. Ibid.
78. Ibid.; *Lansing State Journal*, 24 January 1946.
79. *Lansing State Journal*, 24 January 1946.
80. Ibid.
81. Ibid.; *Battle Creek Enquirer*, 24 January 1946.
82. *Battle Creek Enquirer*, 24 January 1946.
83. *Detroit Times*, 25 January 1946.
84. *Battle Creek Enquirer*, 24 January 1946; *Lansing State Journal*, 24 January 1946.
85. *Battle Creek Enquirer*, 24 January 1946.
86. Ibid.; *Lansing State Journal*, 24 January 1946.
87. *Detroit Times*, 24 January 1946.
88. Ibid.; *Battle Creek Enquirer*, 25 January 1946; *Detroit News*, 25 January 1946.
89. *Battle Creek Enquirer*, 25 January 1946.
90. Ibid.; *Detroit Times*, 25 January 1946.
91. *Battle Creek Enquirer*, 26 January 1946.
92. *Battle Creek Enquirer*, 25 January 1946; *Detroit News*, 26 January 1946.
93. *Detroit News*, 26 January 1946; *Battle Creek Enquirer*, 26 January 1946.
94. *Battle Creek Enquirer*, 26 January 1946.
95. *Detroit Times*, 27 January 1946.
96. *Battle Creek Enquirer*, 3 February 1946.
97. *Battle Creek Enquirer*, 31 January 1946; *Detroit News*, 31 January 1946.
98. *Battle Creek Enquirer*, 31 January 1946.
99. *Detroit News*, 31 January 1946.

100. Ibid.; *Battle Creek Enquirer*, 31 January 1946; *Michigan State Digest*, 30 January 1946.
101. *Detroit News*, 31 January 1946; *Grand Rapids Press*, 1 February 1946.
102. *Detroit News*, 31 January 1946.
103. Ibid.; *Battle Creek Enquirer*, 31 January 1946.
104. *Battle Creek Enquirer*, 31 January 1946; Grand Rapids Press, 1 February 1946.
105. *Grand Rapids Press*, 1 February 1946.
106. Ibid.
107. Ibid.
108. *Detroit News*, 5 February 1946.
109. To show his disdain over Simpson's ruling, Garey interrupted the reading with thirty-seven objections, each of which was overruled (*Detroit News*, 5 February 1946; *Battle Creek Enquirer*, 5 February 1946).
110. *Battle Creek Enquirer*, 5 February 1946; *Detroit News*, 5 February 1946.
111. *Grand Rapids Press*, 1 February 1946; *Battle Creek Enquirer*, 4 February 1946; *Michigan State Digest*, 6 February 1946.
112. *Grand Rapids Press*, 1 February 1946.
113. Ibid.
114. *Battle Creek Enquirer*, 2 February 1946.
115. Ibid.
116. Ibid.
117. Ibid.
118. Ibid. Judge Simpson ruled in Sigler's favor (*Detroit News*, 5 February 1946).
119. *Battle Creek Enquirer*, 2 February 1946.
120. *Battle Creek Enquirer*, 4 February 1946.
121. Ibid.; *Detroit News*, 5 February 1946.
122. *Battle Creek Enquirer*, 5 February 1946; *Detroit News*, 5 February 1946.
123. *Detroit News*, 5 February 1946.
124. *Battle Creek Enquirer*, January 5, 1946.
125. Ibid.
126. Ibid.
127. *Detroit News*, 6 February 1946.
128. Ibid.
129. Ibid.
130. *Detroit News*, 4 February 1946.
131. *Detroit News*, 6 February 1946; *Battle Creek Enquirer*, 11 February 1946.
132. *Battle Creek Enquirer*, 6 February 1946.
133. *Battle Creek Enquirer*, 7 February 1946; *Battle Creek Enquirer*, 11 February 1946.

134. *Battle Creek Enquirer*, 11 February 1946.
135. *Battle Creek Enquirer*, 8 February 1946.
136. Ibid.
137. Ibid.
138. *Battle Creek Enquirer*, 10 February 1946.
139. *Grand Rapids Press*, 9 February 1946.
140. Ibid.; *Battle Creek Enquirer*, 12 February 1946.
141. *Grand Rapids Press*, 9 February 1946.
142. *Battle Creek Enquirer*, 12 February 1946.
143. Ibid.
144. *Grand Rapids Press*, 13 February 1946.
145. Ibid.
146. Ibid.
147. Ibid.
148. *Battle Creek Enquirer*, 13 February 1946.
149. Ibid.
150. Ibid.
151. Ibid.
152. *Battle Creek Enquirer*, 14 February 1946.
153. Ibid.
154. Ibid.
155. Ibid.
156. Ibid.
157. Ibid.
158. Ibid.
159. Ibid.
160. Ibid.
161. *Lansing State Journal*, 14 February 1946.
162. *Battle Creek Enquirer*, 14 February 1946.
163. *Lansing State Journal*, 14 February 1946.
164. *Battle Creek Enquirer*, 14 February 1946.
165. *Lansing State Journal*, 14 February 1946.
166. Ibid.; *Ingham County News*, 21 February 1946.
167. *Michigan State Digest*, 13 February 1946; *Ingham County News*, 21 February 1946.
168. Frank D. McKay to Thomas Burns, 18 February 1946, Frank D. McKay Papers, Bentley Historical Library, The University of Michigan, Ann Arbor, Michigan.
169. Frank D. McKay to William B. Brown, 18 February 1946, Frank D. McKay Papers, Bentley Historical Library, The University of Michigan, Ann Arbor, Michigan.
170. Frank D. McKay to J. B. Whilley, 18 February 1946, Frank D. McKay Papers, Bentley Historical Library, The University of Michigan, Ann Arbor, Michigan. It is possible that McKay's influence was instrumental

in denying Carr that which the jurist most desired—a nomination to the United States Supreme Court from President Dwight D. Eisenhower.

171. Frank K. McKay to Leah Wilson, 19 February 1946, Frank D. McKay Papers, Bentley Historical Library, The University of Michigan, Ann Arbor, Michigan. McKay was not the only financial loser, as the trial cost Michigan's taxpayers more than $300,000 (*Detroit News*, 10 February 1946).

172. *Hastings Banner*, 21 February 1946.

173. *Cheboygan Observer* in *Hastings Banner*, 28 February 1946.

174. *Ingham County News*, 21 February 1946.

175. *Deckerville Recorder* in *Hastings Banner*, 28 February 1946.

Chapter 9 - Notes

1. *Battle Creek Enquirer*, 15 February 1946. Perhaps some of the public support for the probe had been generated by the $150,000 price tag placed on the McKay trial. Kendrick Kimball set forth the details in a 10 February 1946 *Detroit News* article: "Cost to the state goes back many months. Drawing liberally from the $400,000 appropriation voted to the grand jury by the legislature, Kim Sigler, special prosecutor, spared no expense to collect evidence against McKay, McKeighan, and the three men named with them in the conspiracy indictment. The examination last July was long and expensive. Thousands of pages of testimony were taken and transcribed at the cost to the defendants of 85 cents a page, and about that for the state, which got two copies under the contract agreement. Witness fees and expenses were paid and expenses of investigators had to be met. There were two special hearings in the case at Mason and half a dozen Supreme Court appearances. All were costly. Sigler gets $100 a day in expenses. He has three aides. All are on the grand jury payroll. Most of the investigating has been done by State Troopers, who have been paid by the State Police. But the grand jury must pay their hotel and living costs and automobile and gasoline bills.".

2. *Battle Creek Enquirer*, 16 February 1946.

3. Ibid.

4. Ibid.; *Diary of Murl Defoe*, 19 February 1946 (hereafter referred to as *Defoe Diary*).

5. *Defoe Diary*, 19 February 1946.

6. Ibid.

7. *Battle Creek Enquirer*, 26 February 1946.

8. *Michigan State Digest*, 27 February 1946.

9. *Detroit News*, 28 February 1946.

10. Ibid.

11. *Lansing State Journal*, 27 February 1946.
12. Ibid.
13. Ibid.
14. Ibid.
15. Ibid.; *Michigan State Digest*, 27 February 1946.
16. *Lansing State Journal*, 27 February 1946.
17. Ibid.
18. Ibid.
19. *Detroit News*, 28 February 1946.
20. Ibid.
21. *Detroit News*, 3 March 1946.
22. *Battle Creek Enquirer*, 3 March 1946.
23. Ibid.
24. Ibid. Sigler's allegations against Johnston were echoed in a letter to the Senator from the Men's Club of the St. Clair Shores First Methodist Church, in which that body urged the Macomb lawmaker to resign. "Your activity as chairman of the Senate committee does not by the widest stretch of the imagination reflect the wishes of the vast majority of Macomb citizens, especially those who elected you to the Senate. In view of your record of law enforcement in Macomb County, it is our belief that the motives back of your committee's investigation are those of fear and revenge. We believe the only applause you and your committee will receive will come from the vicious vice operator, the gambler, and that most despicable of all, the bribe-taking public official now serving his term in prison or trembling in fear at the prospect" (*Battle Creek Enquirer*, 4 March 1946).
25. *Battle Creek Enquirer*, 3 March 1946.
26. Ibid.; *Flint Journal*, 4 March 1946.
27. *Battle Creek Enquirer*, 3 March 1946.
28. Ibid.
29. *Flint Journal*, 5 March 1946.
30. Ibid.; *Battle Creek Enquirer*, 5 March 1946.
31. *Battle Creek Enquirer*, 5 March 1946.
32. Ibid.
33. *Flint Journal*, 5 March 1946.
34. Ibid.
35. Ibid.; *Battle Creek Enquirer*, 6 March 1946. Foster later recalled that "it wasn't the smartest thing" when Coash "told the State Police to take his [Hemans'] God damn clothes and take them home" (Foster interview, 30 September 1982).
36. *Flint Journal*, 5 March 1946.
37. *Battle Creek Enquirer*, 6 March 1946; *Detroit News*, 7 March 1946.
38. *Detroit News*, 7 March 1946.
39. Ibid.

40. *Flint Journal*, 8 March 1946.
41. Foster interview, 30 September 1982.
42. *Lansing State Journal*, 9 March 1946.
43. Ibid.
44. *Flint Journal*, 10 March 1946.
45. *Lansing State Journal*, 12 March 1946.
46. Ibid.; *Flint Journal*, 12 March 1946; *Flint Journal*, 13 March 1946; *Battle Creek Enquirer*, 14 March 1946.
47. *Flint Journal*, 12 March 1946.
48. *Battle Creek Enquirer*, 13 March 1946.
49. *Hastings Banner*, 13 March 1946.
50. *Lapeer County Press*, 13 March 1946.
51. *Detroit Free Press*, 13 March 1946.
52. *Grand Rapids Press*, 14 March 1946.
53. *Ingham County News*, 14 March 1946.
54. *Michigan State Digest*, 13 March 1946.
55. *Detroit News*, 23 March 1946.
56. *Battle Creek Enquirer*, 21 March 1946.
57. Ibid.
58. *Michigan State Digest*, 27 March 1946.
59. *Detroit News*, 23 March 1946; *Battle Creek Enquirer*, 25 March 1946.
60. *Detroit News*, 27 April 1946; *Michigan State Digest*, 8 May 1946; *Detroit News*, 21 May 1946.
61. *Flint Journal*, 4 June 1946.
62. *Battle Creek Enquirer*, 5 June 1946; *Flint Journal*, 8 June 1946. The convicted gangsters were Harry Fleisher, Mike Selik, Pete Mahoney, Sam Chivas, and William "Candy" Davidson, all of whom had been implicated in the Hooper assassination plot.
63. *Battle Creek Enquirer*, 13 June 1946. Despite lengthy investigation and trial, Johnston never was convicted on any charge.
64. *Michigan State Digest*, 3 July 1946.

Chapter 10 - Notes

1. *Battle Creek Enquirer*, 21 July 1946; *Battle Creek Enquirer*, 22 July 1946; *Lansing State Journal*, 21 July 1946.
2. Ibid. A defense of Stoddard is offered in Richard D. Poll, *Howard J. Stoddard: Founder, Michigan National Bank* (East Lansing: Michigan State University Press, 1980), 115-29.
3. *Battle Creek Enquirer*, 23 July 1946.
4. *Battle Creek Enquirer*, 21 July 1946.
5. *Flint Journal*, 23 July 1946.
6. *Flint Journal*, 26 July 1946.

7. *Flint Journal*, 21 July 1946. In its 24 July 1946 edition, the *Michigan State Digest* ran an editorial by Nelson Brown which portrayed Sigler as being so paranoid that he did not even trust the local justice of the peace in Mason to issue warrants in the bank case because he felt "Frank McKay might be hiding between the bookcase and the safe right behind the big stack of papers in the magistrate's office." Brown added that shortly before Sigler was removed as special prosecutor, he (Brown) asked Victor Anderson when the bank case warrants would be issued. Anderson replied: "I don't know. Honestly, I don't think there is any bank case ready. There has been no progress in weeks." In Brown's own *Ingham County News*, a scathing editorial claimed that "no man in Michigan has done more to undermine the courts than Sigler. But people are beginning to catch on. Many of them now know that Judge Coash, instead of sabotaging the grand jury as was charged by Sigler, was trying to carry out his duties as grand juror [by removing Sigler in order to bring the bank case to trial]" (*Ingham County News*, July 25, 1946).

8. *Battle Creek Enquirer*, 22 July 1946. VanWagoner knew that Ballard was engaged in a conflict of interest of questionable legality. Foster recalled: "We subpoenaed his books and records, and we found instances where he would make a charge against the Michigan National Bank for a conference between him and Murray VanWagoner at the Capitol when he was acting as his legal advisor. It was wrong, and we talked with VanWagoner about it. Hell, VanWagoner once said to me that he never knew which hat Ballard was wearing when he talked to him—that of legal advisor or attorney for Michigan National" (Foster interview, 30 September 1982). VanWagoner steadfastly refused to admit that anything improper happened during his term. In 1982, he wrote: "I was not aware of any corruption in the Michigan legislature" (Murray D. VanWagoner to Bruce A. Rubenstein, 3 September 1982).

9. *Detroit Free Press*, 23 July 1946; *Detroit News*, 23 July 1946.

10. *Detroit Times*, 23 July 1946.

11. *Flint Journal*, 23 July 1946.

12. *Ingham County News*, 5 September 1946.

13. *Detroit News*, 9 September 1946.

14. Ibid.

15. Ibid.

16. Ibid.

17. Ibid. Foster always believed that Hemans had been bought off. "I think he was paid. I can't prove it and never could prove it, and we tried our damndest. He, Charlie Bohn, Howard Stoddard, Denny DenUyl, they were people different from some poor little old legislator. I think he had a different sense of honor, I guess, for people of position or reputation than he did for others. He told me, 'I'll never testify against those guys. They're friends of mine'" (Foster interview, 30 September 1982).

18. *Detroit Times*, 19 September 1946; *Battle Creek Enquirer*, 11 September 1946. Foster later admitted that "I said that, but it was a bit of wishful thinking." Foster interview, 30 September 1982.
19. *Lansing State Journal*, 12 September 1946.
20. Ibid.
21. *Battle Creek Enquirer*, 14 September 1946.
22. Ibid.
23. *Battle Creek Enquirer*, 16 September 1946.
24. Ibid.
25. Ibid.
26. Ibid.
27. *Battle Creek Enquirer*, 17 September 1946.
28. Ibid.
29. Ibid.
30. Ibid.
31. Ibid.
32. Ibid.
33. *Battle Creek Enquirer*, 18 September 1946.
34. Ibid.
35. Ibid.; *Detroit Free Press*, 25 September 1946.
36. *Battle Creek Enquirer*, 18 September 1946.
37. *Battle Creek Enquirer*, 19 September 1946.
38. Ibid.
39. *Detroit Free Press*, 24 September 1946; *Ingham County News*, 26 September 1946.
40. *Detroit Free Press*, 24 September 1946.
41. *Michigan State Digest*, 25 September 1946; *Ingham County News*, 26 September 1946.
42. Ibid.; *Battle Creek Enquirer*, 25 September 1946.
43. *Battle Creek Enquirer*, 26 September 1946.
44. *Detroit Free Press*, 2 October 1946.
45. *Battle Creek Enquirer*, 3 October 1946.
46. *Detroit News*, 4 October 1946. Sigler was very sensitive about his link with Michigan National Bank. Don Gardner of the *Detroit Times* remembered getting a tip about Sigler's background and going to Battle Creek and Hastings to check on it. While there he discovered that Sigler had provided legal counsel for Michigan National Bank. When Gardner returned to Lansing, he was slapped with a summons to appear before Judge Carr and Sigler, who quizzed him about whom he spoke to and information he had learned in his background check of the Special Prosecutor. Carr leaned over to him after the interrogation had concluded, Gardner stated, and said: "Son, I'm very disappointed in you. Why have you been trying to discredit the grand jury?" When Gardner replied he was merely carrying out an assignment from his city editor,

Carr cut him off. "Be that as it may, you are under orders not to reveal anything you've testified about here today or I'll put you in jail" (Gardner interview, 19 November 1982; *Lansing State Journal*, 11 July 1976).

47. *Detroit Free Press*, 4 October 1946.
48. Ibid.
49. *Detroit Free Press*, 3 October 1946.
50. *Detroit Free Press*, 5 October 1946.
51. *Detroit Free Press*, 2 October 1946; *Detroit Free Press*, 12 October 1946; *Battle Creek Enquirer*, 27 October 1946.
52. *Battle Creek Enquirer*, 2 October 1946.
53. *Detroit Free Press*, 3 October 1946.
54. *Battle Creek Enquirer*, 4 October 1946.
55. *Battle Creek Enquirer*, 8 October 1946.
56. Ibid.
57. *Battle Creek Enquirer*, 9 October 1946.
58. *Battle Creek Enquirer*, 11 October 1946.
59. Ibid. Blondy, who had been sentenced to sixty days in jail by Judge Carr for contempt of court in September 1943, achieved somewhat legendary status among his constituents. The maverick Democrat served from 1940 to 1964 and was once chosen Minority Leader of the State Senate.
60. Ibid.
61. *Battle Creek Enquirer*, 16 October 1946; *Detroit Free Press*, 18 October 1946; *Detroit Free Press*, 14 November 1946.
62. *Detroit Free Press*, 18 October 1946.
63. Ibid.
64. *Battle Creek Enquirer*, 18 October 1946.
65. *Detroit Free Press*, 18 October 1946.
66. Ibid.
67. *Battle Creek Enquirer*, 10 December 1946.
68. Ibid.
69. Ibid.
70. *Battle Creek Enquirer*, 12 December 1946.
71. Ibid.
72. Foster interview, 30 September 1982.
73. *Battle Creek Enquirer*, 6 January 1947.
74. *Battle Creek Enquirer*, 3 January 1947.
75. *Detroit Free Press*, 4 January 1947. McCormick revealed the extent of his intimacy with Sigler in a *Free Press* article of 2 December 1953: "I first met Sigler on 13 December 1943 after he had accepted his assignment as special graft grand jury prosecutor. For nearly three years we had our meals together. We took long walks at night to talk over progress of the grand jury. I got to know Kim as few persons have.".

76. *Grand Rapids Press*, 3 October 1953; Rubenstein and Ziewacz, *Three Bullets Sealed His Lips*, 187.
77. *Detroit Times*, 1 February 1947.
78. Ibid.
79. *New York Times*, 19 March 1947.
80. *Michigan State Digest*, 8 October 1947.
81. *Detroit Free Press*, 11 November 1947.
82. *Detroit Free Press*, 15 November 1947.
83. *Michigan Tradesman*, 15 October 1947.
84. Ibid.
85. Ibid.
86. Ibid.
87. Ibid.
88. Ibid.
89. Ibid. This plot was hatched because Brewer had died in February 1943 and could not be called to testify.
90. Ibid. Foster always maintained that Hemans was telling the truth (Foster interview, 30 September 1982).
91. *Michigan State Digest*, 7 April 1948.
92. Ibid.
93. *New York Times*, 20 April 1948.
94. *Detroit News*, 15 June 1948.
95. *Kalamazoo Gazette*, 28 May 1948. Dr. Sherman died a prisoner on 1 June 1949.
96. *Detroit News*, 30 November 1948. Howell died, at the age of eighty-one, on 8 May 1965.
97. *Detroit News*, 10 December 1948.
98. *Detroit News*, 6 January 1949.
99. *Detroit News*, 13 January 1949.
100. *Detroit News*, 14 February 1949. On 22 August 1952 DeLano died as a result of another stroke.
101. Ibid.
102. Ibid.
103. *Detroit News*, 5 November 1949.
104. *Detroit News*, 25 September 1950.
105. Ibid.
106. Ibid.
107. *Detroit News*, 26 September 1950; *Detroit News*, 21 October 1950; *Detroit News*, 15 September 1951.
108. *Detroit News*, 10 April 1951.
109. *Detroit News*, 11 April 1941. Hemans' life continued to follow a somewhat stormy path. His wife divorced him in late 1951, charging that he had been "involuntarily absent" from their home from late 1946 until September 1949, when he was in Lewisburg State Penitentiary. In 1958

he petitioned for reinstatement to the Michigan Bar, but withdrew the request before it was acted on. He lived the remainder of his life on what was left of his family farm running an antique business.

110. *Detroit News*, 29 April 1952.
111. *Michigan State Police Supplement Report*, "Ingham County Grand Jury," 27 October 1947; *Lansing State Journal*, 11 July 1976.
112. *Lansing State Journal*, [n.d.], 1957; Foster interview, 30 September 1982.
113. Foster interview, 30 September 1982.

BIBLIOGRAPHIC NOTE

The investigation into legislative graft took us down many paths, some of which led to open doors and others into brick walls. Ironically, one of our greatest advantages—the passage of time, which permits reflection—also proved to be one of our biggest disadvantages, as many of those most knowledgeable about the times had long since died.

Individual personalities and their idiosyncrasies were revealed to us through interviews with persons familiar with the main characters involved in the grand jury era. Former political correspondents Don Gardner and Al Kaufman, former Ingham County prosecutor Victor C. Anderson, retired Ingham County Circuit Judge Marvin Salmon, grand jury special prosecutor Richard B. Foster, and ex-Michigan Supreme Court Justice Eugene F. Black introduced us to the private sides of Kim Sigler, Leland W. Carr, Louis Coash, John Simpson, Herbert Rushton, Frank D. McKay, and others who passed through the Lansing scene. Gertrude Ludwick, who worked in the Ingham County Clerk's office during the 1940s, recounted the excitement generated by the grand jury trials and helped us locate trial transcripts. Without their aid, our story would have been much less human and more encyclopedic.

Of course, not all our overtures were met with gracious acceptance. Former Governor Murray D. Van Wagoner would not speak with us because, as he stated in his letter of refusal, he "was not aware of any corruption in the Michigan legislature" during the 1940s. Since his lieutenant governor had been indicted for taking bribes, his rationale seemed dubious, but Van Wagoner remained adamant. Likewise, reporter Kenneth McCormick, a Sigler confidante, and former state police trooper Kenneth Templin, who was Sigler's chauffeur, did not respond to our attempts to interview them. Most recalcitrant, however, was Callienetta

Hooper. Despite oft repeated claims that she sought the solution to her husband's killing, Mrs. Hooper not only refused to reply to letters or speak over the telephone, but she would not accept registered mail in which we explained our findings and requested the opportunity to hear her perspectives.

The most informative personal papers were found in the Michigan Historical Collections of The University of Michigan. Among the most useful were those of Donald S. Leonard; Murl F. DeFoe, an ardent Sigler supporter in the state senate; William Cook, editor of the *Hastings Banner* and early political mentor of Kim Sigler; Attorney General John R. Dethmers; and Booth Newspapers Lansing correspondent Guy H. Jenkins, a political foe of Sigler. Unfortunately, the Frank D. McKay collection was of little value as it contained mostly letters of praise for his civic contributions while revealing nothing about his decades of political activism.

Among government documents housed in the Michigan History Division of the State Archives, the most informative were the Records of the Executive Office, Records of the Attorney General-Criminal Law Division, and Records of the Auditor General. Included in these records were letters between Harry F. Kelly, Herbert Rushton, and Leland W. Carr concerning the operation of the grand jury as well as the complete audit of grand jury expenditures.

Published materials, especially newspapers, were extremely helpful. Especially useful were the three Detroit dailies—the *Free Press, News,* and *Times*—because they assigned staff writers to cover every aspect of the investigation and subsequent trials. Other dailies which utilized staff coverage were the *Battle Creek Enquirer, Jackson Citizen Patriot, Grand Rapids Press, Albion Evening Recorder, Lansing State Journal,* and *Chicago Herald-American.* Wire service accounts, supplemented by editorial comment, were selected from the *Flint Journal, Kalamazoo Gazette, Ontonagon Herald, Pontiac Press,* and *Port Huron Times Herald.* These newspapers were chosen because of their circulation and geographic representation. Kim Sigler was lionized in his hometown *Hastings Banner,* while his arch-foe Frank D. McKay was defended vigorously by the *Michigan State Digest.* All the reporters took pride in their accuracy, and when published accounts are compared to the court transcripts, their claims are proven true. Reading the daily newspaper was, in fact, the next best thing to being in the courthouse.

Newspaper stories also provided details unavailable in court transcripts. Reporters detailed everything from the temperature to the clothing of the attorneys and juries to the behavior of the gallery to the facial expressions of witnesses. No movement or sound seemed too insignificant to be mentioned. Consequently, these word pictures, when used in conjunction with photographs and trial records, enabled us to reconstruct courtroom scenes in minute detail.

INDEX

A

Blondy, Charles F., 200, 214, 219, 261n.59
Bloxsom, Paul W., 122
Boggio, Bernard A., 9
Bohn, Charles B., xiii; and anti-chain banking bill trial, 199, 200, 204, 205; and Warren G. Hooper, 82, 90
Bolt, Menso R., 122
Bradley, William F., 36, 51, 65, 107
Brake, D. Hale, 14, 15, 16-17, 57
Bratton, Guy, 37
Brentmeyer, Philip H., 8
Brewer, Joseph, 221, 262n.89
Brown, Abe, 159. *See also*: Leiter, Charles
Brown, Dewey, 145
Brown, Louis, 86, 88
Brown, Nelson, 196, 198, 259n.7
Brown, Vernon J., 196, 198
Brown, William B., 179
Brucker, Wilber M., 230
Buckley, Jerry, 229
Buckley, William G.: and anti-chain banking bill trial, 199, 204, 208; and Charles Hemans, 50, 219; dismissal of charges against, 223; and financing bills investigation, 35, 36, 58, 65; and first naturopathy trial, 119, 128, 131-33, 134; and second naturopathy trial, 135-38
Buhl, Lloyd, 180
Burhans, Earl, 45
Burnett, Elizabeth S., 252n.56
Burns, James A., 106, 199, 219
Burns, William J., 20-21, 77, 129, 218
Bylenga, Harry, 122

C

Callaghan, Miles M.: and Charles Hemans, 45, 50; death of, 122; and financing bills investigation, 36, 39, 40; grand jury payoff of, 190
Carr, Leland W., xiii; appointment as grand juror, 16; appointment to Michigan Supreme Court, 153; and financing bills investigation, 41, 43, 53; and Charles Hemans, 46-47, 67, 186, 187; and Charles Spare, 40; and dental bill investigation, 105, 106, 108, 112, 117; and Don Gardner, 260-261n.46; and Floyd Fitzsimmons trial, 93-94, 96-97; and Frank D. McKay, 148, 255-56n.170; and Herbert J. Rushton, 27-28, 31, 47, 96-97; and investigation of grand jury, 187; and Kim Sigler, 28, 29, 31; life of, 227; and liquor control trial, 147-48, 149-50; and naturopathic bill investigation, 123; and secrecy of grand jury, 24
Chamberlain, Edwin J., 105, 116, 117, 223
Chase, Fred I., 141, 204
Cheboygan Observer, the, 180
Chivas, Sam, 258n.62
Clancy, Michael J., 36, 51
Clark, Dunlap, 207
Clark, Leland, 252n.56
Coash, Louis, xiii; and anti-chain banking bill indictments, 18; and Charles Hemans, 257n.35; and dental bill sentencing, 117; and destruction of grand jury records, 226; and grand jury dissolution, 218, 222, 223; and grand jury funding, 213; and investigation of grand jury, 187, 191; and Kim Sigler, 153, 191-94, 197; life of, 227-28; and liquor control trial, 154
Cobb, Callienetta, 76, 83
Colburn, Harry, 9-11, 12
Comstock, William, 26
Conley, Roy T., 67, 70, 185-86, 188, 189
Cook, Herb, 39. See also: Callaghan, Miles
Cook, William R., 29

270

Cooper, Abraham, 36, 42, 58, 61, 62, 223
Corley, Cecil, 124
Cummins, Charles F., 203

D

Dalton, John, 31, 237n.98
Daniels, Constantine, 140, 141, 142
Davidson, William "Candy", 258n.62
Deckerville Recorder, the, 180
DeFoe, Murl H., 161-64, 176, 184, 198
Dehnke, Herman, 198, 212, 225
DeLano, Carl F., xiii; and anti-chain banking bill trial, 199, 206-7, 209-20, 220; and Charles Hemans, 206-7, 220; commutation of sentence of, 222, 223; death of, 262n.100; and naturopathic bill investigation, 119, 120, 123, 128-30, 133, 134
DeLashmut, Nora, 249n.49
Demmer, Adolph, 42
DeMoss, Orin A., 162, 169, 171
Dempsey, Jack, 98
Dental bill. See House Bill 199
DenUyl, Simon D., xiii; and anti-chain banking bill trial, 199, 205, 206, 210; and Charles Hemans, 210, 219, 220, 221
DeRosa, Thomas, 101
Dethmers, John, 62
Detroit Citizen's League, the, 13
Detroit Free Press, the: and Chester M. Howell, 120; and Frank D. McKay, 24-25, 83, 236n.75; and Kim Sigler, 149, 194-95, 198
Detroit News, the, 149, 196
Detroit Racing Association, the, 139, 142, 250n.17
Detroit Times, the, 54
Deviliers, M. S. "Duke", 105, 106, 114-15, 117
Dewey, Thomas E., 75, 233n.3
Dickinson, Luren, 9, 158, 161, 232

Diggs, Charles C.: and anti-chain banking bill trial, 199; and Charles Hemans, 51, 219; and Charles Spare, 39-40; dismissal of charges against, 223; and financing bills investigation, 36, 51, 58, 61; and naturopathy bill investigation, 128; and pari-mutuel betting bill trial, 139, 140, 141, 143, 145
Dignan, Herman, 143
Dilley, Ronald, 117
Dombrowski, Stanley, 21-23, 24, 35, 44, 50
Doyle, Thurmond B., 211
Duke, Mary, 40, 190. See also: Spare, Charles

E

Earnest, Luella, 42
Elliot, Frederick R., 204
Ellison, Hubert K., 135, 136
Ehrmann, Fred C., 161-62, 164-68, 171, 172, 174, 175, 177
Emergency Appropriation Commission, the, 16
Espie, John, 38

F

Faulkner, Paul, 123, 125, 135
Ferguson, Homer, 8, 199
Financing bills trial, first: jury of, 241n.93; press coverage of, 72-73; pretrial examination, 40-53; trial, 60-71
Fitzgerald, Frank: and Floyd Fitzsimmons, 99; and Frank D. McKay, 26, 157; and Fred C. Ehrmann, 164, 165, 166; and Harry F. Kelly, 229; and the liquor commission, 161
Fitzgerald, George S., 12, 66, 136
Fitzsimmons, Floyd, xiii; charges dropped against, 218; commutation

naturopathy trial, 123, 135, 136, 138; and Warren G. Hooper, 77, 79, 81, 82, 83, 91-92

Grey, Myles F., 205

Groesbeck, Alex, 25, 198

H

Haag, J. M., 252n.56

Hagadorn, Mabel, 252n.56

Haggerty, James, 68, 69

Hamilton, Burritt, 28

Hammel, Godfrey, 159

Hancock, John E., 36, 41, 42, 44, 58, 62, 223, 224

Handy, Gail, 84, 85, 94-96, 101, 246n.24

Harma George O., 200, 208, 225

Harr, Dwight, 252n.56

Hastings Banner, the, 73, 180, 194

Hayden, Charles F., 21-22, 23, 24

Haynes, Alice, 72

Haynes, Ethel, 241n.93

Haynes, Richard, 158-59

Hefty, Genevieve, 249n.49

Hemans, Charles Fitch, xiv; arrest of, 206; black book of, 46, 47, 49, 52-53; and anti-branch banking bill trial, 200, 203-4, 206-8, 212-14, 216, 218-21; and Carl F. DeLano, 206-7, 210; dismissal of charges against, 223; and federal fugitive law trial, 215; and financing bills trial, 48-53, 62, 64, 66-68; and George Harma, 208; hiring as lobbyist, 43; and John E. Hancock, 41, 44; and Kim Sigler, 47-48, 55-56, 57, 203; and Leo J. Wilkowski, 205; life of, 46, 228, 262-63n.109; and Miles Callaghan, 45; payoff of, 47-48, 185-87, 189, 190, 193, 224; press coverage of, 54-58, 120; and Raymond Snow, 208; sentencing of, 225; and Stanley

Dombrowski, 21, 22, 23; and William C. Green, 207; and William C. Stenson, 23-24; and William G. Buckley, 208

Hemans, Lawton T., 46

Hemans, Ruth, 212

Henry, Ernest, 88

Higgins, George N., 18, 80, 139, 207

Hildebrand, Martin, 126, 133, 134

Hooper, Joseph, 76

Hooper, Warren Green, xiv; background of, 75-77; and dental bill investigation, 105-6, 107, 115; and Floyd Fitzsimmons, 77-83, 101; and Frank D. McKay, 77, 79-80, 81, 82, 83; murder of, 88-89, 122, 244n.47; and William J. Burns, 20-21, 77, 80; and William Green, 77, 79, 81, 82, 83

Hooper, William, 76

Hopkins, Samuel, 36, 62, 71

House Bill 22, 80, 84, 139

House Bill 199, 105

Howell, Chester M., xiv; death of, 262n.96; and dental bill investigation, 106, 107, 108-10, 114, 115; and naturopathic bill investigation, 119, 120, 126, 127, 133, 248n.6; and pari-mutuel betting trial, 139, 140, 141-42, 144; press coverage of, 120; sentencing of, 222

Hughes, Florence E., 72, 241n.93

Hull, Ivan, 77

Hunt, Henry, 107

I

Ingham County News, the; and first financing bills trial, 72-73; and grand jury probe, 121-22; and Kim Sigler, 149, 180, 195, 196, 259n.7

Ingham County Press, the, 54

Isbister, Gilbert H., 200, 219

273

J

Jackson, Harry, 86, 88
Jaxtimer, J. P., 106, 107, 108, 110-12, 113
Jeffries, Edward, 197
Jenkins, Guy H., 7, 231, 240n.71
Johnson, Harold, 88
Johnson, Milton, 66
Johnston, Ivan, xiv; indictment of, 198, 258n.63; and investigation of grand jury, 183, 184-85, 187, 188, 189, 190, 193; shady background of, 184, 257n.24
Joint Congressional Pearl Harbor Investigating Committee, the, 199
Jones, Esther, 72, 241n. 93

K

Kane, Edward T., 230
Kaminski, Joseph L., 36, 51, 52
Kaufman, Al, 16, 64, 73, 242n.132
Kelly, Dean W., 234n.33
Kelly, Fred C., 187, 218
Kelly, G. Milton, 135
Kelly, Harry F.: and the anti-chain banking bill, 15; and Frank D. McKay, 27, 62; and Herbert J. Rushton, 25, 62; and Leland W. Carr, 153; life of, 228-29; and Murray D. VanWagoner, 232; and set-up of Ingham County grand jury, 15
Kelly, Raymond J., 197
Keywell, Harry, 3, 86, 88-89
Kimball, Kendrick, 256n.1
Kimmel, Husband E., 199
Kowalski, Joseph Jl, 35, 50, 62, 64, 199, 219
Kronk, Martin A., 35, 36, 50. 65
Kulp, Frank, 211

L

Lantis, Viva, 241n.93
Lapeer County Press, the, 194
Layton, Charles, 160, 218
Layton, Fisher, 151, 160, 161
Lee, Max, 167-68
Leiter, Charles, 150, 158-59, 223, 245n.55
LeMunion, Mattie, 241n.93
Leonard, Donald S., 217-18, 229
Levin, Theodore, 215, 216
Linsey, Jay W., 24-25, 30, 32, 33, 167, 235n.71
Lipsitz, Charles, 160. See also: Layton, Charles
Liquor control trial: cost of, 256n.171, 256n.1; jury of, 252n.56; press coverage of, 180-81
Little Legislature, the, 38, 213-14. *See also*: State Emergency Appropriation Committee, the
Logie, Bessie, 145
Logie, Jerry T.: and Charles Hemans, 52; commutation of sentence of, 223; and first financing bills trial, 36, 65; and pari-mutuel betting bill trial, 139, 140, 141-43, 144, 145
Lovett, William P., 13, 237n.99
Luks, Henry, 86, 87
Lyon, Laurence, 217

M

McCormick, Kenneth: and Charles Hemans, 55, 228; and Francis P. Slattery, 19; and Frank D. McKay, 229; and Kim Sigler, 55, 73, 198, 217, 236n.87; 261n.75; and Stanley Dombrowski, 22
McCrea, Duncan, 8, 9, 10-12, 13
McCurdy, Kathleen, 252n.56
McDonald, Chester B., 135-36
MacDonald, Janet, 8

McDonald, John S., 165, 169
McDonald, Robert J., 183, 188, 189
McElmurray, George, 138
McEwen, Earl, Sr., 200, 219
McGrath, Barney, 9
McGuigan, F. G., 110-11
McGuire, O. R., 215-16
McKay, Frank D., xiv; charges dropped
    against, 218; and Charles Webber,
    169; defeat as Republican National
    Committeeman, 62; and the Detroit
    Free Press, 24-25; and Edwin
    Goodwin, 17, 240-41n.83; and Floyd
    Fitzsimmons, 84, 98, 99, 100; and
    Frank Fitzgerald, 157; and Fred C.
    Ehrmann, 165-66, 174, 175; grand
    jury probes of, 26; and Herbert J.
    Rushton, 33; and Kim Sigler, 148;
    and Leland W. Carr, 148, 179, 255-
    56n.170; life of, 25-27, 229; and
    liquor control trial, 83, 147-81,
    236n.79, 256n.171; and the Purple
    Gang, 245n.55; and Warren G.
    Hooper, 77, 79-80, 81, 82, 83, 86,
    90-91
McKeighan, William, xiv; extradition of,
    212; and Frank D. McKay, 26; and
    Floyd Fitzsimmons, 100, 101; life of,
    229-30; and liquor control trial, 151,
    152, 157, 158; and Charles Layton,
    159, 160
McKinney, Clayton R., 123, 127
McKinney, Harry E., 123
McLaughlin, Robert B., 200, 201
McLean, Charles R., 224, 225
MaDan, George, 185
Mahoney, Pete, 139, 258n.62
Marmon, Ira H., 154, 155
Marshall, Claude, 39, 43, 44-45, 62, 70
Martin, Archibald C., 252n.56
Method, Eugene W., 159
Michigan Bankers' Association, the, 15
Michigan State Dental Society, the, 105,
    110, 113

Michigan State Digest, the: and Charles
    Hemans, 57-58, 120; and Chester M.
    Howell, 120; and D. Hale Brake, 17;
    and dental bill investigation, 106,
    112; and the grand jury, 240-41n.83;
    and Kim Sigler, 195, 259n.7
Millard, R., 47. *See also*: Hemans,
    Charles
Miller, Forest, 252n.56
Moceri, Charles, 233n.19
Mohawk Distillery, the, indictment of,
    59
Morris, Frank, 32
Mulligan, Alma, 233n.19
Munshaw, Earl, 45, 122
Murphy, Francis (Frank), 46, 59-60,
    122, 158
Musolf, Alice, 252n.56

N

Nagel, Ernest G.: and anti-branch banking
    bill trial, 199; and Charles Hemans,
    49-50, 52, 219; and dental bill investi-
    gation, 105, 108, 111-12; dismissal of
    charges against, 223; and financing
    bills investigation, 36, 58, 64
Naturopathy, 247-48n.1
Naturopathy bill, the. *See*: Senate Bill
    269
Naturopathy trial, first, jury of 249n.49
Nelson, Walter, 43, 61, 67-68, 69-70
Nieber, Al, 73, 90, 196, 203
North, Walter, 130
Nowak, Francis J.: and anti-branch
    banking bill trial, 199, 204; and
    Charles Hemans, 44, 51, 64, 219;
    and dental bill investigation, 114;
    dismissal of charges against, 223;
    and financing bills investigation, 35,
    36, 58, 65; and naturopathic bill
    investigation, 119, 128, 131-32, 134,
    135-38; reelection of, 62
Nowak, Stanley, 39, 110-11

O

O'Hara, Chester P.: and anti-branch
banking bill trial, 204-6, 208-9, 210,
212, 215, 216, 218-19, 222; and
Charles Hemans, 210, 215, 218-19;
and Wayne County grand jury probe,
8, 9, 10-12, 13
Olander, Oscar G., 211, 217, 218
Omacht, George: and Abraham Cooper,
42; and Charles Hemans, 62, 65;
dismissal of charges against, 223,
224; indictment of, 36, 58; and
Ralph W. Smith, 43
Otis, Wayne, 42

P

Page, John D., 213
Pari-mutuel betting bill. *See*: House
Bill 22
Parker, Stanley, 62
Parr, Lloyd, 66
Person, Seymour, 212
Pettit, D. C., 86, 88
Phillio, Norman, 140
Pickard, Frank A., 212
Pines, Gustave, 9
Planck, Joseph W., 41, 53
Poirier, Joe, 86
Pomella, Irene, 169
Poole, Floyd J., 178
Prentice, Ruth, 48, 231
Preston, Loomis, 96, 97
Prew, Ernest W.: and Abraham Cooper,
42; and Charles Hemans, 62; and
financing bills investigation, 36, 37,
40, 62, 68, 69
Probert, Marguerite, 252n.56
Pruit, William, 212
Pugsley, Earl C., 8, 12
Pulver, Clarence, 252n.56

R

Richner, Kathryn, 249n.49
Robichaud, Armand, 58, 59, 223
Robinson, Frederick B., 41
Roosevelt, Franklin D., 199
Roosevelt, Joseph, 52, 67, 68, 69, 190
Rosenfeld, Max, 126, 127, 128
Rosenthal, Emmanuel N., 161, 218
Rusch, Roy, 249n.49
Rushton, Herbert J., xiv; and Byron L.
Ballard, 200, 209; and Charles
Hemans, 46-47; defeat as attorney
general, 62; and Floyd Fitzsimmons,
96-97, 102; and Frank D. McKay,
151; and Gail Handy, 85; and grand
jury funding, 38; and Jay Linsey, 24,
25, 30, 32, 33; and John Dalton, 31,
237n.98; and Kim Sigler, 28-29; and
Leland W. Carr, 27-28, 33, 40, 47,
96-97; life of, 230-31; and punishment for legislative graft, 33-34; and
set-up of Ingham County grand jury,
13, 14-15, 16; and Stanley
Dombrowski, 23; and William Green
investigation, 19-20

S

Sallin, Sol, 158
Sanders, Cleyo, 72, 241n.93
Saunder, Carl M., 240n.71
Schemanske, Frank G., 23
Schreier, Samuel L., 60, 218
Schwartz, Isadore, 150, 173, 245n.55
Selik, Myron "Mike", 3, 86, 87, 139,
258n.62
Senate Bill 41, 35
Senate Bill 85, 35
Senate Bill 166, 35
Senate Bill 203, 59
Senate Bill 269, 119, 129
Senate Bill 282, 58

Stockfish, Walter N.: and anti-branch
  banking bill trial, 199; and Charles
  Hemans, 44, 50, 52, 219; dismissal
  of charges against, 223; and financing bills investigation, 35, 40, 58;
  and Stanley Dombrowski, 23
Stoddard, Howard J., 199, 200, 220
Stone, Juanita, 249n.49
Sumeracki, Adam W.: and anti-branch
  banking bill trial, 199; and Charles
  Hemans, 44, 50, 219; and financing
  bills investigation, 35, 40
Summerfield, Arthur, 62

T

Templin, Kenneth, 197
Thompson, Julian H., 43, 58, 59, 223
Toms, Robert S., 9
Toy, Harry S., 9
Traver, Robert, 234n.33
Tripp, Harold D., 183, 188, 189
Trumble, Floyd, 18, 19
Tunney, Gene, 163

V

VanConant, Leo, 47, 124, 185-87
Vandenberg, Harold, 200, 206-7
VanderWerp, Don, 38
VanWagoner, Murray D., xiv; and anti-
  branch banking bill, 15; and Byron
  L. Ballard, 15, 199, 200, 201, 209,
  259n.8; and Gail Handy, 85; and
  Harry F. Kelly, 229; and Kim Sigler,
  211; life of, 232
VerMeulen, Willard B., 236n.78
Voelker, John D., 234n.33

W

Walker, Fred R., 58, 93-94, 96, 166-67,
  173

Walsh, Edward J.: and anti-branch
  banking bill trial, 199; and Charles
  Hemans, 50, 219; dismissal of
  charges against, 223; and financing
  bills investigation, 35, 58, 65; and
  first naturopathy trial, 119, 126, 128,
  133, 134; and second naturopathy
  trial, 135, 136, 138
Warner, Harold H., 40, 185
Warner, John, 249n.49
Watson, Benjamin, 67
Watson, Everett, 9
Watzel, Paul, 130-31, 132
Webber, Charles, 168-69, 170, 171
Weinstein, Abraham H., 60
Wellington, Fern, 249n.49
Wendell, Leo, 47, 224
Wendell, Monroe (Monty), 224
Weza, Isadore A., 36, 40, 51
Whitehead, Warren, 42, 62
Whitliff, J. C., 158
Wickens, Agnes, 79, 243n.17
Wiest, Howard, 153
Wilcox, Florence, 71-72, 241n.93
Wilcox, Thomas, 8, 9, 12, 13
Wilkander, Gunnar W., 123, 135
Wilkowski, Leo J.: and anti-branch
  banking bill trial, 199, 204, 205,
  206; and Charles Hemans, 51, 64,
  205, 219; and dental bill investiga-
  tion, 114; dismissal of charges
  against, 223; and financing bills
  investigation, 36, 58, 65; and
  naturopathy bill investigation, 123,
  126, 135-38; reelection of, 62
Williams, Charles, 151, 158
Williams, Earl, 151, 158
Williams, G. Mennen, 223, 229
Williams, Harry, 125-31, 133, 135,
  136-37
Williams, Louise L., 252n.56
Wilson, Dwight L., 66
Wilson, John A., 154, 155
Wilson, Robert, 86